REMOVING COLLEGE PRICE BARRIERS

SUNY Series, Social Context of Education
Christine E. Sleeter, editor

REMOVING COLLEGE PRICE BARRIERS

*What Government Has Done
and Why It Hasn't Worked*

Michael Mumper

STATE UNIVERSITY OF NEW YORK PRESS

Published by
State University of New York Press, Albany

For information, address State University of New York Press,
State University Plaza, Albany, N.Y., 12246

Production by Cathleen Collins
Marketing by Dana Yanulavich

Library of Congress Cataloging in Publication Data

Mumper, Michael, 1954–
   Removing college price barriers : what government has done and why
it hasn't worked / Michael Mumper.
      p.   cm. — (SUNY series, social context of education)
   Includes bibliographical references and index.
   ISBN 0-7914-2703-X. — ISBN 0-7914-2704-8
   1. Universities and colleges—Unites States—Finance. 2. Federal
aid to higher education—United States. 3. State aid to higher
education—United States. I. Title. II. Series.
LB2342.M76   1996
378'.02—dc20   95-797
                                                                 CIP

10 9 8 7 6 5 4 3 2 1

Contents

Tables

Figures

Acknowledgments

This research has benefitted greatly from the Research Apprentice Program offered by the Honors-Tutorial College at Ohio University. This program pays outstanding undergraduates to serve as junior researchers on a large project with a faculty member. In the summer of 1991 I worked with Jeremy Anderson on the issues of college-savings programs. That collaboration resulted in chapter 7. In addition Jeremy was a great help in conceptualizing the project and organizing the early research. In the summer of 1993 I worked with Kevin Mohr on state spending and state-grant programs. This collaboration resulted in chapter 6. Kevin read the entire manuscript at least twice and offered criticisms and suggestions which aided the final project immeasurably. Along the way we became friends and colleagues in a way that faculty and undergraduate students almost are never able to.

A number of other people made important contributions to my thinking about the complex problems of college affordability. In particular, Robert Berdahl, who introduced me to the study of higher education policy more than a decade ago, and Eric Uslaner, who taught me how to see the links between politics and policy and to think systematically about policy outcomes. At various stages along the way, DeLysa Burnier, Mark Weinberg, and Ann Martino offered advise and encouragement on parts of the project. Susan Pracejus, William Tierney, Gary Orfield, and an anonymous reviewer for SUNY Press each read the entire manuscript and offered useful comments. My deepest thanks to all.

Introduction

In 1947, President Truman's Commission on Higher Education warned the nation that:

> By allowing the opportunity for higher education to depend so largely on the individual's economic status, we are not only denying to millions of young people the chance in life to which they are entitled; we are also depriving the nation of a vast amount of potential leadership and potential social competence which it sorely needs.[1]

The commission's recommendations were simple. The federal government should lead a national effort with the aim of "making higher education equally available to all young people."[2]

By the 1960s, the goal of removing college price barriers had become part of a broad national consensus. In 1964, the Democratic Party platform stated that "Regardless of family financial status . . . education should be open to every boy and girl in America to the highest level he or she is able to master."[3] Four years later, the Republican Party platform echoed this view, recommending that "No American should be denied a quality education because he cannot afford it or find work to meet its costs."[4] Everyone, it seemed, favored knocking down the walls which kept lower-income students out of college.

Support for the goal of equal access to college extended well beyond the rhetoric of policy-makers. Beginning in 1965, and continuing in ever larger amounts throughout the next three decades, hundreds of billions of government dollars were spent to bring higher education within the financial reach of all Americans. In 1994 alone, the federal government appropriated more than $13 billion on generally available student aid programs like Pell grants, guaranteed student loans, Supplemental Educational Opportunity grants, Perkins loans, and College Work Study funds.[5] Today, college student aid represents the single largest education-related item in the U.S. federal budget.

Spending by state governments on higher education was even more substantial. In 1994, state governments spent $65 billion on the operating expenses of public colleges and universities.[6] Much of this was distributed as instructional subsidies which allow public colleges to keep their tuitions relatively low. States spent an additional $2 billion on various forms of student aid to assist lower income students to pay these already subsidized tuitions.[7] When federal, state, and local expenditures are combined, government spending on higher education totaled more than $85 billion in 1994.

But in spite of these substantial efforts, there are now few problems which worry most American families more than how they will pay for their children's education. The reasons for these public concerns are obvious. In 1994, the average annual price of attending a private university was in excess of $20,000. The average annual price of a public university was over $6,700. Even a year at a public two-year college cost $4,000.[8] These prices are all substantially higher, in real terms, than they have ever been.

Rising prices are not the only reason that college is becoming less affordable. Many families now have fewer financial resources available to them to pay those rising prices. Since the early 1980s, family incomes have lagged behind inflation, the buying power of federal grants has been reduced, and unsubsidized student loans have become more difficult to secure. As a consequence, many lower-, middle-, and even upper-income families now feel squeezed from all sides as they struggle to meet rising college prices with a declining set of financial resources. Clearly, in spite of substantial government efforts, the goal of insuring universal access to college is slipping further and further away.

GOALS AND ORGANIZATION OF THE BOOK

This book is a study of government efforts to keep college affordable to all Americans and why these efforts have failed so dramatically. My goal is to determine why the real price of higher education has increased so rapidly in recent years and the implications those price increases have had for students and potential students from disadvantaged backgrounds. Specifically, I attempt to answer four questions:

1. Why have college prices increased so rapidly?
2. What actions have governments taken, both before and since 1980, to try to keep college affordable?
3. Why have these government efforts failed to stem the tide of rising college prices?
4. Given the current economic and political constraints, what reforms are available to policy-makers to reverse these troubling trends?

In attempting to provide comprehensive answers to these important questions, I divide this analysis into eleven chapters. Each focuses narrowly on a portion of the larger issue of college affordability. Chapter 1 examines the various benefits which flow from a college education and illustrates why individuals and communities benefit as their level of higher education increases. I then show how, in the absence of government action, price barriers emerge which place a college education beyond the financial reach of many potential students who have the ability and the desire to attend. Chapter 2 examines the forces which have caused college prices to increase so rapidly since 1980. Chapter 3 compares these changes in the price of attending college with changes in the resources available to lower-, middle-, and upper-income families to meet those changing prices. This shows the differential impact that changes in the affordability of higher education has had on different income groups.

The middle section of the book is an in-depth analysis of the specific efforts of government to remove college price barriers since the mid-1960s. In chapter 4 I describe evolution of the federal student aid programs from their creation in 1965, through their growth in the 1970s, and then through their retrenchment and subsequent transformation after 1980. In chapter 5 I focus on the consequences of these policy changes in the federal programs for lower- and middle-income students. Specifically, I examine why the various federal student loan programs have become so costly, while still not providing sufficient resources to bring college within the financial reach of lower-income families.

While college prices have gone up everywhere, there is substantial variation in the magnitude of those increases from state to state and across types of institutions. Some states have done a much better job of holding down the net price of public higher education than others. Chapter 6 focuses on the various approaches used by the states to equalize educational opportunity. These strategies involve allocating resources, in different combinations, to public colleges as instructional subsidies and to lower-income students as need-based grants. I examine the various combinations employed by the states and compare those strategies to determine which achieved the best results. In chapter 7 I examine some recent innovations in college finance including prepaid tuition, college savings bonds, and assured access programs.

Chapter 8 examines the linkage between changes in college affordability and college participation. Here I show how the reductions in college affordability have translated into reductions in the college-going behavior of specific groups. Chapter 9 draws together the causes of the problems and illustrates in a simple and straightforward way how and why this happened. I show how the combination of limited government resources, rising educational costs, and the failure of policy-makers to target their limited funds to the most needy, caused net college prices to spiral upward. It is this combination which has produced the troubling situation we face today, where governments are spending ever larger amounts on higher education even as college prices are rising rapidly and lower-income families are finding even public higher education to be moving beyond their financial reach.

In the final two chapters I examine what can be done to get the government's college affordability effort back on track. Chapter 10 considers several of the leading reform proposals and speculates as to why they have failed to win legislative or public support. Chapter 11 lays out a series of concrete steps that federal and state policy-makers can take to reaffirm, and, perhaps, to finally achieve, universal college affordability.

LIMITATIONS OF THE STUDY

Removing college price barriers is a complex matter. While I try to provide a comprehensive analysis of the many issues involved, I have limited the focus of this study in three important ways. First, I restrict my discussion to the period between 1965 and 1995. The year 1965 makes sense as a starting point because that is when the federal government first began to make a sustained effort to bring higher education within the financial reach of all Americans. This effort, which culminated in the passage of the "Higher Education Act," established the federal student aid programs in place today.

Second, I define "higher education" and "college education" in a fairly narrow way. I use these terms to refer only to those public or private institutions of higher education which award associate and bachelors degrees, in other words, those schools which are commonly called community colleges, colleges, or universities. I further limit the analysis to undergraduate education. While I recognize the essential role that vocational, proprietary, and graduate schools play in the broad system of American higher education, the financing of these institutions and programs poses different, and largely separate, problems. When the financing issues facing these different sectors are directly related to undergraduate education, as they are in the operation of the federal student loan programs, I discuss both. But, in general, my focus remains narrowly on the operation and effectiveness of government efforts to make undergraduate instruction at two-year and four-year colleges affordable to potential students from all economic backgrounds.

Costs, Expenditures, and Prices

The third, and perhaps most important limitation of this study is found in the way I consider costs and prices. During the last three decades, the expenditure patterns of colleges have changed significantly. College and university faculty members now teach fewer courses, on average, than they did two decades ago. Most institutions now offer their students a far wider array of courses, student services, and extracurricular activities. Many colleges have undertaken expansions, or significant upgrading, of their physical plants and educational infrastructure. And many have undertaken large and expensive capital campaigns or fund-raising efforts. Each of these has required the hiring of new staff and increased expenditures.

To some observers, these new expenditures were merely a reaction to the increasing costs of providing a high-quality college education. Campus leaders had little choice but to make these expenditures or allow their education programs to deteriorate. But to others, many of these new expenditures were seen as imprudent and unnecessary. Campus leaders were unwilling to make the difficult choices necessary to control spending and they were financing their wasteful expenditures through increased tuition.

In this analysis, I have put aside the controversy over the merits of these changing expenditure patterns. I leave it to others to determine whether or not these increased expenditures were necessary to provide a high-quality education. I limit my analysis to describing precisely how college expenditure patterns have changed and reviewing the arguments made by each side about the causes and consequences of those changes.

AGGREGATE ANALYSIS, LEGISLATIVE HISTORIES, AND EVERYDAY LIFE

This study focuses on the economic, social, and political context in which American higher education operates. I trace how and why an important part of that context, college affordability, has changed since 1965 and the impact that these changes have had on the opportunities available to lower-income and disadvantaged students to go to college. In telling the on-going story of government efforts to remove college price barriers, I alternate between examining the actions of policy-makers and evaluating the impacts of their actions. This requires me to provide both detailed accounts of the policy-making process and analysis of policy outputs such as campus revenue structures, government spending patterns, and college participation rates.

These legislative histories and program analyses may seem to be far removed from the everyday lives of disadvantaged families. But, in fact, their impact on such families could hardly be greater. The programs and policy choices discussed here have a direct and lasting impact on the opportunities available to millions of ordinary Americans to attend college. The price of college, the eligibility for need-based grants, and the availability of student loans, are all determined, in large measure, by the actions of state and federal policy-makers. These actions determine how much college will cost and who will have the resources to pay those costs. For many potential students, whether or not they will go to college is a function of the tuition charged and the availability of government-funded student aid. Whether or not they go to college, in turn, has a lasting impact on their career choices, on their lifetime earnings, and on the quality of much of the rest of their lives. I hope that in presenting this analysis, I am able to keep clear the essential linkage between the decisions of policy-makers, and the opportunities to pursue a higher education which are available to disadvantaged children and their families.

1

Why College Matters

I n a 1920 discussion of the value of higher education, Alfred Marshall reasoned that:

> All that is spent during many years in opening the means of higher education to the masses would be well paid for if it called out one more Newton, Darwin, Shakespeare, or Beethoven.[1]

Recently, however, more and more people have begun to openly question the value of additional spending on higher education. Former Secretary of Education William Bennett complained that:

> most colleges promise to make you better culturally and morally, but it is not evident that they do. . . . There are good grounds for suspicion that some students are not getting their money's worth. Some people are getting ripped off.[2]

It is not easy to judge the value of a college education.[3] But in these days of declining wages, slow economic growth, and government budget deficits, individuals and public policy-makers alike must be especially cautious about how they allocate their scarce financial resources. Many families must choose between sending a child to college and paying off the mortgage, or saving for retirement. Governments, too, must choose how much they will spend on higher education. Public monies given to colleges cannot be spent to improve health care, to hire more police officers, or lower tax burdens.

In order to make fair and equitable spending decisions, individuals and governments must carefully consider the benefits they receive for each dollar spent. In this chapter I review the economic and non-economic benefits which accrue to both individuals and to their communities as their levels of higher education increase. My objective is not to produce a quantitative cost-benefit calculus. It is rather to describe in detail those things which individuals and communities receive in return for their spending on higher education.

In the second part of the chapter I explore why, if the benefits from increased levels of higher education are great, individuals and governments are so often unwilling to invest more of their resources in higher education. Specifically, I examine the role that price barriers and neighborhood effects play in discouraging the optimum level of personal and social spending on higher education. The chapter concludes with a look at why governments must act to compensate for the resulting under-investment, and under-participation, in higher education.

THE PRIVATE ECONOMIC BENEFITS OF COLLEGE

Over the past thirty years, economists and social scientists have attempted to measure the economic benefits of a college education in a number of ways. The most common of these approaches is to compare the characteristics of those who have attended college with those who have not. After controlling for other factors, the difference between the two groups is assumed to be causally related to educational experience. These studies ask such questions as: All else being equal, do college graduates earn more? Are college graduates more satisfied with their jobs? Or do college graduates contribute more to the national economy?[4]

While such studies can add a great deal to our understanding of the value of college, their results must be viewed with some caution. The difference in the earnings of the two groups may be the result of some third cause. For example, college may serve as a screening device that identifies individuals with certain qualities and abilities. It could be that these traits, and not the college education, are responsible for the person's success. It is thus possible that college graduates would receive similar benefits without ever attending college.[5]

The Changing Link Between Higher Education and Personal Income

Everyone knows that college graduates earn more than those without a degree, but the size of that wage gap is large and growing.[6] Table 1.1 shows

Table 1.1

Median Annual Earnings of Persons Age 25 and Over by Education and Sex, 1992 (in 1994 dollars)

	High School Graduates	*Some College, No Degree*	*B.A. Degree Or More*
Female	$11,520	$16,611	$26,527
Male	$22,887	$27,850	$42,869

Source: U.S. Department of Commerce, *Money Income of Households, Families, and Persons in the United States, 1992*, table 24.

the 1992 average annual earnings of persons over 25 by education and by gender. Among males, college graduates earn almost 78 percent more than high-school graduates. While women earn less than men at all education levels, female college graduates earn nearly twice that of female high-school graduates.

The economic benefits of a higher education are thus substantial when viewed in the aggregate. Those benefits are even more pronounced when they are broken down by the age of the worker. The economic benefit of a college education seems to accelerate over time. Table 1.2 shows that among male full-time workers with only a high-school diploma, those between 55 to 64 years of age earn 20 percent more than those aged 25 to 34. Among those with a college degree, however, workers aged 55–64 earn 32 percent more than workers aged 25 to 34. At a lower level, the same is true among female workers. Older female workers (55–64) with a high-school degree earn about 5 percent more than younger high-school graduates. But older college graduates earn about 10 percent more than younger college graduates. This is evidence that while a college education helps younger workers secure a higher paying job, it also helps them to move up the earnings ladder once they have begun working.

The private economic returns on higher education have remained substantial since 1970. But, as shown in table 1.3, the size of those benefits has varied widely. In 1970, the mean earnings of a male college graduate were 45 percent higher than those of a high-school graduate. That gap closed throughout the 1970s and reached a low of about 42 percent 1980. For females, the wage gap remained at about 85 percent. This decline in "college wage premiums" for males was sufficient to suggest to some that the market for college-educated workers was saturated and that a college education was no longer a good investment.[7]

Table 1.2

Median Annual Money Income of Persons Age 25–65 by Education, Sex, and Age, 1992 (in 1994 dollars)

	Females		
Age	High School Graduates	Some College, No Degree	B.A. Degree Or More
25–34	$12,948	$16,461	$26,134
35–44	14,937	18,136	29,094
45–54	16,093	20,406	32,159
55–64	13,522	17,767	28,765
	Males		
Age	High School Graduates	Some College, No Degree	B.A. Degree Or More
25–34	$21,137	$22,743	$33,763
35–44	27,020	32,246	46,687
45–54	29,657	36,161	51,515
55–64	25,274	31,292	44,715

Source: U.S. Department of Commerce, *Money Income of Households, Families, and Persons in the United States, 1992*, table 29.

This decline in the gap between the earnings of college and non-college male workers prompted Caroline Bird, among others, to argue that when both costs and benefits were considered, higher education was no longer a sound investment.[8] In her 1975 book, *The Case Against College*, Bird argued that a man who graduated from Princeton in 1972 could be expected to earn $199,000 more over his working life than a man with just a high-school diploma. But if that high-school graduate had taken the $34,000 it would cost to attend Princeton for four years and invested it in an account that earned 7.5 percent interest, he would have more than $1.1 million by the age of 64. In comparative terms, Bird calculated that the high-school graduate would, in the end, have $528,200 more than the earnings of a male college graduate.

Richard Freeman reached a similar conclusion in *The Overeducated American*.[9] Writing in 1976, he attributed the decline in college wage premiums to the large influx of baby-boomers entering the work-force in the 1960s and 1970s and the increasing percentage of those workers who had completed college. Freeman speculated that the number of college

Table 1.3

Median Annual Money Income of Persons Age 25–65 by Education and Sex, 1970–1992 (in constant 1994 Dollars)

	Females		
Year	Four-Years High School	One–Three Years College	Four or More Years College
1970	$12,207	$13,365	$22,170
1975	12,010	14,264	21,984
1980	10,597	13,516	19,796
1985	11,170	15,125	23,660
1990	14,024	18,400	25,527
1992	14,009	17,541	27,896

	Males		
Year	Four-Years High School	One–Three Years College	Four or More Years College
1970	$34,350	$40,150	$49,802
1975	33,536	37,398	47,703
1980	29,102	32,332	41,615
1985	26,079	30,867	43,869
1990	25,285	30,867	42,067
1992	24,040	28,378	42,782

Source: U.S. Census Department, *Current Population Reports*, P-60 Total Money Earnings in 1992 of Persons 25 Years Old and Over by Age, Race, Hispanic Origin, and Work Experience.

graduates was simply growing faster than the number of jobs demanding a college education. The resulting oversupply was driving down wages and reducing the value of college as an investment.

But the predictions of a continuing decline in the value of a college education proved to be dramatically wrong. During the early 1980s, the economic value of a college education began to rise rapidly again. By 1990, the college/high school earnings differential had risen to a record 78 percent for males and 99 percent for females and was continuing to climb.

The widening earnings gap in the 1990s is not entirely good news for college graduates. Table 1.3 also illustrates that the growing difference between the wages of the two groups is not so much that college graduates are doing well, but that the earnings of high-school graduates have fallen precipitously. In 1975, the average annual earnings of full-time year-round workers over 25 with four years of high school was $27,694. By 1992 that same group was earning almost 8 percent less. On the other hand, the full- time worker with four years of college was earning $38,787 in 1975. By 1992, their earnings had risen by a modest 6 percent. As wages of the two groups moved in different directions, the gap between them has grown.

Indeed, what most characterizes the changes in returns to education in the last decade is the dramatic earnings' decline experienced by those without a degree. This development is explored in *The Forgotten Half* by the W.T. Grant Foundation.[10] Here researchers found that the real earnings of male college graduates dropped 6 percent between 1973 and 1986, but high-school graduates lost 28 percent. Men with less than a high-school degree lost a staggering 42 percent in real earnings. In the words of McKinley Blackburn, David Bloom, and Richard Freeman, "For some—mostly young, less educated, and blue-collar men—the 1980s job market was a disaster."[11]

Variations in Family Income by Level of Education

While the impact of education on personal income is substantial, its impact on family income is even greater. More highly educated people tend to marry more educated people and, when both are employed, this reinforces the income differentials. Table 1.4 shows the median family income of American families by the level of education of the householder. The message it presents is unmistakable. When it comes to higher education, more is always better. The income of families headed by someone with an associate's degree is 26 percent higher than families headed by a high-school graduate. The difference is 67 percent between families headed by someone with a bachelor's degree and a high-school graduate.

Higher Education and Wealth Accumulation

Increased personal income is only part of the economic advantages experience by those who have attended college. Frank Levy and Richard Michel estimate that the net wealth of those families headed by a young person (25–34 years old) with at least some college is 66 percent higher

Table 1.4
Median Family Income by Educational Attainment of Householder, 1992
(in 1994 dollars)

Educational Attainment	Median Family Income
Less Than 9th Grade	$19,089
High School—No Diploma	$23,438
H.S. Graduate	$36,003
College—No Diploma	$43,021
Associates Degree	$45,570
Bachelors Degree	$60,129
Masters Degree	$70,689
Doctors Degree	$80,120
Professional Degree	$97,620

Source: T. Mortenson, *Postsecondary Education Opportunity* 19 (January), p. 13.

than that of families headed by a young person with a high-school education or less.[12]

More specifically, Levy and Michel find that college-educated families own a much wider range of assets than the less educated. They were twice as likely to have an Independent Retirement Account and more than twice as likely to have such non-liquid assets as precious metals, jewelry, or art.[13] The value of their liquid assets was more than twice that of the less educated. While they held more investment debt, the size of their retail debt was considerably smaller.[14]

College-educated families also tended to have more expensive homes and the net equity of those homes was 27 percent higher than less-educated families. This is true in spite of the fact that the importance of home equity is greater among the less educated. Home equity accounts for 64 percent of net wealth among the less educated and only 40 percent among the more educated. This leaves the families of the non-college educated as considerably less diversified in their financial assets. So if real housing prices fall, these families will experience a disproportionate decline in their net wealth. As such, this gap in wealth accumulation serves to reinforce and extend the growing gap between the financial situations of those who have attended college and those who have not.

These trends have important implications for both individuals and for the nation. For individuals, a college education has become the key to economic success. As Levy and Michel put it:

For those with the ability and the initiative, a college education seems the surest way to compete in the labor market. The same will be true for the children of today's young parents.[15]

For the nation, increasing the college participation rate is a key to long term economic health, John Bishop and Shani Carter argue that to achieve this, "cost-effective ways of stimulating a substantial increase in the supply of college graduates are needed."[16]

THE PRIVATE NON-ECONOMIC BENEFITS OF HIGHER EDUCATION

Individuals benefit from higher education in many non-economic ways as well.[17] In *How College Affects Students*, Ernest Pascarella and Patrick Terenzini have compiled the findings of 2,600 studies conducted over twenty-five years. Their results show the vast and varied ways in which individuals are affected by higher education. College, it seems, has a major impact on nearly every aspect of the lives of students in both the short and long terms.

There is evidence which suggests that college has a positive impact on the entire character of a student's working life. College graduates have better working conditions,[18] receive greater fringe benefits,[19] have better health and live longer lives,[20] have lower rates of unemployment,[21] lower rates of disability,[22] and make better investment decisions.[23]

But quite apart from its direct impact on their work and earnings, college has been shown to have an important impact on the cognitive development of students. Verbal skills, quantitative skills, oral and written communication skills, and critical thinking skills all improve as a result of college.[24] Students who have been to college simply know more, and can think more clearly, than those who have not. While the consequences of this general intellectual development can be seen very soon upon completion of college, the positive affect remains visible throughout their lifetime.[25]

Not only does college contribute to cognitive growth, but it alters the way individuals see themselves. College has a strong positive impact on a student's self-esteem and sense of psychological well-being.[26] College graduates are more likely to have an internal locus of control.[27] Others studies find them to be more aesthetically and culturally sophisticated, meaning they have an increased interest in art, music, reading, and discussion of philosophical issues.[28]

College seems to impact individuals in ways which positively affect others as well. It has been found to increase a person's tolerance for diversity and to be associated with a greater concern for human rights.[29] Conversely, college graduates are less likely to hold authoritarian or ethnocentric values.[30]

The benefits of a college education even extend to the next generation. College graduates have fewer unwanted children,[31] lower infant and child mortality rates,[32] and their children perform better in school.[33] In summarizing the previous research on the intergenerational impact of college, Parcarella and Terenzini conclude that:

> The more fully an individual develops his or her intellectual faculties and career opportunities through investment in education, the more likely that individual is to believe in the importance of developing similar intellectual facilities and career opportunities in their children. Thus, other factors being equal, highly educated parents are more likely than less educated parents to raise children who themselves recognize the value of education.[34]

Perhaps the most inventive and insightful of the hundreds of studies of the impact of higher education on individuals is David Schuman's *Policy Analysis, Education, and Everyday Life*.[35] Unlike the numbers and formulas which provide the grist for most other studies, Schuman conducted long unstructured interviews with more than a dozen carefully selected people who had been to college many years before. He asked them to explain in their own words the impact that college had had on their everyday lives.

What they said points to the complexity of the college experience and the difficulties of measuring its impact fully. Most of the participants benefitted financially from college, but a few did not. Some were disappointed and frustrated with what they learned or failed to learn. Some wished it would have never ended and others wondered if they would have been better off if they had not gone at all. What is interesting, however, is that college served as a turning point in the lives of almost everyone. It was a time and place where they learned how to better fit into the world and create a meaning for their life.

In his conclusion, Schuman argues that to isolate college as the critical factor in anyone's life is almost always wrong.[36] The impact of higher education cannot, and indeed, should not, be sorted out from countless other influences. He observes that among those people he interviewed:

> Education is one of those things that threads through the public
> and the private. It ties the person to his or her surroundings.
> Education, for those with it, frequently provides a sense of being
> in the world that helps shape and give meaning to a day.[37]

Whether it is a benefit as concrete as reduced crime or as etherial as an aesthetic sense, there is strong evidence that going to college has a positive impact that ranges far beyond simply increased wages and wealth accumulation. While these benefits cannot be translated into a monetary value, it seems clear that for most, attending college significantly enhanced and enriched their lives.

THE PUBLIC BENEFITS OF COLLEGE

Showing that individuals receive benefits from a given activity is not sufficient to establish the need for a public subsidy to make that activity affordable to everyone. Collecting rare coins or exercising at a health club can provide substantial benefits to an individual, but few would argue that the public ought to help bring the costs of these activities down to encourage wider participation in them. In order to justify using public funds to remove price barriers to colleges, it must also be shown that a substantial public or social benefit arises from increased participation in higher education. Next, I examine the many, often unrecognized, benefits that increased levels of higher education have on the health of the economy and the quality of life enjoyed by all Americans.

Higher Education and National Economic Growth

Certainly, educated people bring economic benefits to the societies in which they live. They get better jobs, earn higher wages, and pay more taxes. Raising the educational level of society also tends to raise the productivity of workers in a manner that adds to the economic returns of all factors of production and those benefits extend beyond those who have directly participated in that education.

In his comprehensive analysis of the determinants of national income between 1929 and 1982, Edward Denison finds increases in higher education to be a major source of national economic growth.[38] He observes that the continuous upward shift in the educational background of American workers upgraded the skills and versatility of the labor force and produced a steady and sometimes steep increase in national income. Denison finds that the impact of education can be seen in several ways. Individuals working in a particular occupation perform their work better as a result of more education. The availability of more educated workers also facilitated a shift in the economy from low-skill, low-productivity industries to high-skill, high-productivity industries. Further, Denison notes that education helps workers to find, recognize, and secure the job they do best. He explains how education heightens a person's "awareness of job opportunities and thereby the chances that he is employed where his marginal product is greatest."[39] In sum, a more educated work-force is better able to learn and use the most efficient production practices.

Increasing education levels are a central element behind increases in national income. Denison estimates that between 1929 and 1982, more education per worker was responsible for 23 percent of the nation's economic growth. An additional 20 percent was accounted for by "advances in knowledge," much of which is presumably linked to higher education.[40] Based on a reexamination of Denison's work and ten similar studies, Leslie and Brinkman estimate that "education may contribute as much as 50 percent or more to growth in the economy, and higher education, may constitute almost half of this."[41]

While this is a substantial contribution, G. Psacharopoulos has argued that these "growth accounting" studies actually underestimate the contribution of education.[42] This is because they ignore the necessary support that education provides for the development of technological change. He describes how the interaction between education and other factors of production serves to encourage national economic growth. This raises the productivity of the domestic economy and increases its competitive position in the world economy.

The impact of technological innovations and advances in knowledge is often the direct result of university-based research. So too, the process of technology transfer and application is facilitated and sometimes driven by institutions of higher education. Because of this, increases in the level of higher education in the nation can have the unrecognized benefit of making their less-educated co-workers more productive.

The economic impact of education thus extends well beyond increased personal income. As the international economy becomes more competitive, higher education will be crucial in maintaining America's competitive position relative to the rest of the world.[43] Increased higher education will produce a more skilled and productive work-force that is capable of retaining the high-wage, high-status, jobs that might otherwise move to Europe or Asia. In addition, more education will enable America to stay on the cutting edge of innovation, developing the new products and technologies that determine who wins and who loses in the global marketplace. In the years to come, the United States may not be able to maintain its economic position by simply maintaining its present level of education. Indeed, in the next decades Americans are likely to need more education just to keep up with the rest of the world.

Higher Education and Community Development

There are presently over 3,500 institutions of higher education in the country,[44] not counting the more than 7,000 vocational and proprietary schools. Their combined expenditures are in excess of $100 billion per year.[45] Each of these colleges has an important impact on the economy of the surrounding community and, in sum, on the national economy. Taken together, they form one of the nation's largest industries.

Measuring the economic impact of a college or university involves separating the economic activity attributable to the college from the activity which would have taken place in the absence of the college. While accurately estimating this figure is difficult, the dozens of such studies which have tried to do so have generally reached a common conclusion. Each dollar of expenditure by a college has a local economic impact which is well in excess of one dollar. The magnitude of that impact is a function of both the type of institution and the volume of that institution's expenditures.

Community colleges have the least economic impact on a community. This is because more of their students are already residents and therefore would have been a part of the local economy whether or not there was a community college. Still, economic-impact studies have found that for the average community college each dollar of expenditures by the college (general expenditures plus auxiliary enterprises) produces about $1.60 of business volume in the community. Perhaps even more important, each one million dollars of expenditures (expressed in 1986 dollars) creates fifty-nine local jobs.

The economic impact on the community of four-year colleges is significantly larger. This is because they bring in more external wealth in the form of student spending, private research funding, and net tax revenues. Leslie and Brinkman estimate that for the average four-year college, each expenditure dollar produces about $2.20 of local income and each million dollars of expenditures (in 1986 dollars) produce about sixty-seven jobs. Among private institutions and large research universities, the ratio of spending to local incomes and jobs is still greater.

While most studies find that higher education has a substantial impact on a local economy, Barry Bluestone has argued that they often consider only a portion of the real economic impact of public spending on higher education.[46] Bluestone notes that most of these studies treat the college or university simply as an export base and not as an investment instrument. They identify the number of dollars spent by employees, students, and visitors as they make their way through the community. But colleges also educate a local labor force that remains in the community. As such, the real impact of the college is much greater. Studies need to include a measure of the potential future earnings flow which results from the added earning power to the students, who benefit from having been educated at the college, to gain an accurate picture of the full impact of a college or university on a community or region.

Bluestone conducted a study of the economic impact of the University of Massachusetts–Boston (UMB) on the economy of Massachusetts. In conducting that study, he attempted to determine the overall "rate of return" for the state government from each dollar invested in public higher education. What he discovered was that:

> if you treat the state government as though it were a private bank, one finds that investments in UMB have not only been economically prudent, but indeed highly profitable in a strict business sense. Our best estimate suggests that for every $1 spent by the Commonwealth on UMB including both current and capital spending), UMB students will earn *additional* income over their lifetimes which will generate for the state $1.57 in personal income and sales taxes (in discounted value terms). This is an equivalent to an investment that pays 8.9 percent

nominal rate of return. If the state government were a private bank or industrial concern, it could hardly make a better investment than in the students it implicitly subsidizes.[47]

It is difficult to forecast precisely future increases in income based on increased levels of education. But there is certainly compelling evidence that, in the aggregate, increased education produces increased income for individuals. That increased income, in turn, generates additional tax revenues for the community, the state, and the nation. When the additional state revenues resulting from increased spending on higher education are considered, it is reasonable to conclude that government money allocated to higher education produces a real return to the taxpayers. As such, it is not an expenditure in which all the citizens subsidize those few who are in school. Each tax dollar spent now, generates far more than a dollar increase in future government revenues.

Higher Education and Neighborhood Effects

The social benefits of an educated population extend far beyond the creation of jobs and a more productive work-force. The college experience produces an increase in socially desirable behaviors and a decrease in socially disruptive behaviors. It also has a positive impact on the way people think about themselves and the world. As such, increased participation in college would be beneficial to society even if it produced no increase in individual or aggregate income.

The most elusive benefit to the public from increased higher education is the positive impact it has on the personal values and aspirations of individuals. To the extent that a higher education tends to make one's neighbors more open minded, alert, physically healthy, interested in the community, and more tolerant of differing views, most people believe that a well educated society would be a better society. As such, it is important to most parents not simply to obtain a good education for their own children, but to assure that one's neighbors' children are also educated. Economists call these benefits neighborhood effects—the desire of individuals to exist in a world with good neighbors.

Here again Leslie and Brinkman have compiled an impressive review of the studies which show the benefits to the public of increased rates of higher education.[48] Increases in college education are associated with reductions in many of the major domestic programs which now plague the country. Crime rates fall as education levels increase and the ability to avoid becoming a victim of crime increases.[49] Increases in education are correlated with lower public welfare and Medicaid costs.[50] College graduates are more likely to do volunteer work in community agencies and give to charities.[51] College graduates are more likely to vote,[52] and more likely to be informed about, and involved, in civic affairs.[53]

In summing up the public benefits of higher education, the Carnegie Commission on Higher Education put it quite well:

> Among the more highly educated, there is a greater sharing of aesthetic and cultural values, more political involvement, and a greater sense of tolerance towards diverse points of view. These factors contribute to social cohesiveness and tend to reinforce the procedures of a political democracy.[54]

As such, the rate of college education in a community is the cause of, or at least highly correlated with, many of the factors most Americans associate with a high quality of life.

Future Work Force Needs

There is not an unlimited need for college graduates. If the supply of graduates begins to exceed the demand for graduates in the labor market, employers will bid down wages and the economic premiums will disappear. As such, policy-makers must be careful to recognize the dynamic nature of wages in a market economy. Some studies suggest that the nation may already be producing too many graduates for the needs of the labor market. One recent study found that between 1980 and 1990, about 20 percent of college graduates in the labor force were either educationally under-utilized or unemployed.[55] Moreover, a study by the National Center for Education Statistics indicate that almost 40 percent of the graduates awarded bachelor's degrees reported that *they thought* a degree was not needed to obtain the job they held a year after graduation.[56]

In spite of this evidence, however, most studies reach the opposite conclusion. These studies show that the demand for college graduates has grown rapidly since 1979 and is continuing to grow.[57] In their 1991 study, John Bishop and Shani Carter contended that the demand for college graduates grew extremely rapidly in the 1980s and the resulting shortage bid up the wages of graduates.[58]

Daniel Hecker points to the changes in the U.S. economy which drove the wages of the less educated downward and increased the relative value of a college education.[59] During the restructuring of the U.S. economy which has occurred since 1980, many high-wage jobs which required only a high-school diploma disappeared or were taken by those with more education. Employment in the largely non-collegiate fields of manufacturing and mining peaked in 1979 and 1981 respectively. The number of production jobs in these two areas declined by 2.3 million during the 1980s. During those same years, however, employment growth was above average in retail, finance, insurance, real estate, and health services. While those industries provided many new jobs for high-school graduates, they often paid less than the manufacturing and mining jobs which were lost.

College graduates, on the other hand, have slowly increased their earning level since 1980. This was even true for college graduates employed in fields which did not require a degree a decade ago. Hecker notes that "in every occupational group and in almost every individual occupation" college graduates had a higher increase in earnings during the 1980s.[60] For example, between 1983 and 1990 the earnings of mechanics and repairers with a college degree or more increased by 42 percent. Earnings of those with a high-school degree or less increased by only 21 percent. The economic transformation was thus rewarding college graduates regardless of their field of employment.

These changes point out that the benefits which accrue from higher education are not static. As our social and economic systems change, so too does the demand for, and the benefits of, higher education. Most studies also show that while the benefits of higher education are great today, the benefits of higher education may be even larger in the years ahead.

In *Work Force 2000*, William B. Johnson attempted to predict the labor market demands in the year 2000.[61] While the future occupational mix of an economy is difficult to estimate, Johnson uncovered some important trends which suggest that a much larger percentage of the jobs of the future will have a much greater need for higher education than do today's jobs. Johnson predicts that "job prospects for professional and technical, managerial, sales, and service jobs will far outstrip the opportunities in other fields."[62] The demand for lawyers, scientists, and health professionals will grow even faster. In contrast, jobs for machine tenders, assemblers, miners, and farmers will decline over the next decade.

Among the fastest-growing jobs, the trend toward higher education requirements is striking. The study finds that of all the new jobs created between 1984 and 2000, more than half will require some education beyond high school and almost a third will be filled by college graduates. In 1984, only 22 percent of all jobs created in 1984 required a college degree. That percent increased to 30 percent for jobs created between 1984 and 2000. Johnson also estimates that the median education level required by these new jobs will be 13.5 compared to 12.8 for current workers. These findings are supported by projections made in 1990 by the U.S. Labor Department.[63]

Bishop and Carter go even further. They estimate that in the 1990s, "the shortage of college graduates that prevailed in the 1980s will definitely not end and will almost certainly grow."[64] They go on to warn that:

> Absent a policy response to stimulate the supply of college graduates, difficulties in recruiting highly skilled workers will force the economy off the up-skilling path generated by the growth scenarios we have simulated, and the rapid up-skilling of the 1970s and 1980s may slow considerably.[65]

Moreover, these estimates are based on the assumption that the new jobs created will require the same education levels required for that occupation today. However, recent experience shows that the education requirements are also growing within each job category. If this trend prevails, the level of education needed for the jobs of the next decade will be greater than those projected.

The forces that are shaping the world economy make it increasingly difficult for American workers to succeed in the job market without a college degree. As economic change accelerates in the next decade, more workers will need a higher education simply to have access to useful job training. Economist Lester Thurow makes the point that

> technology has moved in directions that require a much more educated and more skilled work force. To make today's complex semiconductor chips, a company must use statistical quality control. To use statistical quality control, every production worker must master it. To do so requires learning some simple operations research, but to learn what must be taught, workers must know algebra. Americans are not used to a world where ordinary production workers have to have mathematical skills.[66]

From the point of view of the worker, higher education will become a prerequisite to compete in the future labor market. For the nation, having highly educated workers will be an essential ingredient in maintaining a high-productivity/high-wage economy.

WHY COLLEGE AFFORDABILITY MATTERS

Inasmuch as increased participation in higher education creates such wide-ranging benefits, it is in the interest of governments to find ways to encourage college attendance. But this is a difficult task. Most studies find that college participation is largely a function of students' traits such as social class, occupational ambition, or the parent's educational level.[67] Accordingly, a fully effective strategy to increase participation in higher education must address the complex factors which shape the ambitions of young children and structure their opportunities.

But as policy-makers struggle to increase college participation in the short term, there is little they can do directly or quickly to alter these sociological conditions. However, common sense suggests that economic factors also play an important role in the decision to attend college. If this is true, one way to increase participation in higher education is to decrease its price. Focusing on economic incentives to increase college attendance has particular appeal to policy-makers because they have several tools they can use to alter net college prices. Both the tuition levels charged at public colleges and the availability of student financial aid can be readily controlled.

If government efforts to regulate the net price of college can be shown to have the desired impact, they can serve as a means to increasing the private and public benefits which accrue from increased participation in higher education. However, in their efforts to make college affordable to everyone, governments must overcome three separate problems.

Affordability Problem #1: The Cash-Flow Problem

In many ways, the decision to go to college is just like any other personal investment decision. The potential student must balance the price and the risk against the return which accrues over his or her lifetime. Students will attend college if they judge the potential benefit of the investment to be greater than its cost. They will not attend if higher education appears to be a poor investment.

The problem many potential students face, however, is not that they feel the price is too high but that they do not have access to the funds necessary to invest in a college education. They have few personal resources to pay for college and thus must borrow. But such individuals may have a difficult time in securing college loans because they lack sufficient collateral to secure the loan. Both potential borrower and potential lender may recognize the economic value of the investment, but lenders will still be hesitant about making education loans. This is because if the borrower is unable to repay, the lender cannot repossesses their education in the same way it can a car or a business.[68]

The inability of students to pay the up-front price of college results in a net under-investment in higher education. In describing this situation McPherson and Schapiro observe that:

> In the absence of adequate private credit markets, those who do not have access to sufficient personal resources will fail to invest in a college education that will more than pay for itself; as a result, some socially worthwhile investments will not be undertaken, and the productivity of the economy as a whole will suffer.[69]

In solving this problem, the challenge is to develop programs which allow students to invest in their education today and defer payment until later in life when their earnings will be greater. Government help to pay for college is thus more like a cash advance to future wage earners than a public subsidy to lower income families.

One way to correct the problem is for the government to intervene in the operation of private markets to correct the resulting under-investment. This is done by insuring the availability of private loans to potential students and/or their families. Today, this function is performed by the federal government through the provision of loan guarantees and direct loans.[70]

Affordability Problem #2: Paying for Public Benefits

If individuals had to pay the entire price of college, there would be substantial under-investment in higher education, even if individuals could easily finance those costs. Each potential student, when deciding whether or not to invest in a college education, compares the *private* costs with the potential *private* returns. The individual usually does not consider the many public benefits of higher education as a return, since he or she receives no private gain.[71] Thus governments have a compelling interest in keeping the net price of higher education affordable, in order to stimulate college participation.

Today, governments use two forms of subsidies to stimulate private investment in higher education and to increase college attendance. First,
state governments provide subsidies directly to public colleges and universities which allow them to charge tuitions that are substantially below the
actual cost of the education. These subsidies lower the price for everyone,
which makes higher education a more attractive investment for individuals. Second, the federal and state governments provide grants and low interest loans directly to many students. These financial aid programs provide
grants to low-income students that reduce the actual price of college, and
loans to almost all students that provide the up-front money necessary to
enroll. Together, these government subsidies reduce the posted price of
higher education, and give more students the resources to invest.

While the public subsidies are available to all college students they
go largely to younger citizens and are paid largely by older citizens. Thus,
they represent a redistribution of wealth not only between income groups
but also between generations: each generation pays for the education of
the next. As members of each successive generation graduate and enter
the work-force, they become the taxpayers that continue the cycle. The
result is a kind of reversed Social Security system, in which one generation of workers provides the education for the next generation. As Allan
Ostar describes the process:

> The parental generation pays, primarily through state taxes, for
> the education of young people who attend public postsecondary
> institutions. Then, members of the younger generation, as col-
> lege graduates, enter the work force, earn income, quickly be-
> come taxpayers, and in their productive years pay, in turn, for
> the higher education of the next generation. The investment in
> education is thus constantly renewed: by paying taxes each gen-
> eration accepts responsibility to increase educational opportu-
> nity for successive generations.[72]

Affordability Problem #3: An Equal Opportunity Society

At least since the 1960s, it has been the explicit objective of the federal
government to insure that every American has an equal opportunity to
participate in the economy and the society. In this regard, college price
barriers pose two separate obstacles to the creation of an equal opportu-

nity society. First, the very existence of price barriers denies lower-income and disadvantaged students the opportunity to attend college. For those who view education as a right, this alone is enough to justify government efforts to insure that all Americans have access to the resources necessary to attend college.

The second obstacle to equal opportunity posed by college price barriers is even more important. Increasingly, a college education has become a prerequisite necessary to take advantage of many other social and economic opportunities. Either implicitly or explicitly, a college degree is now necessary to enter most professions, to obtain most high-paying jobs, and to hold many positions of status within the community. If lower-income or disadvantaged students are systematically denied access to college because they lack financial resources, they are also denied access to the lifetime of opportunities which follow from going to college.

In order to reach the goal of providing an equal opportunity to find a good job, earn a good living, and become full participants in community affairs, all Americans must first have access to the education necessary to compete for these rewards. This, in turn, requires that a college education be within the reasonable financial access of everyone. This does not mean that everyone should go to college. Many people have neither the desire nor the ability to pursue a higher education. It simply means that all those who have the ability and the desire to attend college, must have the financial resources necessary to meet the price. Put simply, as long as college price barriers remain, the goal of equal opportunity can never be achieved.

PUBLIC UNDERSTANDING OF THE VALUE
OF HIGHER EDUCATION

In this chapter, I sought to show the wide range of benefits, often unrecognized, which accrue to individuals and communities as levels of higher education increase. Next, I explained how, in the absence of corrective government actions, there will be an under-investment in higher education especially among low- and middle-income families. This occurs because potential students may lack the liquid capital necessary to pay college prices and because potential students are unwilling to bear the full costs without a public subsidy. The result is that the national goal of building an equal opportunity society cannot be achieved.

The evidence examined here points to the next set of questions. If increasing college participation produces such benefits, and if governments have at their disposal mechanisms which have been shown to compensate for the under-investment in higher education and raise college participation rates, why are public subsidies not more effectively used today? Put another way, if removing college price barriers is so important, why have government efforts to achieve that goal been so ineffective? The rest of this book is devoted to answering these questions. In the following chapters I examine the many and varied government efforts to remove college prices barriers. I examine how those programs have attempted to overcome the affordability problems outlined here and, in turn, how they have altered college participation rates over the past three decades.

A NOTE OF CAUTION

Removing college price barriers, and hence increasing participation in higher education, is not the only step which needs to be taken to increase the wages of American workers and improve the productivity of the American economy. It may not even be the most important step. Not everyone has the abilities and motivation to succeed in college. Moreover, even studies which predict an increased demand for college graduates in the future recognize that a large percentage of jobs will never require conventional higher education.

The point made here is much more narrow. Increasing college participation brings substantial benefits, both economic and non-economic, to individuals and communities. But today, price barriers limit the college attendance rates of lower-income students and result in a national under-investment in higher education. Removing those price barriers will certainly increase participation in college. But it will not mean that everyone can, or should, go to college. As price barriers are removed, those who have the ability and the desire to go to college, but who had previously found college to be unaffordable, will now have the opportunity to enroll. Those young people who had become discouraged by their family's inability to pay the price of college, might be encouraged now that higher education is within their reach. Simply removing price barriers, however, will have little impact on those who lack the skills, intellect, or motivation to attend college.

2

UNDERSTANDING COLLEGE PRICES

The price of higher education has been rising rapidly in recent years.[1] Since 1980, college tuition has increased faster than the cost of food, energy, new cars, new houses, and even medical care.[2] Newspapers, news magazines, and television programs are filled with horror stories of talented young people who were forced to stay home because they could not afford the higher tuitions. Concerns about college prices are not limited to the poor. Today, middle- and even upper-income families are worried about how they will pay for their children's higher education.[3] Financial columnist Jane Bryant Quinn summed up the view of many families when she described paying for college in the 1990s as the "Matterhorn of personal finance."[4]

Often, the stories about rising prices conclude with speculation that if tuitions continue to increase at the present rate, college will soon be beyond the financial reach of many, if not most, American families. A widely cited study by the investment firm of Paine-Webber estimated that by 2005 "the price of a college education is likely to climb to $62,894."[5] A 1991 article by Andrea Trachtenberg speculated that by "the year 2007—when today's two-year-old is ready for the ivy halls, four years at a private college could easily cost in excess of $200,000.[6] Such stories heighten and reinforce the public's fears over rising college prices.

THE CHANGING COURSE OF COLLEGE PRICES

Because of all of the recent attention to college price increases, it is easy to assume that these prices have been increasing steadily for a long time.[7]

Table 2.1

The Price of Colleges and Universities: Selected Years, 1970–1993
(in constant 1994 dollars)

	Average Annual Undergraduate Tuition and Required Fees			
	1970	1980	1990	1993
Private 4-Year Universities	$7,117	$7,792	$12,097	$13,812
Private 4-Year Colleges	5,743	6,144	9,634	10,151
Public 4-Year Universities	1,755	1,661	2,413	2,822
Public 4-Year Colleges	1,182	1,296	1,949	2,368
Public 2-Year Colleges	640	692	1,016	1,114

	Average Annual Undergraduate Price (Including Tuition, Required Fees, Room, and Board)			
	1970	1980	1990	1993
Private 4-Year Universities	$12,262	$11,867	$18,652	$20,027
Private 4-Year Colleges	9,170	9,482	$14,018	$14,702
Public 4-Year Universities	5,319	4,909	6,386	6,709
Public 4-Year Colleges	4,254	4,314	5,785	6,160
Public 2-Year Colleges	3,615	3,546	3,870	4,006

Source: Digest of Education Statistics 1994, Table 305 (Washington D.C.: GPO, 1992).

But that is simply not the case. Table 2.1 shows that both the average tuition and the average total price of attending a two- or four-year college increased very little during the 1970s. In fact, the average annual price of public college's actually dropped by about 5 percent between 1971 and 1981. To be sure, tuitions were rising during these years, but they were increasing at about the same rate as consumer prices. Hence the real, or constant dollar, price of higher education increased only slightly.

In sharp contrast to the 1970s, however, college prices started on a relentless upward spiral in 1980. While the rate of that increase slowed somewhat in the second half of the 1980s, it has accelerated again in the 1990s. Even when adjusted for inflation, the price of public universities rose more than 50 percent during the 1980s. The total price of a year at private university increased by 60 percent during the decade. That price stood at more than $20,000 in 1994. Many elite private colleges had annual prices of more than $25,000 a year.

The price of all types of higher education has increased since 1980. Private institutions experienced the most rapid tuition inflation. The total yearly price of the average private university rose by 57 percent between 1980 and 1990. The price of a private college rose by 47 percent. The rate of increase was much slower at public universities and four-year colleges, 30 percent and 34 percent respectively. In contrast to the rapid tuition inflation experienced at four-year colleges and universities, the total yearly price of public two-year colleges increased a modest 9 percent over those ten years.

These differences in the absolute price of higher education, and in the recent rates of tuition inflation, provide an important caution throughout the rest of this study. By focusing too much attention on the very high prices of a few elite institutions, it is possible to exaggerate the rate of increase in college prices. This caution notwithstanding, by the early 1990s the total price of attending a college or university was greater than it has been at any time in at least two decades and it was increasing steadily.

EXPENDITURES, REVENUES, AND ENROLLMENTS: THE TRIPLE BIND OF COLLEGE FINANCE

Measuring changes in the annual price of colleges and universities is a straightforward matter. Determining their causes is much more complex. Indeed, several factors played important roles in the college price increases since 1980. Predominant among these were the increasing costs of providing high-quality post-secondary education, the changing revenues available to colleges and universities, and a decline in the number of traditional college-age students. In both the public and private sectors, these forces placed colleges in a triple bind of rising costs, declining resources, and competitive pressures to attract students from a declining pool of 18–24-year olds.

The interaction of these factors and their impact on college prices can best be seen by looking at a typical college budget. The principle expenses of a college are for instruction, administration, research, student services, the operation of their physical plant, and the cost of providing institutional scholarships to students. Colleges and universities meet those expenses with revenue derived primarily from government support, private gifts, endowment income, and the tuition and fees charged to students. Public colleges, of course, receive more funding from state governments and less from gifts and student charges, while private colleges rely more on tuitions and gifts and less on government, particularly state government, support.

In building its annual budget, a college must generate enough revenues to cover its expenditures. When expenditures go up, colleges need to find new ways to generate revenue. When revenues go down, colleges must either cut spending or find new revenues. At most colleges it is tuitions which are used to fill the gap between expenditures and revenues. When the combination of government support, private gifts, and endowment income comes close to covering the operating expenses of the college, it can hold its tuitions down. But when the gap between revenues and expenditures widens, institutions must increase tuitions to generate the revenue necessary to cover their expenses. As David Martin describes it:

> Many colleges and universities build their budgets from the expense side, first adding up everything they need to run the institution for the next year and only then looking to potential revenues to see how they are going to cover expenses. If endowment income, investments, and government support aren't enough to cover expenses, the only resources left to make up the difference (and the only one over which the institution has control) are tuition and fees.[8]

During the 1970s, real tuitions at many colleges decreased because they were able to hold their expenditure growth to less than the inflation rate. Moreover, increasingly generous government support provided institutions with additional revenues to cover these expenditures. Additionally, the rapid growth of the number of college-age Americans, which occurred as the baby-boom generation left high school, allowed colleges to spread their expenses over an ever larger number of students. College leaders were thus faced with the pleasant combination of declining expenditures, rising revenues, and increasing numbers of students.

But all this turned around in the early 1980s. College expenditures began to increase rapidly. Many of the non-tuition revenue sources available to colleges began to dry up, and a decline in the number of traditional college-age students set off an expensive competition among schools to attract new types of students to college. In short, a reversal of the same factors which had allowed college prices to drop in the 1970s, were responsible for their rapid increase since 1980.

Table 2.2
Current Fund Expenditures of Institutions of Higher Education
Per FTE Enrollment by Purpose: Selected Years, 1975–1990
(in constant 1994 Dollars)

	Public Colleges and Universities				
Purpose	*1975*	*1980*	*1985*	*1990*	*15-Year Change*
Instruction	$3,583	$3,750	$4,209	$4,418	+ 23%
Administration	1,261	1,365	1,668	1,870	+ 48
Research	810	966	1,071	1,319	+ 63
Student Services	420	493	562	620	+ 47
Physical Plant	813	932	997	978	+ 15
Scholarships	300	270	303	379	+ 26
Libraries	309	300	259	238	– 23
All Other	533	564	626	697	+ 31
Total Expend.	8,030	8,639	9,776	10,479	+ 30
	Private Colleges and Universities				
Instruction	$4,492	$4,531	$5,159	$6,161	+ 37%
Administration	1,958	2,218	2,700	3,415	+ 74
Research	1,422	1,400	1,541	1,779	+ 25
Student Services	641	738	925	1,146	+ 79
Physical Plant	1,162	1,340	1,369	1,486	+ 28
Scholarships	1,053	1,109	1,457	2,120	+101
Libraries	501	441	489	429	– 14
All Other	469	505	599	798	+ 70
Total Expend.	11,697	12,302	14,237	17,325	+ 48

Source: *Digest of Education Statistics 1994*, Table 326 (Washington D.C.: GPO, 1992).

BIND #1: CHANGING EXPENDITURE PATTERNS

Since the mid-1970s there has been a substantial change in the expenditure patterns of colleges and universities.[9] Table 2.2 shows that not only do colleges spend a great deal more per student today than they did in 1975 but that they allocate their expenditures in different ways. Between 1975 and 1990, expenditures per full-time equivalent student (FTE) increased by 30 percent at public colleges. Per FTE expenditures at private colleges increased by 48 percent. The vast majority of those increases have occurred since 1980.

There was no single reason which can explain why the level of college spending increased so rapidly. Spending growth was not confined to one purpose or evident in only one type of institution. With the sole exception of spending on libraries, there were substantial increases in every spending category at both public and private colleges. In the following section I examine some of the areas where spending has increased the most rapidly since 1980 and review the leading reasons offered to explain them.

Increasing Instructional Expenditures

Instruction is the largest expenditure category for almost every college and university. It accounts for more than 40 percent of total expenditures at public colleges and more than 35 percent at private colleges. As a consequence, the aggregate cost of operating a college or university is very sensitive to changes in its instructional costs. During the 1980s, increasing faculty salaries, changes in the distribution of faculty, changes in student demands, and increasing benefit costs combined to drive up college instructional costs. Institutions were then forced to pay more for the same amount of instruction.

Increasing Faculty Salaries. Since college instruction is such a labor-intensive activity, faculty compensation represents the largest portion of a college's instructional costs. As such, changes in the overall instructional expenditures closely mirror changes in the levels of faculty salaries. Table 2.3 shows that the salaries of college and university faculty, as measured in real terms, declined sharply during the 1970s. By 1980, salaries for faculty members at all ranks stood a full 30 percent below where they had been in 1970. Some of this decline was experienced as cuts in current dollar wages. But most of it occurred as wage freezes or modest salary increases allowed the rapid consumer price inflation of the 1970s to erode the purchasing power of wages.

While this reduction in real salaries during the 1970s was bad news to faculty members, it was good news to the balance sheets on most colleges. Because they could now purchase the same amount of instruction at a lower price, colleges could pass those savings on to the students in the form of lower real tuitions, or at least lower rates of tuition inflation.

Beginning in the early 1980s, the downward trend in faculty salaries

Table 2.3
Average Salaries of Full-Time Faculty Members by Rank
(in constant 1994 dollars)

Year	Assistant Professor	Associate Professor	Full Professor
1970	$40,750	$49,250	$65,038
1980	31,402	38,568	51,054
1990	37,134	44,653	59,864
1993	38,817	46,607	62,802

Source: Academe, "Annual Report on the Economic State of the Profession," in March/
April of each year.

came to an end. Throughout the 1980s and into the early 1990s, faculty salaries increased steadily, although they still remained below their high point of the early 1970s. From the perspective of the budget office, higher average salaries meant colleges were paying more for the same amount of instruction.[10]

There are several reasons for the change in direction of faculty salaries since 1980. Colleges are judged based on the abilities and the reputation of their faculty and institutions must compete with one another to attract the most highly qualified professors. In many fields, they also compete directly with private industry. As salaries stagnated in the 1970s, the gap between the compensation of college professors and their counterparts in industry increased. Many schools worried that they were in danger of losing their best faculty members to non-academic positions or that they would be unable to recruit top graduates into academic positions. As a consequence, during the 1980s these colleges felt compelled to bid up salaries in order to attract better faculty.[11]

Interestingly, faculty salaries also increased in fields where there was no competition with industry or non-academic employment. In fact, salaries in some fields began to rise even as conditions in the academic labor market continued to deteriorate. In explaining this unusual phenomenon, Hauptman observes that:

> the growth in tuition revenues in the 1980s no doubt permitted institutions to improve their employee compensation more than if those additional revenues had not been available, including for faculty and other employees for whom the labor market did not materially improve in the 1980s.[12]

Faculty Career Progression. During the 1980s, the distribution of faculty members by rank changed in a way which produced even greater increases in instructional costs. Faculty salaries increased for all ranks, but more faculty were also moving into the higher, and more highly paid, ranks.

Table 2.4 shows that the portion of faculty members who are full professors increased steadily for two decades while the portion who are assistant professors, instructors, and lecturers declined. In many cases, the faculty which had been hired in the 1960s and 1970s, as the children of the baby boom attended college in record numbers, were now tenured and moving steadily up the salary ladder. This shifting alone increased college expenditures as lower paid employees were promoted to higher-paying positions.

Increasing Benefit Costs. The increases in the levels of faculty compensation were not all in the form of higher salaries. Since the mid-1980s, the fastest-growing expense at many colleges has been fringe benefits such as Social Security taxes (or contributions to state retirement systems) and health care costs. Workers compensation contributions and various types of malpractice insurance also have increased rapidly. While such costs have risen in all sectors of the economy, because college instruction is so labor-intensive, increases in the costs of faculty benefit packages have a disproportionate impact on instructional expenditures.

Table 2.5 shows how the cost of these fringe benefits has increased over twenty years both in real dollars and as a percent of average salary. The pattern is steadily upward. In 1992, the average price of the benefit package provided to faculty members had increased by more than 147 percent in two decades to more than $12,400. The value of these benefit packages now stands at one-quarter of the average faculty salary.

These increases in benefit costs created a paradoxical situation for many colleges and their faculties. In real terms, the purchasing power of faculty salaries increased relatively little during the decade. But because of the increases in the costs of fringe benefits, colleges were paying larger and larger amounts for overall faculty compensation. The result was that, from the point of view of the college, compensation costs were rising rapidly even as faculty were seeing only modest change in their take-home pay.

The Shift to Higher-Cost Majors. A final reason that college instructional expenditures have increased was driven by a shift in the types of courses and degree programs demanded by students since 1980.[13] As labor

Table 2.4

Distribution of Faculty by Rank: Selected Years, 1970–1993

Year	Instructor, Lecturer	Assistant Professor	Associate Professor	Full Professor
1970	16%	36%	24%	25%
1975	11	33	28	28
1980	10	29	29	32
1985	9	26	29	35
1990	9	27	28	36
1993	8	27	28	37

Source: *Academe*, "Annual Report on the Economic State of the Profession," in March/April of each year.

Table 2.5

Average Fringe Benefits of Faculty: Selected Years, 1970–1992
(in constant 1994 Dollars)

Year	Average Faculty Benefits	Benefits as a Percent of Average Faculty Salary
1970	$5,039	10%
1975	6,014	15
1980	7,210	18
1985	9,328	22
1990	11,086	24
1992	12,454	25

Source: *Academe*, "Annual Report on the Economic State of the Profession," in March/April of each year.

markets and student's interests shift, colleges must adjust their offerings accordingly or lose enrollments.

Among the fastest-growing fields during the 1980s were the higher-cost majors of computer science, engineering, and engineering technology, which require large capital outlays for equipment and laboratories.[14] The number of degrees awarded in business and communications also increased rapidly. As students shift into these high-demand fields, colleges must compete with business and industry to attract and retain qualified faculty. As a consequence, institutions must not only hire new faculty to staff these growing programs, they often must pay higher salaries in these growing fields.

Conversely, the lower-cost fields of study like education, letters, and the social sciences all experienced significant declines. The problem these trends presented is clear. Since all students pay the same level of tuition, these shifts in student demands presented colleges with higher costs without generating additional tuition revenues. Moreover, tenure rules and staffing policies make it nearly impossible for colleges to rapidly reduce their faculty in areas when student demand is declining. Colleges must continue to pay the staff in declining areas even as they add new staff in growing areas.[15]

Increasing Administrative Expenditures

Administration, as defined by the Department of Education, includes spending on student services and all academic support services except libraries. Next to instruction, administration is the largest expenditure category for most colleges and universities. It is also among the most rapidly growing. In real terms, expenditures for administration increased 48 percent at public colleges between 1975 and 1990. They increased a startling 78 percent at private colleges.

A substantial portion of these increases in administrative expenditures went towards developing new and expanded student services. Today most colleges provide career placement offices, tutoring and mentoring services, computer labs and computer support systems, child care centers, adult learning services, handicapped services, and honors programs. These administrative activities did not exist at most colleges twenty years ago, but now they are essential elements of even the smallest college.

Similarly, as government support has been reduced in the 1980s, both public and private colleges have been forced to more aggressively seek outside funding sources. Fund-raising campaigns are now large and permanent operations at most colleges and universities. In order to organize and carry out these efforts, development, foundation relations, government relations, and alumni affairs offices have been expanded.[16] These units have also professionalized their operations, and increased their status within the higher education community. As such, the cost of these activities has risen even more rapidly than their sheer numbers would indicate. In the long term, successful fund-raising campaigns may generate enough revenue to support their operation and more. But in the short term they are expensive undertakings which require staff and equipment, and add to a college's administrative expenditures.

To many observers, this growth of administrative expenditures seemed like an odd trend since the budget pressures of the last decade might have been expected to force colleges to seek ways to reduce administrative overhead.[17] To others, it seemed a genuinely dangerous development. Barbara Bergmann, past president of the American Association of University Professors (AAUP), argues that:

> the bloating of college administrations over the past decades has made administrative performance worse rather than better. It has bogged us down in reels of time-consuming and despair-creating red tape. It has fostered delusions of grandeur among some administrative higher-ups, whose egos have grown along with the size of their staffs under their supervision.[18]

Putting aside arguments over the merits of this administrative growth, there is little doubt that per-student spending on administration has increased rapidly since 1980 and that, at least in the short term, these increases have translated into higher prices for students.

Unfunded Government Mandates. A second source of higher administrative costs is the burden of responding to government regulation. In areas such as safety, health, pollution control, and financial accountability, government regulatory requirements are growing and additional professional and clerical staff are necessary to respond to new government requirements.[19] Examples of this are numerous. The Americans with Disabilities Act mandated that institutions make facilities accessible the disabled, but provided colleges with no funds to pay for the required improvements. Some of these costs were then passed on to the students. A similar pattern was evident in federal laws requiring new expenditures on pollution reduction equipment, on energy conservation programs, on hazardous waste disposal procedures, and on equal employment opportunity offices.

Many states have also passed laws which mandate such things as recycling programs, implementation of affirmative action guidelines, or more rigorous accounting procedures. These state mandates also require colleges to do more, but provide no new resources to cover their costs. Such laws and regulations may advance socially important goals. But by adding to the administrative costs of operating a college or university, they inadvertently contribute to rising college prices.

Increasing Research Expenditures

Colleges also rapidly increased their expenditures for research during the 1980s. This increase was particularly evident at public colleges and universities where research became a higher priority on many campuses. Certainly a part of this was that more public colleges began expecting their faculties to engage in research in order to secure promotion and tenure. This, in turn, required them to make additional expenditures in order to provide the human and physical capital necessary to allow the faculty to fulfill these expanded expectations.

But even universities with long traditions of research experienced rapid increases in the costs of their scholarly enterprises. The need to purchase new technology, and to hire and train staff to operate that technology, greatly added to the costs of many types of research. Equipment, laboratories, libraries, and even faculty offices all needed to be overhauled to accommodate technological advances. New equipment, even if donated, brings with it additional maintenance and training costs. As Carol Francis notes:

> New technology has added enormously to the capital costs of higher education on the administrative side as well as the teaching side. New technology has affected libraries, administrative services, student record keeping, and telecommunications. Not only did colleges and universities have to purchase new computers, but some of them had to rewire old buildings on campuses to handle the electrical loads.[20]

Certainly, all colleges have needed to make additional capital expenditures if they were to continue to attract the best faculties and advance the frontiers of knowledge. But research investments made by colleges and universities are fundamentally different than are private business investments in research. As Kent Halstead notes, industrial and commercial enterprises expect new investments in workers and technology to pay for themselves through increased productivity and profits. But in colleges and universities similar research investments in faculty and equipment generally do not produce corresponding increases in institutional revenues. Keeping up with the latest technology, providing faculty and students with state-of-the-art labs and facilities, and insuring that faculty have the opportunity to continually update their knowledge and skills are all essential if a college is to pursue a productive research agenda.[21] The question colleges have had to face since 1980 is how to finance these necessary, but costly, investments. The answer was often through higher tuitions.

Increased Institutional Student Aid Expenditures

As college tuitions increase, the costs of providing scholarships to a fixed number of students rises proportionately.[22] Higher tuitions also mean that a larger number of students, or potential students, cannot afford to attend without financial aid. These two factors have forced colleges to increase their spending on institutionally awarded financial aid.[23] As a consequence, such financial aid was the most rapidly growing expenditure category for private colleges, increasing by 129 percent between 1975 and 1992. Even at public colleges, expenditures on scholarships per FTE increased by 26 percent in that seventeen year period.

In aggregate terms, the growth of institutional student aid is even more stark. Between 1970 and 1980, total institutional aid awarded by colleges and universities fluctuated between $2.7 billion and $3.1 billion per year (in constant 1994 dollars). But by 1985, that figure had risen to $4.0 billion and was beginning to grow rapidly. As shown in table 2.6, institutionally awarded student aid mushroomed to $7.2 billion in 1992. This is an increase of 160 percent over twelve years. As a consequence, the National Institute of Independent Colleges and Universities estimated that today, "the amount of grants provided by independent institutions to undergraduates was greater than the amount of all federal grants combined."[24]

As colleges increase the amount of internal financial aid they award, they must find revenues to cover these new expenditures. The ironic consequence has been that institutional efforts to provide grants to disadvantaged students have driven up college costs and, in turn, driven up tuitions. This forces more students to seek institutional aid and puts additional pressure on colleges to provide more such aid. Many private colleges thus find themselves trapped in a cycle where the more need-based student aid they award, the more demand they create for additional need-based aid.

Table 2.6

Institutionally Awarded Student Aid: Selected Years, 1970–1992
(in constant 1994 Dollars)

Year	Institutionally Awarded Student Aid (in millions)	Institutionally Awarded Student Aid Per FTE Enrollment
1970	$3,123	$464
1975	3,124	369
1980	2,780	316
1985	4,038	451
1990	6,376	642
1992	7,250	691

Source: College Board, *Trends in Student Aid: 1983–1993* and author's calculations.

WERE THESE INCREASED EXPENDITURES NECESSARY?

Looked at in one way, this long list of increased expenditures provides a clear explanation for the rapid increases in the per-student expenditures of colleges since 1980. But, looked at in another way, these increased expenditures are not really a cause at all. Simply because college leaders chose to increase their spending does not mean those increases were necessary or justified. Many expenditure decisions are, more or less, under the control of college presidents, trustees, and/or state legislatures. Certainly increased expenditures associated with shifting faculty ranks or student majors, and those resulting from rising benefit costs and government mandates are difficult for campus and state policy-makers to control in the short term. But increased expenditures on administration, student services, faculty salaries, new technology, or institutionally awarded student aid are the result of explicit decisions by college leaders to spend more. These decisions were often followed by the implicit decision to pass those spending increases on to students in the form of higher tuitions.

Taking this view, Thomas Sowell argues that "[W]hen a college expends its range of expenses first, and then calls it 'increased costs' later, when seeking more money from various sources, this tends . . . to erode the very concept of living within one's means."[25] Sowell goes on to observe that:

> when parents are being asked to draw on the equity in their homes to pay rising tuition, it is not simply to cover the in-

creased cost of educating their children, but also to underwrite the many new boondoggles thought up by faculty and administrators, operating with little sense of financial constraints.[26]

College leaders counter that since 1980 they have been forced to pay more in order to provide a high-quality education. If they had chosen to spend less, they would have risked losing the best faculty to non-academic careers, providing students with inferior and outdated educations, compromising their standards, and tarnishing their reputations. As such, the long-term costs of reducing spending would be far greater than the rising tuitions they were forced to charge.

BIND #2: CHANGING REVENUE SOURCES

Changes in college's expenditure patterns account for only a portion of the tuition increases experienced since 1980. At least as significant were declines in the non-tuition revenues available to public colleges and universities. Public institutions of higher education derive their revenues primarily from student tuitions, state subsidies, federal aid, private gifts, and institutionally operated enterprises such as dormitories, food services, and hospitals. Private institutions receive their revenues from the same sources as public colleges albeit in a very different mix.

Table 2.7 shows how the revenue sources of both public and private higher education changed between 1970 and 1990. Public colleges and universities receive the majority of their revenue from state governments. The largest of these are instructional subsidies awarded to public colleges based on their enrollments. While the level of subsidy varies widely from state to state, the overall level of state support to higher education increased during the 1970s. The portion of public college revenues derived from state governments increased from 41 percent to 46 percent.

This increasing state support, along with a small increase in federal support, had an important impact on public college tuitions. As combined government revenues accounted for a larger share of public college revenues in the 1970s, institutions were able to reduce their reliance on tuition and fees. Indeed, during this period, the percent of total public college revenue derived from government increased from 58 to 63 percent and the percent derived from tuitions decreased from 15 to 13.

The reverse occurred after 1980. As states and the federal government decreased their share of total revenues, colleges increased the

Table 2.7

Revenue Sources of Institutions of Higher Education:
Selected Years 1970–1990

Percent of Current Fund Revenues by Source

	Public Colleges and Universities				
Revenue Sources	1970	1975	1980	1985	1990
Tuition and Fees	15%	13%	13%	15%	16%
Federal Government	12	15	13	11	10
State Government	41	45	46	45	42
Local Government	5	6	4	4	4
Private Gifts	2	2	3	3	4
Endowment Income	1	1	1	1	1
Sales & Services	18	18	20	20	22
Other Services	6	2	4	5	4

Percent of Current Fund Revenues by Source

	Private Colleges and Universities				
Revenue Sources	1970	1975	1980	1985	1990
Tuition and Fees	35%	37%	37%	39%	40%
Federal Government	15	19	19	18	16
State Government	1	2	2	2	3
Local Government	1	1	1	1	1
Private Gifts	10	10	9	9	9
Endowment Income	5	5	5	5	5
Sales & Services	24	23	23	23	23
Other Services	6	3	4	4	4

Source: *Digest of Education Statistics 1994*, Table 317 (Washington D.C.: GPO, 1992).

percent of their total revenue derived from tuition. But increased tuitions were not the only way public colleges responded to reductions in government support. Increased fund-raising produced increases in gift revenues. Expanded marketing and better financial controls have helped to increase the revenues derived from sales and services revenues. But these factors are relatively small when compared to changes in government support. Indeed, when government support is reduced, public colleges have little recourse other than to raise tuitions or cut programs.[27]

At private colleges, the changes in the revenue patterns were quite different. As a percent of total revenues, tuitions at private colleges increased steadily throughout both decades. This increase seemed to occur independently of changes in the level of government support. By 1990, private colleges derived 40 percent of their revenues from tuition.

Private colleges were also hit hard by the recession of the early 1980s. Private colleges receive a much smaller percent of their revenues from government. That percentage rose from about 17 in 1970 to about 22 in the 1970s but fell back to 20 by 1990. Private colleges, however, also experienced small reductions in the percent of revenues received from private gifts and from sales and services. As with public colleges, the contraction of non-tuition revenues left private institutions with little choice but to raise tuitions or reduce expenditures.

In attempting to explain the rising costs of private higher education since 1980, several studies have suggested that there was a subtle change in the pricing strategy employed by private college leaders during these years.[28] Michael O'Keefe has suggested that in the 1980s a few leading private institutions concluded that they had been underpriced relative to market value and that many of their students could pay more than they were being charged.[29]

Other institutions raised prices because they felt they needed to keep up with their competitors in the heightening competition for new students. In this regard, Halstead observes that:

> Some highly selective colleges believe they must match every improvement of their peer group if they were to remain competitive. Legitimate upgrading requirements always exist. In some areas, however, further improvements may be inconsistent with the institutions mission or sense of responsibility. Some may even be superfluous or extravagant. Matching the competition leads to what might be labeled a "price spiral" from which an individual institution may have difficulty breaking away.[30]

Changes in pricing policies at a few highly visible private colleges set off a chain reaction which was quickly followed by other private colleges. Large price increases were thus not confined to a small group of expensive institutions as a broad range of institutions shifted to the high-tuition/high-aid pricing strategy.

Trends in State Support for Higher Education

State governments supply more than 40 percent of the revenues available to public colleges. However, the level of state support has varied considerably over time. Table 2.8 shows how that aggregate state spending on higher education increased steadily throughout the two decades. While state support accounted for 41 percent of public college revenues in 1970, that percentage increased to 45 in 1980. On a per FTE basis, state support increased from $3,472 to $3,981. This rapidly growing state support was one of the principle reasons public colleges were able to hold the line on tuition increases during the 1970s.

While state support continued to grow in the early 1980s, it did not increase fast enough to compensate for the rapid increases in college expenditures taking place at that time. The portion of public college revenues derived from states dropped back to 42 percent in 1990, virtually the same place it had been in 1970. As a result of this leveling off of state support coupled with rising expenditures, public colleges began to shift a larger portion of their costs on to their students in the form of higher tuitions. Between 1980 and 1990, the percent of public college revenue derived from tuitions increased from 13 percent in 1980 to 16 percent in 1990. Thus, students were not simply paying more because colleges were spending more, but because of declining government support they were paying for a larger share of the total cost of their education.[31]

Trends in Voluntary Support of Higher Education

Colleges have always relied on the voluntary support of benefactors whether they were alumni, private philanthropists, corporations, or private foundations.[32] In 1992, voluntary contributions to higher education amounted to $10.7 billion. This was more than $1,000 per full-time equivalent student enrolled in a college or university. These dollars are used to fund capital improvements, subsidize current operations, and build endowments. They provide both public and private institutions with an important supplement to government support and tuition revenues.

As shown in table 2.9, aggregate voluntary support of higher education declined in the early 1970s. While private giving rebounded in the later part of the 1970s, voluntary support per student was 16 percent lower in 1981 than it had been in 1972. Because this decline came during

Table 2.8
State Support for Higher Education (in constant 1994 dollars)

Year	Total State Spending For Higher Education (in billions)	State Higher Education Spending Per FTE Enrollment
1970	$23.5	$3,472
1975	30.9	3,642
1980	35.1	3,981
1985	39.4	4,410
1990	41.6	4,195
1992	43.2	4,113

Source: Adapted from Edward Hines, *Appropriations: State Tax Funds for Operating Expenses of Higher Education* (Washington D.C.: National Association of State Universities and Land Grant Colleges, Annual). FTE data from *Digest of Education Statistics, 1994.*

Table 2.9
Voluntary Support for Higher Education (in constant 1994 dollars)

Year	Voluntary Support for Higher Education (in billions)	Voluntary Support for Higher Education per FTE Enrollment
1972[a]	$6.9	$945
1975	6.1	736
1980	7.1	815
1985	10.6	1,169
1990	10.7	1,079
1992	10.7	1,029

Source: *Voluntary Support for Higher Education, 1992* (New York: Council for Aid to Education, 1992). FTE data from *Digest of Education Statistics, 1994.*
[a] Earliest year for which data are available.

a period of decreasing college expenditures, increasing government support, and increasing enrollments, it did not translate into tuition increases.

Spurred by aggressive fund-raising efforts in the early 1980s, voluntary support increased in the early 1980s. In fact, voluntary support per FTE increased a dramatic 43 percent between 1980 and 1985. Again, the impact of private giving on tuitions was not immediately obvious.

Because state support was leveling off and college spending was increasing, tuitions were rising rapidly in spite of increasing private support.

The link between voluntary support and tuitions is most evident in the last half of the 1980s. After 1985, driven largely by changes in the tax code resulting from the Tax Reform Act of 1986, voluntary support for higher education slowed and the amount of voluntary support per FTE declined. While more colleges were devoting more time and attention to fund-raising during this period, those efforts were producing fewer dollars. This gave colleges even fewer resources to cover their increasing expenditures. Private gifts dropped from 9.3 percent of revenues at private colleges to 8.8 percent in the 1980s. Just as public colleges responded to reductions in state support by raising tuitions, private colleges compensated for the decline in voluntary support by expecting students to pay more.

BIND #3: FEWER COLLEGE-AGE STUDENTS

Arthur Hauptman and others have documented the central role that the decline in the number of traditional college-age students played in the rapid price increases at both public and private colleges. Table 2.10 shows that the number of 18–24-year-old Americans peaked around 1980 at about 30 million. Since that time the number began to decline and continued to decline until 1991 when it reached a low of about 24 million.

In his study of the causes of the tuition inflation of the 1980s, Hauptman notes that the fact there were fewer 18–24-year-olds forced colleges to work harder and to spend more in order to maintain or expand their enrollments. He notes that:

> institutions today invest much more in marketing than they ever did before. Today's colleges commonly send packets of printed materials to applicants, have enlarged their admissions staffs, and have taken other steps designed to lure students to their campuses. No doubt, these steps have accelerated the steep rise in the administrative costs of many institutions over the past decade.[33]

As a result of this increased attention to marketing and retention, the decline in the number of traditional college-age students has not translated into declining enrollments in the higher education system broadly. Indeed, in 1992 there were more students enrolled in America's

Table 2.10
Traditional College Populations: 1970–1993 (in thousands)

Year	All Persons 18-24 Year's Old	Annual High School Graduates	College Enrollment Rates of High School Graduates[a]
1970	23,688	2,889	51.8%
1980	28,965	3,020	49.3
1990	24,574	2,503	59.7
1993	26,133	2,513	62.6

Source: U.S. Census Bureau *Current Population Reports*, P 25-1104. High school graduates and college enrollment rates from *Digest of Education Statistics, 1994*.
[a] Enrollment in college as of October of each year for individuals, age 16–24, who graduated from high school in the previous twelve months.

colleges and universities than in any previous year. What has happened, however, is that colleges have increased the number of non-traditional students enrolled and increased the college participation and retention rates of their traditional students. Both of these efforts have required costly additions in marketing and recruitment programs, expanded campus child-care services, increased academic counseling and tutoring programs, and the development of off-campus programs.[34]

This decline in the number of traditional college-age students also set off an expensive competition among colleges to attract students. This competition put pressure on many colleges to continue to offer a full range of academic programs or even expand their offerings in order to appeal to the widest audience.[35] Under other circumstances, cost pressures might have led some colleges to reduce staff and programs. But institutions now feared that such reductions would diminish their ability to attract new students. Colleges thus may have raised prices to maintain programs and offerings rather than eliminate them and running the risk of losing enrollments to their competitors.[36]

CHANGES IN PRICING STRATEGIES

Faced with increasing expenditures and demands on the one hand, and declining revenues and a diminishing pool of traditional college age students on the other, colleges and universities struggled to find the best way to use their limited resources to hold down the net price they charged lower-income students, while maintaining the quality of their educational programs. This prompted a rexamination of tuition setting practices both on campuses and in statehouses. Many colleges chose to abandon the traditional low-tuition strategy in favor of a high-tuition/high-aid pricing strategy.

The Debate over Low-Tuition Pricing

Traditionally, most colleges attempted to keep their tuitions relatively low.[37] The logic behind this pricing strategy was lower prices would maximizes enrollment from all economic groups. That high enrollment should, in turn, produce a diverse student body and encourage upward social mobility for low-income residents.[38] The low tuition approach to achieving college affordability has a long and distinguished history. In 1947, President Truman's Commission on Higher Education recommended the elimination of all tuition and required fees for the first two years of public higher education.[39] The Carnegie Commission on Higher Education put forth a similar plan in 1973.[40]

Recently, however, a number of analysts have began to question the continued value of the low-tuition approach to college affordability.[41] Frederick Fisher, for example, argues that:

> A low tuition policy by itself does not promote equal opportunity. Just the opposite. It provides a subsidy that increases as income rises, while providing insufficient assistance to provide the poor with real opportunity. It is manifestly and grossly inequitable.[42]

This criticism of the low-tuition approach to college affordability is based on two factors. The first is the growing difficulty many colleges now face in attracting the non-tuition revenues necessary to keep tuitions low. This is exacerbated by rising costs and increasing student demands. Given the fiscal strains facing colleges today, a low-tuition policy may simply be too expensive to maintain. Thomas Mortenson, for example, argues that:

> There is not enough money available to continue subsidizing the higher educations of students from affluent family incomes who do not "need" those subsidies when those subsidies compromise higher education opportunity for those from low and middle in-

come family backgrounds. The time for low tuition has clearly passed, if indeed there ever was a sound argument for it.[43]

The other factor which has drawn the low-tuition approach into question is the growing realization that costs other than tuition are the major economic barrier to higher education for lower-income students.[44] Accordingly, even if a college could afford to limit tuition increases, potential lower-income students would still face significant price barriers to college. The bills for room, board, books, transportation, child care, and medical insurance may well be too great for many low- and middle-income families to afford, even when tuitions are low.

High-Tuition/High-Aid Pricing

To some, a more cost-effective way to improve college affordability is to allow (or even encourage) tuitions to rise and then channel the resulting revenue to lower-income students as need-based financial aid. By awarding need-based grants, colleges can reduce the net price facing their lower-income students.

For public colleges, one advantage of providing grant aid directly to students is that the states do not provide a subsidy to upper-income students who do not need the assistance to attend college. Another advantage of need-based aid is the amount of choice it provides to lower-income students. Whereas students must attend a public institution to benefit from instructional subsidies, students can often apply need-based grants to private and out-of-state schools.[45]

By allocating a larger portion of their tuition revenues to student grants, colleges can improve affordability for lower-income students even as their tuitions are rising. But this occurs only if they increase their need-based grant programs by an amount sufficient to compensate for the higher tuition rates. If, on the other hand, a college increases its grant spending more slowly than tuitions rise, that college will become less affordable to their lower-income residents instead of more affordable.

This high-tuition/high-aid funding strategy also has its critics. Their concern is not that grants are an inefficient mechanism to target dollars to lower-income students. They are. Rather, critics argue that the high-tuition/high-aid strategy ignores important psychological and political realities. As such, a plan which may look good in an economics class may prove counterproductive in the real world of college finance. In this view, lower-income students are likely to become discouraged by rapid increases in the "sticker price" of higher education.[46] This occurs because information about tuition levels is much more widely known and available than is information about financial aid programs. Moreover, the amount of aid any student is eligible to receive is not determined until the year before that student enters college. Because of the perceived high prices, prospective students may judge college to be beyond their families' financial reach years before they can even apply for student aid. The result might thus be a reduction in a state's college participation rate, even as the net price of public higher education in that state declines.

Perhaps a more serious concern is whether or not a college can maintain the consensus necessary to fully fund a high-tuition/high-aid strategy over several years. The danger here is that in the years after campus leaders let public tuitions rise, the grant programs could begin to erode due to lack of political support.[47] In the annual (or biennial) budget battle, any program needs powerful supporters to survive. Grants for lower-income students may lack that support. If this happens, the promise of a high-tuition/high-aid strategy could easily be transformed into a high-tuition/low-aid nightmare. Rather than purchasing increased access at a bargain price, the result could be decreased access for lower-income and disadvantaged students.

THE CONSEQUENCES OF THE TRIPLE BIND: SHIFTING PAYMENT RESPONSIBILITIES

There is thus no single reason for the rapid college price increases since 1980. The combination of increasing costs, new demands, and changing demographic forces drove up the costs of operating public colleges and universities more rapidly than the non-tuition revenues available to these institutions to meet those costs. Increasing compensation and technology costs as well as expensive efforts to attract and retain an ever scarcer number of students drove college expenditures up. Simultaneously, federal support was declining and increasing state and voluntary support was insufficient to make up the difference. Faced with this triple bind, many college leaders abandoned the traditional low-tuition pricing strategy and

Table 2.11
Changing Percentage of Financing Burden for Postsecondary Education: 1970–1990

| | Percent of Total Burden | | | | |
	1970	1975	1980	1985	1990
Federal Gov't	17	24	18	12	11
State & Local					
Government	23	25	25	24	23
Philanthropy	6	5	5	5	6
Family	48	39	43	49	49
Parent	34	23	23	29	31
Student	14	16	20	20	18
Other	4	7	9	10	11

Source: National Commission on Responsibilities for Financing Higher Education, *Final Report: Making College Affordable Again.*

shifted to the high-tuition/high-aid model. The result was rising tuitions at all types of colleges and rapidly rising tuitions at most.

These changes in the system of college finance fundamentally altered the way that the nation, families, and students pay for higher education. In 1992, the National Commission on the Responsibility for Financing Higher Education issued its final report.[48] Part of what they found, shown in table 2.11, illustrates how colleges have adjusted to the problems of increasing cost, declining government revenues, and a changing student body.

The commission estimated that the proportion of the total cost of college paid by families declined from 48 percent to 43 percent in the 1970s. This decline in the share paid by the family was the direct result of aggressive government action to remove cost barriers to college. But as governments moved away from that commitment after 1980, the share of total cost paid by the family increased to 49 percent. That percent is now higher than it had been at any time in twenty years.

When examined in the context of the rising tuition rates of the 1980s, the pattern is clear. Colleges and universities are in the process of shifting the costs of their operations from governments to students and their families. Historically, of course, the U.S. system of higher education always has placed the primary financial responsibility for paying for college with the family. But beginning in 1965, the federal government began to relieve that burden through increased funding of student aid. State governments also began to assume a larger portion of the overall costs of higher education by increasing their spending on both student aid and instructional subsidies to public colleges and universities. These impressive government efforts during the 1970s significantly reduced the price burdens placed on families. However, these government gains were almost totally undone in the 1980s and 1990s. Today, in spite of the continuing efforts of federal and state governments, families are paying an ever larger share of higher education costs through increased tuitions.

THE FUTURE OF COLLEGE PRICES

The future of college prices leaves little reason for lower- and middle-income families to be optimistic. The factors driving college prices up—rising expenditures, reduced non-tuition revenues, and a declining student base—will be very difficult to change. The development of new technologies and the emergence of new fields of study should continue to drive college expenditures up. Faculty salaries, which have increased steadily since 1980, still remain below 1970 levels and upward pressures on salaries are likely to continue. Rapidly rising health care costs will continue to drive up the price of providing benefits to faculty and staff. And each additional tuition hike increases the cost of institutionally awarded student aid and heightens the pressures on college leaders to expand their aid programs to mitigate the impact of increasing prices.

The revenue picture facing colleges is even more bleak. State governments are burdened with rising costs for health care, prison construction and operation, elementary and secondary education, and rebuilding their crumbling infrastructures. Higher education must compete with these other pressing social needs in a statehouse environment of fiscal restraint. In the search for private funding sources, institutions must now compete with other colleges, with private charities, and with a growing number of non-profit organizations. This will make fund-raising both more expensive and potentially less productive.

The number of traditional college-age students does present a ray of hope. The number of Americans between 18 and 24 years of age will begin to increase slowly during the last half of the 1990s and rapidly thereafter. If this growth leads to increased enrollments it will allow colleges to spread their fixed costs out over a larger number of students. It will also reduce the intense pressure to compete for new students.

But even the demographic trends are a mixed blessing. The labor market demands of the next decade will force more non-traditional students back to college. These returning students will demand that colleges provide them with high-tech educational facilities, offer courses and programs to accommodate their work schedules, meet their child-care needs, and often provide remedial English and English as a second language programs. As Carol Francis noted in a recent study conducted for the American Association of State Colleges and Universities:

> On balance, there will be considerably greater external economic pressures pushing tuitions higher in the 1990s than there are restraints holding them down. Consequently, in establishing tuition levels, management's challenge will be to balance the internal educational imperatives and aspirations against the external economic trends.[49]

In this context, colleges are left with two unpleasant choices if they hope to hold down tuitions and still maintain the quality of their academic programs. First, they can seek to greatly increase their revenues either from new or expanded government programs or from philanthropic or corporate sources. This will be difficult because more and more colleges will be competing for the same funds.[50]

Alternatively, colleges can find ways to improve efficiency or control costs which allow them to keep expenditures stable. This will also be difficult. Many of the forces which are driving college expenditures up are beyond the control of campus or state leaders. Even those forces which can be controlled, such as salary and administrative costs, cannot be reduced in the short term due to legal constraints and political pressures.[51]

In the absence of either of these alternatives, more colleges are likely to embrace the high-tuition/high-aid funding model which implicitly shifts the financing burden to middle- and upper-income students and their families. If colleges continue to experience rapid increases in their costs of operation and are unable to devise effective ways to control administrative, institutional, and research expenditures, tuitions will continue their upward spiral. As a consequence, the real question of the next decades won't be whether tuitions will go up, but rather how fast will they go up and how will families and society pay those costs.

3

THE CHANGING COURSE
OF COLLEGE AFFORDABILITY

The fact that college prices have risen dramatically in recent years is undeniable.[1] But the view that these price increases are a cause for concern is not universally shared. The affordability of higher education is determined by much more than just the price listed in the college catalogue. It is also a function of the ability of families to pay for those prices. Terry Hartle, for example, argued that college prices did not present families with an appreciably higher burden relative to income in 1986 than they did in 1980.[2]

Similarly, in a study commissioned by the State Higher Education Executive Officers, John Wittstruck and Stephen Bragg concluded that the problem of college affordability had been exaggerated. They provide evidence that:

> tuition and fees at public institutions of higher education represent a lower percentage of per capita disposable income in 1988 than it was in 1973. And student financial aid is much more prevalent in 1988 than it was in 1973.[3]

Wittstruck and Bragg argue that during the 1970s, incomes increased far more rapidly than college prices. It was not until the 1980s when these trends reversed and college price surpassed family incomes. But the cumulative outcome of these two decades of change was that college prices and incomes were left, in 1988, in about the same relative positions as they had been in 1973. As such, concerns over affordability may be little more than an artifact of the public's "short-term memory."[4] This view is sup-

51

ported by the annual survey of the attitudes of college freshman. In 1988, the percentage of freshmen who expressed concern over their families' financial ability to pay for college remained almost the same as it had been in 1968.[5]

COMPARING COLLEGE PRICES WITH FAMILY RESOURCES

In order to shed some light on changes in the real price of higher education, I compare trends in the price of college with trends in the principal financial resources available to low-income families to pay for college: family income and savings, Pell grants, federally guaranteed student loans, and grants from state governments. My objective here is to look beyond the posted college prices and trace the more important course of net college price, or what might be called college affordability, in light of all of the major resources available to families between 1970 and 1992.

Family Income: Selecting the Proper Measure

Most families pay for college with their income, either from their present earnings or from savings taken from their past earnings. But while college prices are relatively easy to measure, income trends are not. The two most commonly used income measures are per capita income and median family income. The former is calculated by dividing national pre-tax income by the total of every man, woman, and child in the country. It reflects changes in the incomes of families and individuals. The latter is found by locating the mid-point in the distribution of family incomes.

During most times, the two measures move in the same direction. But since the mid-1970s, demographic forces have caused these two measures to diverge sharply. Per capita income increased at a steady pace, while median family income remained stable. During the 1970s and into the early 1980s, birth rates began to fall, the age of first marriage increased, labor force participation increased, and the baby-boom generation left home and entered the work-force.[6] As a consequence, family size decreased and more individuals lived outside of traditional family units. Moreover, incomes at the top of the distribution increased at a very rapid rate.[7] Each of these forces caused measures of per capita income to continue to increase while median family income did not.[8]

There is no question that the drop in family size produced an increase in the purchasing power of family income. As Gillespie and Carlson point out:

> Mean family size dropped about 12 percent from 1965 to 1981. A decline in family size means that income is spread over a smaller number of family members. All other things being equal, a 12 percent decrease in family size means that about 13 percent more income is available to each family member.[9]

In the following analysis I use measures of family income rather than per capita income. This is because I view family income to be a more accurate indicator of changes in the income available to a family of the same size at different points in time. Indeed, from the perspective of the family who hoped to send a child to college, the growth in per capita income was of little comfort. The fact that fewer people were having children and living in traditional families did not mean that traditional families had more financial resources. It only meant that the per capita measure of income made it appear as if they did. What was of greater consequence to lower-income families was what had happened to family incomes.

Trends in Family Income

As was the case with college prices, when trends in median family income are examined, two distinct periods can be seen.[10] Beginning after the Second World War and continuing through the early 1970s, the incomes of American families increased at a steady pace. In 1950, the median income of American families was less than $20,000. By 1970, it had risen to $36,468. This increase allowed each succeeding generation to afford a standard of living which had been beyond the reach of their parents. It also placed public higher education within the unassisted financial reach of an ever larger number of American families.

As shown in table 3.1, however, since 1970 growth in family income had slowed considerably. In 1992, the median income of an American family was $40,051. This was an overall increase of less than ten percent in twenty-two years.

Not only has the median family income stagnated since the mid-1970s, families at the bottom of the distribution experienced real declines

Table 3.1

Median Family Income: 1970–1992 (in constant 1994 dollars)

1970	$36,468
1975	37,263
1980	38,992
1985	39,346
1990	41,290
1992	40,051

Source: U.S. Census Department, Money Income of Households, Families, and Persons in the United States, 1992.

Table 3.2

Mean Family Income by Quintiles: 1970–1992 (in constant 1994 dollars)

Year	Lowest Fifth	Second Fifth	Third Fifth	Fourth Fifth	Highest Fifth
1970	$10,837	$24,304	$35,142	$47,402	$81,515
1975	11,102	24,177	36,026	49,332	84,284
1980	11,094	24,915	37,741	52,366	89,670
1985	10,524	24,705	38,217	54,777	98,584
1990	11,146	25,999	40,039	57,582	107,013
1992	10,252	24,644	38,837	56,353	104,810

Source: U.S. Census Department, Money Income of Households, Families, and Persons in the United States, 1992.

in their income. Table 3.2 shows the changes in the distribution of American family income by quintile. The declining position of low-income families can be seen examining the incomes of the lowest fifth of the income distribution. The mean family income of this group stood at $11,102 in 1975. By 1992, it had dropped to $10,252.

To a lesser degree, the same pattern was evident among lower-middle income families. In 1970, the mean income of this second-fifth of the distribution was $24,304. It increased to $24,644 in 1992. This was an increase of less than 2 percent in twenty-two years.

In terms of college affordability, these family income trends paint a disturbing picture. Between 1970 and 1992, the incomes of the lowest-income families declined and the incomes of lower-middle-income families remained stable. When college prices began to rise after 1980, these families were required to spend an increasingly large portion of their incomes to purchase the same amount of higher education.

Table 3.3
Savings as a Percent of Disposable Personal Income: 1970–1992

Year	Personal Savings Rate
1970	7.4%
1975	7.7
1980	7.9
1985	6.4
1990	4.2
1992	5.3

Source: Council of Economic Advisors, *Economic Indicators: Report of the Congressional Joint Economic Committee*, published monthly.

Family Savings Rates

Income is not the only personal financial resource families use to pay for college.[11] Indeed, very few families are able to meet the entire price of college out of their current year income. They use the savings they have accumulated over the years. By saving progressively larger portions of their incomes each year, it is possible that some families were able to increase their wealth in spite of a stagnant income. Recent evidence, however, indicates that savings rates have, instead, declined over the past twenty years and thus further exacerbated the college affordability problem.

The U.S. government calculates what is generally called the "national savings rate." This figure is determined by subtracting taxes and spending from aggregate personal income. The remainder is said to constitute total national savings. This figure is then converted to a percent of national after-tax income. While this national savings rate is not directly comparable to the income figures discussed previously, it does provide a reasonable estimate of changes in the savings patterns of Americans over time.

Table 3.3 shows that during the 1970s, the national savings rate held steady at between 7 and 8 percent of disposable income. But since 1980, the national savings rate has dropped steadily. By 1990 the national savings rate was less than less than 5 percent. While the savings rate increased slightly in the early 1990s, American families today were able to save a smaller percentage of their stagnant incomes to pay for college than they had two decades ago. Moreover, this reduced savings rate creates an even greater concern for college affordability in the future. Because today's savings are used to pay for tomorrow's college education, this decline may mean college will pose an ever greater strain on family resources in the years ahead.

GOVERNMENT EFFORTS TO IMPROVE AFFORDABILITY: AN OVERVIEW

Governments have two principle mechanisms to help families and individuals pay for college.[12] First, states provide subsidies to public colleges to allow them to keep tuitions low. But in spite of these subsidies, public college prices have been increasing rapidly since 1980. Second, the federal government also plays a role in keeping college affordable. By providing grants to lower income students and subsidized and guaranteed loans to low- and middle-income students. These grant and loan programs were created with the explicit purpose of removing price barriers to college. In judging changes in the affordability of a college education, it is critical to examine the impact of the student aid and student loan programs.

The Federal Student Aid Programs

As recently as thirty years ago, the federal government provided almost no general purpose assistance to the families of lower-income college students. Except for special programs which provided federal aid to veterans or to students studying in areas judged to be of critical national interest, paying for college was the responsibility of the family and the student.

In 1964, direct federal aid to college students amounted to less than $0.5 billion. But since 1965, the federal government has developed several programs to assist the children of low- and middle-income families to attend college. The primary vehicle to achieve this improved access was Title IV of the Higher Education Act of 1965, which created grant, loan, and loan-guarantee programs intended to target federal dollars to college students. Since 1965, the federal government has made more than $200 billion in direct aid available to lower-income students. This aid was awarded primarily in the form of Pell grants which go directly to students from low-income families and student loans which allow lower-income students to take out subsidized and guaranteed loans.

Table 3.4
Pell Grants: 1975–1993 (in constant 1994 dollars)

Year	Grant Recipients (in 1,000s)	Grant Dollars Per Recipient	Maximum Grant Award
1975	1,228	$1,975	$3,742
1980	2,708	1,598	3,023
1985	2,813	1,728	2,863
1990	3,405	1,596	2,544
1993	4,177	1,534	2,392

Source: The College Board, *Trends in Student Aid: 1983–1993* (Washington D.C.: The College Board, 1993); and D. Gillespie and N. Carlson *Trends in Student Aid: 1963–1983* (Washington D.C., The College Board, 1983).

Pell Grants and Low-Income Students

The Pell grant program, originally called the Basic Educational Opportunity Grant, was created in the Education Amendments of 1972. It was intended to be the primary source of federal aid to needy college students. The amount of the grant is calculated by a needs-test in which the estimated financial contribution of the family is subtracted from the price of the college chosen. The difference between the estimated family contribution and the college price is the amount of student need.

The actual Pell grant awarded is not always the same as the student need. Pell grants can only be used to cover a fixed portion of college prices. The limit was 50 percent from the creation of the program until 1986, when it was increased to 60 percent. As such, even the most needy students attending the lowest-priced colleges must use other resources to pay for 40 percent of the cost of their higher education.

Between its creation in 1972 and 1980, the Pell grant program was expanded several times to provide larger grants to more students. Table 3.4 shows that the number of federal Pell grant recipients increased from 1.2 million to 2.8 million between 1975 and 1980. That growth in the number of recipients continued to more than four million in 1993.

But in spite of the rapid growth in the number of Pell grant recipients, the value of the program to the most needy students has declined since 1980. The size of the average Pell grant dropped by more than $400 between 1975 and 1993. Similarly, the size of the maximum Pell grant, the grant awarded to the most needy students, declined by almost one-third since 1970. Thus, as the price of college was rising, the size of most Pell grants was actually declining.

Even the increasing number of grant recipients was a mixed blessing to most lower-income students. Changes in program eligibility made it easier for students with higher family incomes to qualify for Pell grants. As a consequence, even as the total number of recipients was rising, the percent of lower-income students who were receiving grants was dropping. In a 1988 study, Thomas Mortenson estimated that among first-year college students from families with incomes below the poverty level, the proportion which receive a Pell grant declined from 49 percent in 1980 to 34 percent in 1986. Among families from "modest" incomes (defined in the study as families with an income of between 101 to 200 percent of the poverty line), the proportion receiving Pell grants declined from 44 percent to 28 percent. But families with "comfortable" incomes (those earning 200 percent of the poverty level), the percentage of students receiving Pell grants declined by only five percentage points[13]. Mortenson concludes that the changes in the Pell grant program "shifted the focus of Pell grants away from lowest resource aid applicants towards applicants from more middle income backgrounds."[14] The outcome of these changes was a significant loss of Pell grant purchasing power for those who were the original focus of the program.

There is no doubt that since its creation, the Pell grant has provided the children of low-income families with an important new financial resource to pay for college. This was especially true during the 1970s when the size of the grants was growing faster than college prices. But since 1980, as college prices increased much more rapidly than the incomes of lower- and middle-income families, the Pell grant program did not grow in ways which compensated for those reductions. More students were receiving Pell grants each year, but the purchasing power of both the maximum grant and the average grant were declining. As a consequence, the already limited value of the program has been badly eroded.

Federal Student Loans and Lower-Income Students

Since 1980, both family incomes and federal grants have lagged behind college prices for those at the lower end of the income distribution. As a

Table 3.5
Stafford Loans: 1970–1993 (in constant 1994 dollars)

Year	Borrowers[a] (in 1,000s)	Loan Dollars Per Borrower	Maximum Loan Per Year[b]
1970	1,017	$3,124	$8,500
1975	922	3,079	6,241
1980	2,904	3,057	4,250
1985	3,536	3,040	3,260
1990	3,689	2,841	2,836
1993	4,071	2,750	2,650

Source: The College Board, *Trends in Student Aid: 1983–1993* (Washington D.C.: The College Board, 1993); and D. Gillespie and N. Carlson *Trends in Student Aid: 1963–1983* (Washington D.C., The College Board, 1983).
[a]Borrowers through the Stafford loan, PLUS and SLS loans. Borrowers through the Perkins loan program are not included.
[b]Maximum Subsidized Stafford loan available to first year students.

consequence, a larger percentage of these families began borrowing a larger amount of money to pay those prices.[15] Federally guaranteed student loans were the principle source of this capital.

The original federally guaranteed student loan program was created in 1965 in order to allow middle-income students to more easily finance the price of higher education through private lenders. It was envisioned by its creators as a small, supplementary program which would operate at a small cost to the federal treasury.[16] But as the gap between family resources and college prices increased, public pressure mounted to make guaranteed loans available to more families.

Responding to this public pressure, federal policy-makers took a series of actions to increase eligibility for federally guaranteed loans during the 1970s. This expansion culminated in 1978 when, with the passage of the Middle Income Student Assistance Act, Congress removed the needs test and made all full-time students eligible for federally subsidized college loans. This set off a dramatic increase in the number of students participating in the program. As shown in table 3.5, between 1970 and 1980, the number of student-borrowers increased from 1 million to 2.9 million. But even as the number of borrowers increased, the real value of the average loan remained stable at about $3,000 per year.

As the total costs of the federal student loan programs spiraled upward after 1978, federal policy-makers moved to cap program eligibility and control costs. Among other limitations, the needs test to qualify for a loan was reinstituted in 1981. In spite of these efforts, however, the number of student loans and the total cost of the program continued to grow throughout the 1980s and into the 1990s.[17] This caused concern that the rapidly rising student loan costs were diverting funds away from the grant programs.[18] In the early 1980s, each additional dollar going to student loans seemed to result in a dollar less for the grant program.

While more and more students have borrowed through the guaranteed student loan program, it too has become a progressively less valuable resource for low- and lower-middle-income families. This is because the real value of the maximum subsidized guaranteed student loan has decreased steadily since its creation. Between 1972 and 1987, the maximum amount which any undergraduate student was allowed to borrow in a year was frozen at $2,500. In 1987 that amount was raised to $2,650/year for first- and second-year students and $4,000/year for second- and third-year students. In 1992 that amount was increased to $3,500 a year for second-year students and $5,500 a year for third- through fifth-year students. This increase was not enough to keep pace with consumer inflation, let alone tuition inflation.

In a study of the impact of increased loan utilization by low-income students, Mortenson argues that:

> Higher education is a far riskier investment decision for low-income students because they characteristically demonstrate less promise for academic success, and hence are less likely to earn the higher incomes following graduation that enable them to repay their loan obligations.[19]

The pre-college family income of students is strongly correlated with their eventual success in college. Students from lower-income families are much less likely to finish college and those who finish are less likely to do well.[20]

The impact of increased borrowing among potential students from low-income families goes beyond the dampening effect it has on their propensity to enroll in school. Students from disadvantaged groups may be just as willing to borrow as other students, but because of continuing disparities in income between white males on the one hand and women and minorities on the other, even after adjusting for differences in education and work experience, the latter will eventually find their loans more burdensome to repay. Put simply, they must use a larger portion of their income to repay a loan of the same size.

Another impact the increased reliance on college loans may have on low-income students is that, unlike grants, they must be repaid with interest. An undergraduate student who takes out the maximum guaranteed student loan for four years would face a debt of almost $18,000 after graduation.[21] For a low-income student, the prospect of such large debt re-inserts the price barriers to higher education which the financial aid programs were designed to remove.[22] Worse still, such loans actually add to those price barriers by adding interest charges to the amount borrowed.

Finally, Carol Francis estimated the impact college borrowing might have on the post-college asset positions of students.[23] She compared the situations of two similar students, one who borrowed $10,000 to attend college and the other who did not. She found that at the end of the fifteen year term of the loan, the non-borrower would hold four to six times more in assets than the borrower. This capital can be used to buy a house or start a business. Thus, while student loans were designed to provide potential students with the choice of a wider range of institutions, the growth of these programs as a principle way for low-income students to pay for their education may serve to "exacerbate the income inequality that the education was supposed to mitigate in the first place."[24]

TRENDS IN STATE STUDENT ASSISTANCE

State governments also operate financial aid programs which students can use to pay for college.[25] The various state student-assistance programs are not nearly as large as the federal aid programs. In 1994, for example, states awarded a total $2.0 billion in grants to college students. This compares to $6.1 billion in Pell grants and $15.0 billion in federally guaranteed loans awarded during the same year. Still, despite their relatively small size, it is possible that as the growth in incomes and federal aid slowed after 1980, the states were able to provide enough new college aid to make college more affordable for lower-income families.

Finding trends in the state programs which provide grants to college students is a difficult matter. There is much variety in the structure, operation, and eligibility requirements of the programs from state to state. Since an identical student would be eligible for a grant in one state and

Table 3.6

State Grant Dollars Awarded per State Resident (in constant 1994 dollars)

State	1970	1980	1990	1992
Alabama	–	$0.57	$3.24	$3.43
Alaska	–	1.08	4.42	3.59
Arizona	–	1.36	1.06	.95
Arkansas	–	1.95	2.26	5.03
California	2.77	7.23	6.09	7.84
Colorado	–	4.33	6.80	8.40
Connecticut	1.87	4.20	11.37	11.48
Florida	.64	2.41	5.07	5.90
Georgia	–	1.53	3.85	3.56
Hawaii	–	1.24	6.00	6.25
Idaho	–	1.05	.71	.79
Illinois	10.48	13.70	19.90	19.29
Indiana	2.15	7.84	12.09	9.67
Iowa	4.23	10.16	23.95	23.44
Kansas	.21	3.84	3.43	2.81
Kentucky	–	3.39	4.18	7.86
Louisiana	–	.38	2.44	3.97
Maine	–	2.03	1.89	4.32
Maryland	2.51	2.51	5.18	4.89
Massachusetts	2.23	5.13	25.13	6.98
Michigan	5.03	6.21	8.81	9.45
Minnesota	1.40	14.15	18.29	19.07
Mississippi	–	2.69	.82	.51
Missouri	–	3.72	3.85	4.09
Montana	–	.99	.59	.62

not be eligible in another, it is impossible to talk about the grant a typical student would receive. As such, the discussion of state aid cannot be folded directly into a comprehensive discussion of college affordability.

The 1970s were a period of unparalleled growth in state student aid programs. In 1970, only twenty-one states had programs which provided state appropriated funds to college students in the form of grants. By 1975, all fifty states were operating such programs. The principle stimulus for that expansion was the creation of the State Student Incentive Grant (SSIG) program in the Higher Education Amendments of 1972.[26] This

Table 3.6 (*continued*)

State	1970	1980	1990	1992
Nebraska	–	1.33	1.46	1.56
Nevada	–	.81	.43	.33
New Hampshire	–	1.13	1.75	1.47
New Jersey	8.69	10.72	13.25	16.28
New Mexico	–	1.15	5.85	9.60
New York	13.19	27.23	26.92	28.18
North Carolina	–	5.31	8.91	5.61
North Dakota	–	1.67	2.76	3.17
Ohio	2.87	5.26	8.04	8.31
Oklahoma	–	1.42	11.19	12.98
Oregon	.29	4.92	4.42	4.38
Pennsylvania	15.63	12.60	12.78	14.09
Rhode Island	6.21	8.64	13.62	10.03
South Carolina	–	7.20	6.37	5.49
South Dakota	–	.32	.95	.51
Tennessee	–	2.71	4.58	3.69
Texas	–	2.07	7.25	8.42
Utah	–	2.07	6.79	.85
Vermont	10.59	18.06	23.09	21.12
Virginia	–	3.90	4.90	4.52
Washington	.39	2.46	3.47	5.26
West Virginia	.50	2.93	7.17	8.63
Wisconsin	2.44	8.90	9.65	9.84
Wyoming	–	1.11	.54	.51
Nation	3.34	6.74	9.56	11.44

Source: National Association of State Scholarship and Grant Programs, *Annual Survey Report* Annual 1970–1992.

federally funded program provided dollar-for-dollar matching funds to states for the expansion of grants to undergraduate students.

The growth in state spending on student grants was evident almost everywhere. By 1980, all fifty states were awarding more grants, and appropriating more dollars for those grants than they had a decade before. As shown in table 3.6, all states, except Pennsylvania, increased their grant spending per resident between 1970 and 1980. Indeed, state grant spending per resident more than doubled during the decade. This expansion in state grant spending mirrored the growth in the federal student aid programs. Moreover, because that growth came at a time when college prices were largely stable, the purchasing power of state grants did not erode throughout the decade. The result was that during the 1970s, state grants provided students in nearly every state a significant new resource to pay for college.

Unlike the federal student aid programs, state spending on student aid continued to grow steadily, at least in the aggregate, during the 1980s. By 1990, every state was spending more on student aid than they had in 1980 and thirty-seven states were spending more per resident. In combination, state spending on student grants increased by 50 percent over the decade. Yet, this growth was not as rapid as was tuition inflation. As a result, the purchasing power of those grants was declining even as state spending was increasing.

The 1980s also produced wide variation in the size of state grants. Some states, such as Connecticut, Iowa, Massachusetts, and Oklahoma, increased their grant programs quite rapidly. Residents in these states received substantial increases in their resources to pay for college. At the same time, Arizona, Kansas, Mississippi, and Oregon, among others, reduced their grants spending per resident even as their public colleges were significantly increasing their tuitions. Residents in these states thus experienced resource reductions during the decade.

The early 1990s brought an even more troubling trend in state grant spending. In aggregate, state grant spending per resident continued to increase. But nearly half of the states experienced reductions in their grant spending per resident between 1990 and 1992. These states were unable to maintain their level of grant spending even as they were raising public college tuitions. Of greater concern, Massachusetts, Utah, and Rhode Island experienced such dramatic reductions in their grant programs that it called in to question their commitment to removing college price barriers.

By the mid-1990s, states were providing more money for student grants than at any time in history. But those increases were not large enough to compensate for combination of rapid tuition inflation and stable levels of federal student aid. Increased state grant spending produced important new resources to help lower- and middle-income students pay for college. In some states, those new resources may have opened college opportunities for students who could not otherwise afford college. But in most states, these programs grow far too slowly to provide lower- and middle-income students with sufficient additional resources to cover their rising college costs.

COLLEGE PRICES AND FAMILY RESOURCES:
PUTTING THE PIECES TOGETHER

In order to get a clearer view of how these trends in prices and resources have altered the overall affordability of higher education, it is useful to consider their cumulative impact on some hypothetical families. There is, of course, no such thing as a typical family. Each family possesses a unique set of resources in their efforts to pay for college. But based on some simple assumptions, I compare college prices with the resources available to a low-, middle-, and upper-income family considering sending one dependent child to a private university, a public university, or a public two-year college in 1970, 1980, and 1992.

Case #1: The Low-Income Family

As used here, a "low-income family" is one with an income equal to the mean income of the lowest quintile of American families. In each of the years considered, this income level would qualify a student from such a family for the maximum Pell grant. The analysis further assumes that the student is willing to finance as much of the remaining price as possible.

The net price of college is defined here as the average college price minus the actual Pell grant. Seen another way, net price is the total a family must pay or borrow in order to meet college prices.[27] This change in college affordability is shown in table 3.7.

In 1970, the situation facing the low-income family considering private higher education was discouraging. The average price of a private four-year university was $12,262. The Pell grant program had not yet been established, so the family would need to borrow the entire amount. But in order to pay for a year at a private university, even the maximum federally guaranteed student loan would not be nearly enough. In 1970, even with the maximum loan, that family would still face $3,762 of unmet need in order to pay the price of a private university.

By 1980, the picture for this low-income family had improved greatly. Family income had declined. However, a combination of lower-college prices and the now available Pell grant had reduced the financial burden facing the low-income family. To attend a private university, a student with the maximum Pell grant would face a net college price of

Table 3.7

Affordability of Higher Education to Low Income Families: 1970–1992
(in constant 1994 dollars)

	Private Four-Year University			
	1970	1980	1990	1992
Average Price[a]	$12,262	$11,867	$18,652	$20,027
Available Pell Grant	–	3,023	2,544	2,392
Student Loan[b]	8,500	4,250	3,260	2,650
Net College Price (price minus grant)	12,262	8,844	16,108	17,635

	Public Four-Year University			
	1970	1980	1990	1992
Average Price	$5,319	$4,909	$6,386	$6,709
Available Pell Grant	–	3,023	2,544	2,392
Student Loan	5,319	1,886	2,836	2,650
Net College Price (price minus grant)	5,319	1,886	3,550	4,317

	Public Two-Year College			
	1970	1980	1990	1992
Average Price	$3,615	$3,546	$3,870	$4,006
Available Pell Grant	–	1,773	2,322	2,392
Student Loan	3,615	1,773	1,548	1,614
Net College Price (price minus grant)	3,615	1,773	1,548	1,614

[a]Average college price includes tuition, room, and board.
[b]Maximum Subsidized Stafford loan available to first year student.

$8,844. This was nearly $4,000 less than that same student would have paid to attend that same private university in 1970.

The net price of a public higher education also become dramatically more affordable in the 1970s. The creation and expansion of the Pell grant program substantially reduced the net price of both public universities and at public two-year colleges between 1970 and 1980. Moreover, that amount was now low enough that a student willing to finance the remaining price cost of their education would be eligible to borrow the full amount through a federally guaranteed student loan. By 1980, the loan necessary to pay for a year at a public university was $1,886. For a two-year college it was $1,773.

After 1980, college affordability began a steady and often dramatic decline. By 1992, college prices were up sharply and the value of Pell grants was down. For the low-income family in 1992, the combination of the maximum Pell grant and the maximum Stafford loan was now more than $17,000 short of the average price of a private university. This is an increase in net price of a frightening $8,791 between 1980 and 1992.

That same reduction in affordability was evident at public universities. By 1992, the maximum Pell grant of $2,392 was $4,317 short of the average cost of a public university. Even the maximum subsidized student loan of $2,650 was insufficient to cover that price. The net price of a public university more than doubled between 1980 and 1992. But that net price was still lower than it had been in 1970 before the creation of the Pell grant.

The affordability of public two-year colleges has followed a slightly different pattern. During the 1980s, the net price of a public two- year college declined by more than $200. But as college prices continued to spiral upward in the early 1990s, net price of public two-year colleges increased to more than $1,614 for a student receiving the maximum Pell grant. In both 1980 and 1992, the combination of federal student aid was sufficient to meet the entire price of a two-year college. But in 1992, the amount the student was required to borrow was greater.

When college prices are compared with the resources of low-income families, a sharp dichotomy emerges. During the 1970s, stable college prices, the creation of the Pell grant, and the expanded availability of student loans produced significant progress toward removing college price barriers. But after 1980, rising college prices, the declining value of the Pell grant, and tightened student-loan eligibility, dramatically reduced college affordability for lower-income students. Indeed, by 1992 these factors left even those low-income families who qualified for the maximum Pell grant and the maximum Stafford loan without sufficient resources to cover their college costs.

For two-year public colleges, the progress toward improved college affordability evident during the 1970s continued into the 1980s. By 1990, the net price of a two-year college was lower than it had been in 1980 or 1970. But as college prices continued to increase in the early 1990s, the net price of two-year public colleges also began to rise. As a consequence, by 1992, the net price of all types of higher education was greater for lower-income families than it had been in more than two decades. And those net prices were rising rapidly.

Case #2: The Middle-Income Family

Concern over college affordability is not restricted to low-income families. Many have argued that middle-income families are also under pressure by the combination of slow increases in family incomes and rapid increases in college prices. In order to examine this assertion, the following analysis examines the changing situation faced by a family earning the median family income in 1970, 1980, and 1992.

Because they are unlikely to qualify for a Pell grant, the calculus facing the middle-income family is relatively simple. Although they may defer a substantial portion of college price through loans, either the family or the student must eventually pay the entire price of college. Accordingly, to a middle-income family, the relationship between income and the price of college is a reasonable measure of college affordability. If family incomes are growing at a faster rate than prices, college will be judged to be more affordable. On the other hand, if prices are rising faster than their incomes, college will be less affordable.

As shown in table 3.8, the average price of a private university was about 30 percent of the median family income in 1970. The price of a public university was about 14 percent. By 1980, these percentages had dropped to 28 percent and 10 percent respectively. In spite of the fact that the median family income was growing quite slowly, college prices were growing even more slowly. As a result, both public and private universities were becoming more affordable to middle-income families.

But since 1980, the price of both public and private universities has risen more rapidly than incomes. In 1992, the average annual price of a private university as 51 percent of the median family income. For public universities, prices rose to 18 percent of median income. This made both private and public universities less affordable to middle-income families in 1992 than they had been since at least 1970.

The affordability of two-year colleges to middle-income families also declined, albeit at a much slower rate. Between 1970 and 1990, the price of a two-year college as a portion of median family income held steady between 9 percent and 10 percent. But in 1992, that increased to 11 per-

Table 3.8

Average College Price as a Percentage of Median Family Income: 1970–1992

Year	Four-Year Private University	Four-Year Public University	Two-Year Public College
1970	30%	10%	10%
1975	29	13	10
1980	28	12	9
1985	37	14	10
1990	43	15	9
1992	51	18	11

Source: Author's calculations from table 2.2 and table 3.1.

cent. Thus, the affordability of two-year colleges to middle-income families was only slightly greater in 1992 that it had been in 1970.

Case #3: The Upper Income Family

Not much attention is usually given to college affordability for upper-income families (defined here as the mean income of the top quintile). But it is useful to look at how trends in incomes and college prices affected high-income families as well those with middle or low incomes.

Table 3.9 shows that the affordability of the average priced private university to an upper-income family increased slightly during the 1970s and decreased rapidly after 1980. College prices increased over this period but so did the resources available to those families. The result was that affordability for upper-income families was at roughly the same level in 1985 that it had been in 1970. But since 1985 the average price of a private university increased even more rapidly than did the incomes of those in the top quintile. By 1992, that price stood at 19 percent of the mean family income of the top quintile.

The affordability of public higher education to upper-income families also increased slightly during the two decades. The annual price of the average priced public university increased from 5 percent in 1985 to 7 percent in 1992. The price of a two-year college never exceeded a meager 4 percent of the mean income of the top quintile. Thus even the most wealthy families experienced the declining affordability of both public and private universities since 1980.

Table 3.9

Average College Price as a Percentage of Mean Family Income of Top Quintile: 1970–1992

Year	Four-Year Private University	Four-Year Public University	Two-Year Public College
1970	13%	5%	4%
1975	13	6	4
1980	12	5	4
1985	14	5	4
1990	16	6	3
1992	19	7	3

Source: Author's calculations from table 2.2 and table 3.2.

SUMMING UP:
COLLEGE AFFORDABILITY TODAY

This analysis has been limited to only four major family resources: income, savings, federal grants, and state grants. But financial aid officers at public and private colleges are not so limited. They are able to draw upon college work-study aid, Perkins loans, the various institutionally based aid programs, as well as private scholarships in order to package student aid for the unique needs of individual students. Such creative packaging of financial aid can serve to mitigate the trends discussed above. But these other resources are quite small. When family income, savings rates, Pell grants, federally guaranteed student loans, and state grants lag behind college prices, even the best financial aid office can do little to make college more affordable.

When trends in college prices are compared to trends in the resources considered here, the years between 1970 and 1992 divide into two sharply different periods. In the 1970s, the incomes of the poorest families declined, but college prices declined even more. In addition, several public programs were developed and/or expanded to make new financial resources available to low-income families. The federal government established the Pell grant in 1972 and dramatically expanded the federal student loan program in 1972, 1976, and again in 1978. State governments, stimulated by the SSIG, also moved to assist low-income students. Low-income families thus saw all of the financial resources available to them increase at a more rapid rate than college prices and all sectors of higher education became more affordable to them.

But all of these trends begin to change after 1980. The price of attending college accelerated rapidly and the resources available to low-income families to meet those prices did not keep pace. Family incomes, Pell grants, and state grants all increased more slowly after 1980 than did the average price of a public or private university. The price of attending two-year colleges also increased, but not as rapidly as did the price of public universities. As a result, students from low-income families were left to borrow the growing difference between their diminishing resources and the spiral costs of higher education.

Middle-income families also experienced changes in the affordability of public higher education. During the 1970s, median family income increased more rapidly than did the price of higher education. Moreover, 1978 changes in the federal student loan program had made all students eligible for a subsidized student loan. After 1980, however, all types of higher education became less affordable to middle-income students. Family incomes climbed, but at a slower rate than college prices. Additionally, tightened federal student loan requirements made many such families ineligible for subsidized loans.

Paradoxically, upper-income families experienced the least change in college affordability over the past twenty years. College prices as a percent of family income remained largely stable. Up until 1990, while unable to qualify for most direct student aid, upper- income families compensated for rising college prices with rising incomes. But since 1990, even upper-income families have seen sharp increases in the portion of their incomes required to pay for private universities.

POSING THE NEXT QUESTION: WHY HAVE GOVERNMENT EFFORTS FAILED?

Since 1980, spending by federal and state governments to remove college price barriers has continued to increase. But, despite these efforts, the affordability of public and private four-year colleges has still declined precipitously for lower- and middle-income students. The affordability of public two-year colleges has improved only slightly.

These trends in net college prices bring us to the troubling question which is at the heart of the rest of this book. Why have government efforts to remove the price barriers to college had so little success? In order to find the answer, it is necessary to tell two separate stories. The first is about the federal effort to remove the price barriers to higher education over the past three decades. This story, about the growth and transformation of the student aid programs, is told in the next two chapters. The second story, about the actions of the various state governments to help families to pay for college, is told in chapters 6 and 7.

4

THE CREATION AND TRANSFORMATION OF THE FEDERAL STUDENT AID PROGRAMS

The view that higher education should be accessible to everyone, regardless of their financial situation, has been the explicit objective of American policy since the enactment of the Higher Education Act in 1965.[1] But from the perspective of the mid-1990s, the goal of universal college affordability still seems far beyond reach. As shown in chapter 3, not only do lower-income families continue to face substantial price barriers to college, but higher education has become progressively less affordable to most American families since 1980. Somewhere between the high hopes of the 1960s and the reality of the 1990s, something clearly went wrong.

In order to understand how and why this happened, it is necessary to examine the legislative history of the continually changing federal student aid programs. In telling this story here, I describe the ways in which policy-makers struggled to establish the various programs, and then to adapt them to changing economic, political, and social circumstances. In this chapter, I recount the creation, expansion, retrenchment, and transformation of the programs from 1965 to 1995. My goal is to describe what happened in federal student-aid policy and to consider the consequences of those actions on college affordability for disadvantaged students.

What makes these events especially interesting, and often confusing, is that in their efforts to remove college price barriers, policy-makers did not act as a unitary force carefully implementing a comprehensive plan. Rather, the growth in the student aid programs emerged from more or less constant negotiations among an ever changing cast of characters making small, periodic, incremental revisions. As new problems or circumstances emerged, adjustments were made in each of the programs and in the relationships among them. As these events unfolded over three decades, no one individual or viewpoint was able to dominate the process. Hence, today, no side can claim credit for the program's successes and none must accept full blame for their failures.

THE FEDERAL GOVERNMENT AND HIGHER EDUCATION: AN OVERVIEW

For most of American history, the federal government had little to do with higher education. It neither regulated the activities of the nation's colleges nor provided them with much money. This separation was no accident. Prior to the late 1950s, the prevailing view among both public officials and academics was that the government should keep its hands off college affairs.[2] Certainly there were exceptions like the Morrell Act of 1862 and the National Defense Act of 1916. But these were exceptions to a general pattern of separation.

As a consequence, the national government was not organized to address higher education issues. In Congress, for example, prior to 1946 there was no education committee. There was no higher education subcommittee until several years later. In the executive, there was almost no administrative apparatus through which to carry out the limited federal initiatives. As recently as 1963, the Office of Education employed only twenty-six professionals assigned to higher education (in 1940 there were only eight). The primary function of these officials was simply the collection and publication of rudimentary data about the nation's colleges.[3]

With little policy being made in Washington, colleges and universities found no reason to involve themselves in national politics. There were few national groups or associations representing the views of higher education to national policy-makers. The absence of an active higher education lobby, however, was not simply the result of a lack of national policy. Most colleges and their national associations were committed to avoiding political entanglements regardless of the level of government. Many higher education groups refused to hire lobbyists on the grounds that it would compromise their academic freedom and drag them into the "messy" world of national politics.[4] In short, for most of American history, higher education was the domain of the states and college boards of trustees and it was in statehouses and on campuses where the direction of American higher education was shaped.[5]

Early Federal Student Aid Programs

In this same vein, paying for college was viewed as the responsibility of students, their families, and, to a lesser extent, state governments. Prior to the late 1950s, the federal government had no programs which provided generally available financial aid to college students. There were, however, several programs which provided some college aid to select populations. The largest of these was the post–World War II Serviceman's Readjustment Act, popularly known as the G.I. Bill of Rights. It provided college grants as an entitlement to those who had completed military service. The G.I. Bill, however, was not viewed as a student-aid program. To its many supporters, it was a benefit program for military service that was merely disguised as college aid.[6]

Similarly, the federal government periodically provided aid to college students with talents in areas of special social need. In times when the nation was in need of scientists, for example, aid to prospective scientists was considered an appropriate antidote. The same was true, at various times, of doctors and engineers. Such federal aid was not distributed as an entitlement to a particular group, as veterans' aid had been. It was provided as a scholarship to students of exceptional merit or potential in a designated area.

While these limited types of federal student aid were sporadically available to a select group of college students throughout the 1940s and 1950s, neither provided any general purpose aid to the vast majority of students who were not a part of a special group or did not possess a skill that the government designated as a special need. Senator John Kennedy summed up the view of most members of Congress when he said in 1957:

> It seems to me that there are quite adequate funds for any student to get either a scholarship or an education in the state university and that federal efforts should be directed towards providing funds so that colleges can expand their facilities and the schools can expand their school buildings rather than in the area of scholarships.[7]

Rudiments of a Federal Policy: 1958–1964

In the late 1950s, the federal government first began to consider broader efforts to remove college price barriers. Much of this reflected the changing role of the national government in all spheres of American life. As Washington began to assume more and more responsibility for advancing science and technology, insuring equality of opportunity for the disadvantaged, and stimulating economic growth, the resulting national policies inevitably thrust the government into the previously alien world of higher education finance.

The Cold War of the late 1950s served as the backdrop for an event which would, quite unexpectedly, lead to a lasting change in the long-standing hands-off relationship between the federal government and the nation's college students. It began in 1957 when, after the launching of the Soviet Sputnik, there was a sudden public fear that America was losing the competition in space technology because of deficient science education in the schools and colleges. In response, President Eisenhower asked Congress to spend $1.6 billion to improve education in the sciences and foreign languages. After significant modifications, Congress passed the National Defense Education Act (NDEA) in 1958.[8]

The NDEA was multifaceted. Its principle provisions dealt with elementary and secondary education, vocational training, and teacher education. But the act also contained a suggestion that all potential students ought to have an opportunity to attend college and that it was the job of the federal government to guarantee that opportunity. The preamble to the NDEA stated:

> The security of the nation requires the fullest development of the mental resources and the technical skills of its young men and women . . . the nation requires . . . that the federal government give assistance for programs which are important to the nation's defense.[9]

While such a statement is a long way from a federal promise to remove price barriers for all lower-income students, it provided an important symbolic breakthrough by articulating a clear national interest in achieving equal educational opportunity.[10]

The NDEA also created the first generally available federal student aid program: the National Defense Student Loan, now called the Perkins loan. This program provided colleges with capital that they could lend directly to students at exceptionally low interest rates. The federal share of the capital was to be 90 percent with the rest provided by the institution. Colleges could collect the loan and recycle the principle and interest. Each participating campus was, in effect, told to identify needy students, lend them money for college, collect those loans after the student had graduated, and then re-lend the money to another needy student.

While the NDEA and the Perkins loan program marked the first step toward the development of federal student aid, they hardly constituted a significant federal commitment to remove college price barriers. Yet, by stressing the link between education and national security, they recognized an implicit imperative to find and educate talented individuals. Meeting this need required federal assurance that no student of ability would be denied a higher education because of financial need.[11]

Equal Opportunity and College Affordability

The long-standing opposition to broad federal aid to college students began to weaken in the early 1960s. Following the landslide victory of Lyndon Johnson and the Democratic party in 1964, momentous social legislation was enacted by the Congress. In 1964, the Equal Opportunity Act began the War on Poverty. This was followed in 1965 by the Voting Rights Act, Medicare, and the Elementary and Secondary Education Act. The rights of the poor and disadvantaged were at the top of the political agenda and congressional leaders had both the political opportunity and the financial resources to take action.[12]

The Great Society was an aggressive federal effort to achieve equal opportunity for all income groups. Insuring an equal opportunity to go to college was a central part of that effort. The logic behind the first equal educational opportunity programs was simple, and perhaps a bit simplistic. By removing college price barriers, it was assumed that lower-income students would be able to attend college in greater numbers. This would lead to their finding better jobs, earning higher wages, and moving out of poverty. Based largely on this economic rationale, the federal government jumped headlong into the business of providing financial aid to needy college students in 1965 with the passage of the Higher Education Act.

THE HIGHER EDUCATION ACT OF 1965:
ESTABLISHING A FEDERAL ROLE IN STUDENT AID

The Higher Education Act (HEA) of 1965 was sweeping legislation intended, among many other things, to provide disadvantaged students with the financial resources to attend college. The act established a new federal role and purpose in higher education—promoting equality of opportunity.[13] The federal government was, for the first time, going to accept partial responsibility for finding ways to overcome the barrier which college costs posed to low-income students. Specifically, the act sought to both "increase the supply of trained manpower" and to remedy "the appalling frequency with which a student is presently forced to forego the opportunity of post-secondary education because of inability to meet the costs."[14]

The act contained five major titles. Title I created community service and continuing education programs directed primarily to urban areas. Title II involved the upgrading of college and university libraries. Title III provided aid to historically black colleges. Title IV, the centerpiece of the act, were the provisions for college student aid. And Title V established the National Teacher Corps. In combination, these programs drew the federal government into the funding of higher education to an unprecedented degree and, for the first time, explicitly articulated the clear national goal of making college affordable to all Americans through federal student aid.

The Title IV Programs

Title IV of the Higher Education Act established three types of student assistance: (1) direct "opportunity grants" were to be given to the neediest students, (2) federally guaranteed loans, which were capitalized by private lenders, would be available to both lower- and middle-income students and, (3) the existing campus-based programs, like the Perkins loan and College Work-Study aid, were continued. Campus officials were expected to "package" these different types of aid in ways which would match the individual needs and circumstances of each student.

Opportunity Grants. The centerpiece of Title IV, and indeed the entire HEA, was a program of Educational Opportunity Grants (EOG) available to students of "exceptional financial need" in order to allow them to attend college. Fred Hechinger described the EOG as "a natural extension of the G.I. Bill."[15] These grants were to be the first step in the process of insuring that all Americans had the financial resources to attend college.

But the 1965 act left many of the specific provisions of EOG unclear. Determination of eligibility was decentralized to the colleges. The act required that the size of the grants be determined by the college (or a needs-analysis service) based on family need and the cost of the college. Yet the act left unclear the criteria by which colleges would determine eligibility.[16] It was not clear whether the phrase "exceptional financial need" used in the act meant students from poor families or students who had very high costs of attendance. Each institution was left to make their own interpretation of who qualified as exceptionally needy.[17]

Guaranteed Student Loans. Of the various student-aid provisions included in Title IV of the HEA, President Johnson personally was interested in the Guaranteed Student Loan Program (GSLP). As a young man, Johnson had struggled to pay his way through Southwest Texas State Teachers College. Only a loan from a family friend, and a willingness to get by with very little, allowed him to stay in school. He felt strongly that the opportunity to borrow for college ought to be widely available.[18]

Under this new GSLP, the federal government would encourage private lenders to make loans available to qualified student-borrowers at below market interest rates.[19] The program provided several incentives to encourage lenders to make such loans. After the loan is made the lender receives a subsidy payment from the federal government to compensate for the low interest rate charged. The federal government also pays the full interest on the loan during the time the borrower remains in school. Finally, the loan is fully guaranteed against default by the federal government. This structure virtually insured that a participating lender would make a profit on each GSL they made.

The GSLP also had several features which made it attractive to potential students. Not only was the loan available at a low interest rate, the student-borrower paid no interest at all until twelve months after they were no longer in school. All eligible students could borrow any amount up to the difference between the cost of attendance and the expected family contribution as long as the amount did not exceed program limits.

Campus Based Aid. In addition to the EOG and student loan program, the Higher Education Act reauthorized the College Work-Study program, and the Perkins loan program which were already in existence. The College Work-Study program was transferred from the Office of Economic Opportunity to the Office of Education. The Work-Study program sprang from the Equal Opportunity Act of 1964 and was originally considered an anti-poverty measure rather than a student aid program. In the College Work Study program, the federal government furnished about 80 percent of the funds to pay the wages of needy students employed by the college. The college was required to pick up the remaining 20 percent.

The Perkins loan program was also reauthorized and expanded in 1965. But it was still relatively small. In 1964, for example, slightly more than 200,000 students were borrowing through Perkins loans. The average loan was less than $500.

LIMITS OF THE TITLE IV PROGRAMS

Title IV of the HEA was unquestionably the largest single development in the federal effort to remove college price barriers.[20] It laid out a set of programs and responsibilities which remain largely intact today. But almost from their creation, there was dissatisfaction with the effectiveness of the Title IV programs as a vehicle to achieve universal college affordability.[21] As the EOG was being put into place in the late 1960s, that dissatisfaction grew.

By the end of the decade, it was clear that the goal of equalizing college opportunity was just too big for these relatively small efforts. A 1969 report by Alice Rivlin, then an Assistant Secretary of Health Education and Welfare, laid out the situation in stark terms.[22] Rivlin reported that even with the new federal aid programs, the probability of an 18- to 24-year-old being enrolled in college remained strongly tied to family income. For those from families with 1970 incomes of less than $3,000 per year, the proportion enrolled in college was 14 percent. However, among those from families with annual incomes of $15,000 or more, the proportion enrolled in college was 60 percent. In other words, individuals from high incomes were more than four times more likely to be enrolled in college than were individuals from low-income families.

Additionally, there were several features of the way the EOG operated which made the distribution of funds inequitable across income groups and between campuses. Even if a student knew that the EOG program existed, he or she first had to be admitted to a particular college before they knew whether or not they were eligible for a grant.[23] This was because eligibility standards differed widely from institution to institution and the act had established no precise eligibility requirements. Funds were distributed to the states based on the number of students enrolled and not on the financial status of those students. Thus states with more low-income students would be able to help a smaller portion of them. This created wide differences among states in the family income levels which qualified a student for an EOG. As Hansen notes:

> Theoretically, a low cost state university with many poor students could find itself with insufficient EOG funds to aid all who were clearly low-income while an expensive private college might have few low income students and yet, because of high costs, have lower-middle or even middle income students with larger levels of need than their low income counterparts in the state university.[24]

Through the late 1960s and into the early 1970s, such concerns over the effectiveness and the equity of the Title IV programs grew. But in the face of the fiscal and political constraints imposed by the Vietnam War, national policy-makers were generally not in the mood to expand the Great Society commitments.[25] In addition, student rioting and general campus unrest had soured many people on aid to higher education in general and on student aid in particular. The Title IV programs remained in place, but they proved only to be small first steps toward insuring equal educational opportunity.

THE EDUCATION AMENDMENTS OF 1972:
MAKING HIGHER EDUCATION A RIGHT, ALMOST

It was not until 1972 that Congress again turned its full attention to college affordability and student aid issues. The Higher Education Act was due to expire in 1972 and Congress was compelled to reauthorize it.[26] For those who felt the act was not working well, the reauthorization provided an opportunity to attempt to fundamentally recast the various student aid programs in order to expand the access they provided to low-income students.

In this effort, the chair of the Senate Subcommittee on the Arts and Humanities, Claiborne Pell, took the lead. Pell put forth a proposal that called for a fundamental shift in the focus and the structure of the Title IV programs. He was convinced that the EOG was simply not big enough to achieve equal opportunity for low-income students. In its place he proposed the creation of a much larger "Basic Education Opportunity Grant" (BEOG) which would be administered in Washington and targeted more carefully to the most needy students. These grants would provide a foundation of support upon which a comprehensive and reliable system of student aid could be built. After much intrigue, Senator Pell, with the support of John Bradamas and Albert Quie in the House, was able to persuade the Congress that the time had come to dramatically expand and recast the federal student aid efforts.[27]

The Logic of the Pell Grant

The centerpiece of the Amendments to the Higher Education Act of 1972 was the newly created BEOG, renamed the Pell grant in 1980, that authorized students to receive up to $1,400 each depending on their estimated costs and family income. But no student could receive a grant larger than half of the cost of attendance.[28] Cost was defined to include room, board, books, and transportation as well as tuition and fees.

The new Pell grant differed from the old EOG in several fundamental ways. Determination of eligibility would be made in a centralized way in Washington and not on each campus. This insured that students from similar economic backgrounds and attending similarly priced colleges would receive the same size grant. Moreover, Congress made clear that Pell grants were meant for students of relatively poor families and awards were to be carefully targeted to the most needy. Pell grants were not awarded on the basis of competition, but only on the basis of need. That need was determined by a formula that considered both the resource level and the level of expenses of the recipient. A student who qualified for aid (that is one whose family could not afford $1,400 of the cost of college) automatically received up to the $1,400 maximum in the form of a Pell grant.

The Pell grant was to give students a predictable, guaranteed foundation of federal support. The theory was that such an assurance of aid, and early knowledge of it (hopefully in the junior year of high school), would encourage lower-income students to entertain the idea of going to college. It was hoped that students who would benefit from some form of postsecondary education, but had not considered it for lack of money, would perceive that opportunity and take advantage of it.[29]

Limits of the Pell Grant

While the Pell grant was a significant improvement over preceding federal efforts, it still contained several features which limited its ability to advance the cause of equal opportunity. Despite the rhetoric of its supporters, the program was not a true entitlement at all. The government was not obligated to meet all of the needs as outlined in the statute. If appropriations fell below the entitlement amount, individual grants would simply be reduced by the percentage that the total appropriation was deficient. Indeed, there was not a full appropriation until 1976. Thus, low-income students still could not be certain that the floor of educational aid would be there when they needed it.

Another feature which limited the ability of the Pell grant to fully address the college affordability problem was the half-cost limitation on the amount the grant awarded. This provision, retained from the EOG, required all students to find other sources for half of their college expenses, even at a low-cost institution. Thus, as Sally Davenport noted, "the same uncertainties and inequalities, horizontal (across campuses) as well as vertical (among income groups) still existed" despite the improvements in the program.[30]

These limitations notwithstanding, the Pell grant quickly grew in both the number of grants given and their overall costs. In 1974–75, the first year that the program was fully operational, more than 1.2 million, 16 percent of all undergraduates, received such grants. This included an estimated 21 percent of all college freshman.[31]

Supplements to the Pell Grant

In addition to the Pell grant, the 1972 amendments also created the State Student Incentive Grant (SSIG) program. This program provided federal matching funds for state scholarship programs. SSIG funds were allocated to the states according to a formula tied to total enrollments. The states were given wide latitude to design and manage their own programs. The SSIG met with widespread acceptance. In 1965, only about ten states had programs which provided aid to low-income students. Under the stimulus of the SSIG, such state aid increased rapidly. By 1975, all fifty states were operating student aid programs that would qualify for federal SSIG grants.[32]

While the Pell grant and SSIG were entirely new student-aid programs, the 1972 amendments did not abandon the patchwork of existing programs. With minor adjustments, the amendments reauthorized the College Work-Study, Educational Opportunity Grants, and Perkins loan programs. But while these older programs were continued, their original purpose had been fundamentally changed. They were now to serve as supplements to the Pell grant. To emphasize this new purpose, the EOG was renamed the Supplemental Educational Opportunity Grant (SEOG).

A Diminished Role for the GSLP

The federally guaranteed student loan program was also amended during the 1972 reauthorization so as to play a secondary role to the Pell grant. Congress had anticipated that the creation of the foundation grant program would reduce the need for students to borrow for college. As such, the GSLP was not expected to grow much beyond its 1972 size and, at least at first, it did not. In 1970, for example, about $1.0 billion dollars ($3.8 billion in constant 1994 dollars) in federally guaranteed student loans were awarded. In 1975, about $1.3 billion ($3.4 billion in constant 1994 dollars) were awarded.[33] Similarly, while about one million students were borrowing through the program in 1970, that number declined to 922,000 in 1975.[34]

The logic of the 1972 act was to shift a larger portion of the college costs from low-income students and their families to the federal government. In keeping with this spirit, the act sought to both increase the amount of aid available to low-income students and to lessen the volume of student borrowing and replace it with a system of direct grants.

The 1972 amendments proved to be a tremendous success when judged by these two objectives. In 1970, just over $1.6 billion in generally available federal student aid was awarded (this includes Pell grants,

SEOG, College Work-Study, Perkins loans, and guaranteed student loans). Of that, less than $0.5 billion was in the form of grants and $1.0 billion in loans. By 1976, more than $4.0 billion in such aid was awarded. But the distribution had changed such that $1.4 billion were now in grants and $1.3 billion in loans.

MINOR ADJUSTMENTS PRODUCE MAJOR GROWTH:
1973–1978

After the 1972 amendments were passed, the problems of college affordability and equal opportunity to higher education again moved off the national agenda. This was partly because it took several years for the various new programs to be implemented and to gauge their impact. The first Pell grant was awarded in 1974, but the program was not fully operational until 1976. This inattention to college affordability also reflected broader national conditions. The real price of both public and private higher education was remaining stable and college participation rates were rising. The gap between the participation rates of upper- and lower-income students was closing. Further, President Nixon was preoccupied with Vietnam and later with Watergate. The president's attention to education was limited to the controversy over forced busing in elementary and secondary schools.[35]

It was not until the HEA was due to expire again in 1976 that national policy-makers returned to the problems of college affordability. But quite unlike the situation four years before, as the 1976 reauthorization approached, the consensus was that the new student-aid programs were working reasonably well.[36] This confidence in their effectiveness fostered a desire to do little more than maintain and expand the programs. Accordingly, the subsequent debate over the reauthorization of the Title IV programs focused narrowly on what minor changes were needed and exactly how the programs should be expanded.[37]

As a consequence, as college groups bickered with each other over formulas and technical adjustments, Congress did not feel any strong demand to change the basic student aid programs. Apart from increasing the size of Pell grants and loosening eligibility for GSLs, the only course of action that was acceptable to everyone was to leave things as they were. On the surface, at least, that is what the 1976 amendments did.

The 1976 Reauthorization

The scope of the changes which resulted from the 1976 reauthorization was modest. Neither the ends nor the means of federal student aid were restructured. These modest adjustments, however, carried a large price-tag. The act liberalized eligibility for the Pell grant and increased the size of the grants available to students at all income levels. A new method of calculation was introduced which made many new students eligible. In 1975 about 16 percent of all students, or 1.2 million, were receiving Pell grants. By 1978 the number of recipients had increased to more than 25 percent of all students, or 1.9 million.[38]

In dollar terms, the growth was even more stark. The 1976 adjustments increased the costs of Pell grants by 60 percent, in just two years. The increasing costs of the program were not the product of larger grants to the most needy students. Indeed, the maximum grant actually declined in constant dollars during these years. The expansion occurred because the new eligibility rules made many less needy families eligible for the Pell grant.

The GSLP was also significantly expanded. The 1976 reauthorization increased the total a student could borrow from $10,000 to $15,000. This produced an expansion in the GSLP, but not of the magnitude experienced by Pell grants. The number of borrowers remained stable at about 12 percent of all students between 1976 and 1978. However, the size of the average loan and the total cost of the program increased steadily. In 1976, the average GSL was about $1,400. Two years later it had increased to more than $1,700. This increased the total amount of aid awarded in the form of federally guaranteed student loans from $1.3 billion in 1976 to $2.4 billion in 1978.

The cumulative result of the 1976 amendments was thus an impressive growth in the size of the student aid programs. Perhaps as important as the aggregate dollars spent on student aid was the overall improvement it created in college affordability for lower-income students. The combination of stable college costs, an expanded Pell grant, and an easily accessible system of federally subsidized and guaranteed loans, was substantially reducing the net price of higher education facing lower-income students.

RESPONDING TO THE MIDDLE-INCOME SQUEEZE

The next major event in the federal effort to improve college affordability came in 1978, two years before the HEA was due to be reauthorized. Driving the renewed attention to the problem of college affordability were broad public pressures to expand the availability of federal student aid to middle- and even upper-income families. It is paradoxical that public concern over the problem of college affordability emerged at a time when college tuitions were relatively stable and the net price of higher education for lower income students was declining. Indeed, the timing of this public pressure was especially odd since it came on the heels of more than a decade of rapid growth in all types of student aid.[39]

The Challenge of Tuition Tax Credits

As congressional attention turned to improving college affordability for middle-income students, a disagreement developed over the best mechanism to use. The most direct approach would be to expand the existing student aid programs so as to make middle- or even upper-income students eligible for grants and loans. This would address the problem facing middle-income students without the need for new federal programs.

The alternative approach was to use the tax system to provide relief for middle-income college students. This could be done by offering a tax deduction against adjusted gross income for college expenses. Supporters of this tax-credit approach believed that it was the best way to keep federal authority out of education and to assist middle-income families without forcing them "to go hat in hand and plead poverty to get an education grant or loan from the federal government."[40]

Tax-credit supporters were careful not to present their plan as a substitute for federal grants and loans. Indeed, many tax-credit supporters were vocal advocates of the existing grant and loan programs. Senator Moynihan, for example, maintained:

> I reject out of hand the proposition that this society cannot afford both need based aid for impoverished students AND relief through the tax system for all students. The concepts are not in conflict. Indeed, they are entirely compatible.[41]

However, opponents of tax credits, including President Carter, argued that they were too costly and that they provide an unjust and wasteful subsidy to upper-income students. In addition, opponents viewed the proposed credit as both too small to help the most needy students and not large enough to have any impact on the education choices of wealthy students.

Defeating Tuition Tax Credits

Given the stagnate economy and the growing concern over the federal budget deficit, President Carter made it clear that he would not accept even the smallest tax-credit measure. He announced that he was opposed to "tuition tax credits under any circumstances, even if it is at a very slight level, because they would inevitably grow with each succeeding budget."[42] It was Carter's oppostion to tax credits, as much as public pressure for increased federal aid to college students, which fueled the push for increasing the traditional student-aid programs.

Working closely with President Carter, opponents of tax credits scrambled to put together an alternative way to provide additional federal aid to middle-income students.[43] Termed the "Middle-Income Student Assistance Act" (MISAA), Carter's plan would significantly increase the amount a family could earn and still remain eligible for federal grants and loans. It retained the basic structures of the programs, but adjusted them to make many more students eligible for awards.[44] Overall, Carter's plan would increase federal spending on student aid by almost 40 percent in one year and raise the number of students receiving aid from 3 million to 5 million. In fact, the plan was so generous it would have made 94 *percent* of all students eligible for federally subsidized loans. Rep. William Ford described the plan as "the biggest single infusion of funds for middle-income students since the adoption of the G.I. Bill."[45]

The politics which unfolded during the debate over student aid in 1978 amounted to little more than a bidding war between supporters of the two approaches. Proponents of each side continued to expand their package to appeal to ever larger numbers of middle- and even upper-income families. The two bills raced through the Congress and each appeared to have enough support to pass in both houses, but President Carter continued to threaten a veto of any tuition tax-credit bill.

In the end, the tuition tax credit plan bogged down in a conference committee dispute over their size and scope. This paved the way for the enactment of MISAA.[46] As such, the president and supporters of the traditional student-aid programs won a major victory. But they had done so at a very high cost. Students from families earning between $15,000 and $26,000 were now eligible for Pell grants. The act also provided that the asset exclusion for independent students with dependents be the same as for the family of a dependent student. This change allowed a great many independent students to qualify for Pell grants who had previously been shut out. Much more significant, however, were the adjustments MISAA made to expand eligibility for GSLs. The legislation entirely removed the income ceiling (previously $25,000) for subsidized student loans. These simple alterations set off a chain of events that soon drove the costs of the programs far beyond what the government could afford. Indeed, no one fully anticipated the explosion in student borrowing that was to follow.

FEDERAL STUDENT AID AND COLLEGE AFFORDABILITY: A VIEW FROM 1980

As the 1970s came to an end, the situation of the lower-income student hoping to go to college was better than it had been at any time in more than twenty years. As a direct result of the Higher Education Act of 1965 and the expansions to the Title IV programs which took place in 1972, 1976, and 1978, lower-family-income students could make use of a wide array of financial resources in their efforts to pay for college. In addition to their earnings and savings, they could now receive Pell grants, SEOGs, and College Work-Study aid. They could borrow directly from their school through the Perkins loan program or from a private lender through the GSLP. These resources combined to significantly reduce the net price of college facing low-income students.

Similarly, the situation of middle-income families was also greatly improved. After years of being ineligible for most federal student aid, MISAA made all families eligible for federally subsidized GSLs. There were certainly price barriers to college which remained. Private colleges were still beyond the financial reach of many families. And, in a less visible way, the expanded availability of student loans allowed many parents to shift the responsibility for paying for college to their children. These limitations not withstanding, by 1980 the federal efforts to achieve universal college affordability were achieving significant, albeit costly, success.

THE TRANSFORMATION OF THE FEDERAL PROGRAMS: 1980–1995

The year 1980 was a watershed in the efforts of the federal government to remove college price barriers. During the late 1970s, President Carter and the U.S. economy faced the devastating combination of high inflation, high unemployment, and high interest rates. As Carter's term unfolded, Republicans in Congress joined with conservative Democrats to press Carter to cut federal spending as the first step in reducing inflation and stimulating economic growth. Carter's opponents were determined to make this issue the focal point of the 1980 presidential election campaign. With his approval ratings sliding downward, the president faced what appeared to be a clear choice between reining in federal spending or losing the election.

When seen in light of the huge federal budget, the student aid programs involved almost insignificant expenditures. But while small, the cost of these programs was growing rapidly in the late 1970s. In 1978, the federal government appropriated $10.6 billion (in constant 1994 dollars) in generally available college student aid. That amount had increased to $16.8 (in constant 1994 dollars) by 1982.[47] Virtually all of this 66 percent price increase was the result of increasing participation in the student loan programs resulting from MISAA. Indeed, in 1978 about 1 million GSLs were made with an average size of about $3,380. By 1982, the number of loans had mushroomed to 3.1 million annually. But the size of the average loan remained less than $3,500. This produced a 300 percent increase in the costs of the GSLP to the federal treasury in only four years.

This growth in the costs of the GSLP was the result of a complex interaction between the adjustments Congress made in the program in 1978 and the unusual conditions of the financial markets in the late 1970s. Together, they created the right conditions for an explosion in student lending. MISAA had simplified the loan programs for the banks. Now that the needs test had been removed, they were free to make loans to any of their customers. Moreover, they no longer had to cope with the paperwork of previous years. This increased the supply of capital available for student loans.[48]

Removing the needs test and allowing all students to participate caused the demand for student loans to increase as fast as the supply. The 7 percent GSLP interest rates were about half of market rates in 1978. This made the program attractive to many students that might not have been interested in borrowing when market rates were lower. The program was such a bargain that *House and Garden* magazine ran an investment column "How you can make a substantial profit from a student loan."[49]

Given the budget constraints of the day, it was clear that the federal government could not afford the mushrooming growth in expenditures mandated by MISAA. As a result, less than a year after implementation the huge expansion of student aid programs in 1978, a powerful consensus was developing to reduce the cost of those programs. A *New York Times* editorial echoed this view when it noted that "one way to save a great deal of federal money is for the Congress to reform the college student aid programs. The present system is getting out of hand."[50]

Concern over Program Management

Another factor which contributed to the pressure to cut spending for federal student aid was the mounting evidence of fraud and waste in the programs. The record of the Department of Health, Education, and Welfare (HEW) in the administration of the GSLP was dismal. Prior to 1978, loan records were kept on index cards in shoe-boxes in several regional offices. In others, what little computer programming existed was woefully inadequate.[51] The backlog of alleged fraud cases in the GSLP alone equaled three years of work for the entire investigative staff of HEW.[52]

This concern over the administration of the GSLP was not the product of an increase in the number of defaulted loans or even increases in the costs of loan defaults to the federal treasury. In real terms, both these figures remained largely unchanged between 1978 and 1982. But the growth in loan volume was driving up the financial obligations that the government was incurring for future years. Unless Washington greatly improved collection procedures, the costs of defaulted loans could soar over the next decade.

The GSLP was not the only program which was producing concerns over waste and fraud. The Pell grant program, which had been run largely through outside contractors, had an equally lax administrative history. In 1978, although the program was providing aid to more than two million students, the government had never undertaken any systematic efforts to validate the information supplied on the grant application. In the first effort to screen the 3.4 million applications for the 1978–79 school year, 1.3 million were rejected for inaccuracy, incompleteness, or internal inconsistencies. At this time the Carter administration estimated that $100 to $150 million had been given to ineligible students each year since the program began operation in 1974.[53] In light of these revelations, and the on-going search for federal budget cuts, even supporters of the student aid programs agreed that it might be necessary to tighten up their management.

THE 1980 REAUTHORIZATION:
PUTTING THE BRAKES ON STUDENT AID

As the 1980 reauthorization was beginning, and the 1980 presidential election campaign was beginning to heat up, the orientation of federal policy-makers toward the student aid programs had shifted. For the first time since their creation, there was now substantial sentiment in Washington to scale back the federal commitment to student aid. That viewpoint did not represent a rejection of the goal of universal college affordability, but was the product of concern over the costs and effectiveness of the programs designed to achieve that goal. As a consequence, the debate over the extension of the Higher Education Act in 1980 took a far different shape. The focus of reauthorization no longer revolved around ways to expand the Title IV programs. Instead, it focused on how, and how much, to reduce or redesign them.[54]

The 1980 amendments to the Higher Education Act produced some reductions in student-aid eligibility, but it did little to reverse the massive growth which had begun in 1978. Specifically, it increased the interest rate paid by new GSL borrowers from 7 to 9 percent and shortened the after-school grace period before loan payments begin. It also transferred some of the costs of subsidizing loans from the government to parents. It did so by establishing a new loan program called Parent Loans for Undergraduate Students (PLUS), to allow parents to borrow up to $3,000 for each dependent child, but under less attractive terms than the GSL.

Despite its more restrictive character, President Carter used the bill signing to reaffirm the goal of the program as equal educational opportunity. He presented the act as the culmination of a long march toward the removal of financial barriers to higher education when he said:

> We've brought college within reach of every student in the nation who's qualified for higher education. The idea that lack of money should be no barrier to a college education is no longer a dream—it is a reality.[55]

Clearly, the national goal of universal college affordability remained intact, even as the pressure to reduce spending on the programs designed to achieve that goal was accelerating.

Doing Too Much?

The debate over the 1980 Higher Education Amendment was animated by a struggle between student-aid supporters and budget cutters. When viewed this way, the outcome was a clear victory for the budget cutters. But by failing to adjust to the emerging economic and political realities, Congress had promised students much more aid than they would be able to afford.

Lawrence Gladieux, one of the most perceptive observers of federal higher education policy, argued at the time:

> In 1980 Congress cannot fairly be accused of doing too little for higher education. The question is whether by trying to do *too much* the recent legislation may blunt the effectiveness of federal efforts to equalize educational opportunity, the overriding objective of higher education policy for more than a decade. There is a real danger that federal benefits will shift increasingly towards the relatively well-off at the expense of the neediest.[56]

Gladieux warned that this drift was occurring not because anyone explicitly favored shifting the focus of aid from low- to middle- and upper-income families. It was occurring because, by failing to reign in the costs of the GSLP, there would not be enough money remaining to fund the need-based student-aid programs. By continuing the promise to give loans to everyone, and expanding the promise of grants to the disadvantaged, Congress had made commitments that they simply could not afford to keep.[57]

The full extent to which such a drift in policy would have resulted from the 1980 amendments will never be known. The 1980 election of Ronald Reagan and a Republican majority in the Senate, made the issue moot. Beginning almost as soon as he took office in 1981, President Reagan mounted a much more extensive effort to reduce spending on student aid. As such, many provisions of the 1980 act were amended or abandoned before they were ever put into place. Still, Gladieux's observation is no less correct. The pressures to reduce student-aid spending predated the election of Ronald Reagan and were certain to accelerate regardless of the outcome of the 1980 election. The levels of loan and grant spending mandated by MISAA, and largely reaffirmed by the 1980 amendments, could not be sustained. Different presidents, or Congresses, may have focused the efforts to reduce that spending in a different way. But it was the state of the economy, the federal budget, and the growth in student loan costs, which were driving the need for spending cuts.

REAGANOMICS AND COLLEGE AFFORDABILITY

When Ronald Reagan was sworn in as President in January of 1981, he had an unusually clear vision of the changes he thought were necessary in American domestic policy. He wanted to lower federal income taxes, reduce government spending in non-defense areas, and transfer the authority for many social programs back to state governments.

Reagan wasted no time in proposing swift and substantial cuts in the student aid programs as part of his overall effort to reduce federal spending. In submitting his first budget to congress, Reagan called for wide-ranging cuts in the programs which, if enacted, would amount to a 20 percent reduction (about $1 billion) in spending on federal grants and loan guarantees. In describing the logic behind President Reagan's 1981 budget proposal, David Stockman, Director of the Office of Management and Budget at the time the plan was drafted, recalled that:

> Our controversial and draconian scaleback of middle-income student grant and loan aid . . . was based on my general critique of middle class welfare. It was absolutely the right thing to do if you wanted low taxes, low spending, and more justice. Why should some steel-worker pay taxes to help his plant manager send his kid to a private school out of state?[58]

Specifically, the president's plan called for reinstituting a needs test in the GSLP for all students with family incomes above $30,000. It also called for the discontinuation of the federal payment of interest while borrowers were in school. It proposed requiring parents borrowing under the new PLUS program to pay market interest rates. And it would require all Pell grant recipients to contribute at least $750 a year to their own education. While limiting the number of students who could borrow and expecting others to repay more, the proposal also added a new cost. For the first time, it would allow banks to charge student-borrowers a 5 percent "origination fee" to be deducted from the amount of each loan at the time it is made.[59]

The opposition to these proposed cuts and fee increases was, to say the least, substantial. Claiborne Pell described the president's plan as "penny-wise and pound-foolish."[60] Rep. Peter Peyser estimated that as many as 700,000 students could be forced out of college and that many small schools would be forced to shut down.[61] Even Secretary of Education T.H. Bell admitted that these reductions would cause some short-term pain, but that they were necessary to "put the program on sound financial footing" and help to get inflation under control.[62]

Despite this vocal opposition, Congress buckled to the demands of the new president and agreed to accept most of his proposed cuts. It reinstituted a GSLP needs test for families earning more than $30,000. Students with incomes above that limit would be allowed to borrow only the difference between their educational costs and their expected family contribution. Students with incomes below $30,000 could continue to borrow an annual maximum of $2,500. It also accepted the 5 percent origination fee and increased the interest rate on PLUS loans.[63]

While congress did fend off some of the president's proposed cuts,[64] the administration and budget cutters had won a substantial victory. They had redefined the debate over the federal effort to improve college affordability. As John Wilson, former president of the University of Chicago, explains it:

> the Reagan administration has set a course to reestablish the traditional view that the primary responsibility for the costs of higher education should rest with the student and his family. When family support is not available under strict limiting conditions, presumably the government will help the needy segment of the student population. For the rest of the student population the administration rejects the two decade liberal consensus that called for a family-school-government partnership in financing a student's education but that had, in President Reagan's view too generously shared governments funds in the cost of financing higher education.[65]

Higher Education Fights Back

The 1981 Reagan budget battle was only the first of literally dozens of efforts by the Reagan administration to cut back student aid during his two terms in office. However, none of the president's subsequent proposals met with same degree of legislative success. In 1982, President Reagan again proposed huge reductions in federal funding for all areas of higher education.[66] But this time the higher education lobby was prepared for the president's attacks. Confronted by massive opposition from colleges, students, and parents, Congress passed a bill that rejected nearly all of the president's reductions in the Title IV programs.[67] Reagan vetoed it as a "budget buster," but congress overrode the veto.[68]

This same pattern was repeated in 1983, 1984, and 1985. The administration proposed dramatic cuts in the Pell grant program, elimination of the SEOG, doubling the loan origination fee, requiring a needs test for all federally guaranteed student loans, and raising loan interest rates. But again the well-organized efforts of the higher education lobby derailed the president's efforts.[69]

By 1986, the stalemate between Reagan and the Congress over student aid was firmly established. Despite determined efforts on both sides, the president was unable to assemble the coalition necessary to cut the aid programs further and student-aid supporters in Congress were unable to muster the support to expand them. But the resulting six-year stalemate did not mean that the student aid programs did not change. External forces were causing precisely the changes Gladieux had warned about in 1980. The rapid tuition inflation of the early 1980s meant that even as federal support was holding steady, the purchasing power of that support was eroding. Also, each year a larger percent of the total federal aid was going to support the rising costs of the GSLP, leaving fewer dollars for grants. As a consequence, the federal student-aid programs were changing, but not as the result explicit policy choices. They were being transformed as a result of legislative deadlock and programmatic drift.[70]

THE 1986 REAUTHORIZATION: FACING THE HARD CHOICES

The Higher Education Act was again set to expire in 1986. Reauthorizing it presented Congress with a variety of challenges other than simply how much to spend on student aid. Since the act had last been reauthorized in 1980, the net price of attending college had increased by more than 60 percent and was rising steadily. The median family income was falling. The national savings rate was at an historic low. The price gap between public and private colleges was at an all-time high and the number of older students attending college part-time was reshaping the profile of the typical undergraduate. The act needed to be adjusted to address all of these new circumstances.

Increasing Demands, Diminishing Resources

In spite of growing concern that the Title IV programs were failing to achieve their intended objectives and might be in need of fundamental reform, the mid-1980s was a poor time to be reforming any major domestic policy. It was not only the Reagan administration which was putting pressure on Congress to reduce spending, the deteriorating budget situation was casting a dark shadow over almost every federal program. Rep. Thomas Coleman euphemistically described it as "working within an atmosphere of reduced expectations."[71]

In this context, the effort to reform the student aid programs in 1986 revolved around ways to make the existing programs work better to help an increasing number of lower-income students to cover their rapidly rising college costs. One approach was to say that the college affordability problem had become so severe that additional spending was going to be necessary to solve it. Specifically, William Ford, chair of the House Postsecondary Education Subcommittee, advocated increasing the level of the maximum Pell grant and broadening eligibility to include part-time students.[72]

This approach was challenged by those who argued that the price of such an expansion was simply too great. In its place, they favored a more limited plan which would make it harder for middle-income students to qualify for a Pell grant but would expand the grants of those students who did qualify. This would target that aid more carefully to the most needy students. To compensate for the tightening of eligibility for middle-income students, they would allow such students to both borrow more money each year and to accumulate a significantly larger aggregate debt.[73]

The final compromise which emerged from the debate over these two positions included a reinstatement of the needs test for loan eligibility, and it limited student borrowing to the amount of their need. The 1986 act also included several other features to reduce the cost of the programs. Family assets were to be considered in the needs assessment as well as family income. All borrowers were now to be charged an insurance premium of 3 percent of the principle to be used to reduce the costs of program defaults to the government.[74] But bowing to the demands of middle-income students who were struggling to pay their rising college prices, the loan limits were relaxed to allow students to borrow more.[75]

Few people were happy with the final package. It promised no reduction in the overall cost of the still growing student aid programs. It did nothing to reverse the declining value of the Pell grant to low-income students. It increased the dependence of many students on borrowing for college. It increased the long-term costs of the program, and it accelerated the shifting character of federal aid toward loans and away from grants.

The Stalemate Continues

Frustrated with their inability to break the stalemate over student aid, the Reagan administration shifted its tactics in the mid-1980s. Their new approach was to argue that student-aid cuts were necessary to restore accountability in the use of federal funds. Federal student aid was no longer portrayed as simply too expensive, it was now attacked as wasteful and unnecessary.[76] Led by Secretary of Education William Bennett, this new approach focused directly on the abuses of the student aid programs. In his first press conference after taking office, Bennett sarcastically warned that his proposed reductions in federal student aid may require some students to undertake a "divestiture of certain sorts: stereo divestiture, automobile divestiture, three-weeks-at-the-beach divestiture."[77]

Bennett's attacks generated equally strong responses from college leaders and student groups. John Bradamas, then president of New York University, called Bennett's assertions a threat to an entire generation of scholars,[78] and Senator Paul Simon accused the Secretary of "trivializing a very important national issue."[79] Even former Secretary Bell wrote an essay in the *New York Times* in which he blasted the new assault on student aid and argued that further cuts in student aid would strain the budgets of the states and effectively preclude able students from "setting their sights on our most distinguished institutions."[80]

In the end, the new attacks on the student aid programs proved to be no more successful than the first. The Reagan administration was not able to persuade the public, or Congress, that the government should cut back on spending for middle-income student aid. To the contrary, rising college prices were bringing public pressure to expand that aid, not to reduce or redirect it to lower-income students. As Reagan left office in 1989, the federal government was spending more money on student aid than it ever had before. But the purchasing power of that aid was declining, the portion going to higher-income students was increasing, and rising price barriers were driving down the participation rates of disadvantaged students.

THE EDUCATION PRESIDENT AND COLLEGE STUDENT AID

The election of George Bush in 1988 was seen as a hopeful sign by those who sought to bring an end to the dramatic declines in college affordability experienced since 1980. Bush, who had promised to be the "Education President," did not have the record of opposition to student aid of his predecessor. Indeed, during the 1988 election campaign, Bush had expressed an interest in addressing the issue of college affordability. In an August 1988 speech, then-Vice-President Bush said:

> In higher education today the question is just as much access as it is quality—economic access. . . . Many middle-income families are panicked by the high costs of four years of college—the specter of $100,000 per child.[81]

Once elected, however, Bush devoted much less attention and effort to the issues of college affordability than had either Carter or Reagan. And, to the disappointment of those who hoped he would bring a fresh approach to the student aid programs, Bush continued to press Congress to reduce spending on middle-income student aid and to redirect those funds to lower-income students in the form of larger Pell grants.[82]

But Bush had no more success with his proposals than had Reagan. Senator Pell, speaking for most others in Congress, continued to regard any effort to redirect aid from middle- to lower-income students as "moving in precisely the wrong direction" and felt that the real answer was "larger Pell grants for more students, not larger grants for fewer students."[83] As a consequence, the stalemate over how to reform student aid continued into the early 1990s. The bitterness and passion which characterized student-aid policy-making during the Reagan years may have been gone, but the results were largely the same.

The Continuing Deterioration of the Loan Program

By the early 1990s, the combination of rising college prices and the ten-year stalemate over student-aid reform had taken its toll on the federal student-aid programs. The maximum grant was no longer large enough to provide low-income students with sufficient resources to have access to even moderately priced public colleges. The student loan programs were not providing middle-income students with access to the capital necessary to afford rapidly rising private college prices. Yet, even as the Title IV programs were proving to be less and less successful in achieving their original objectives, their costs to the government were continuing to rise rapidly. Students, parents, and colleges, were demanding that the programs be expanded. But budgetary realities made such expansions politically impossible.

The GSLP, in particular, seemed to be on the verge of a total collapse. In 1991, Senator Edward Kennedy warned that the "student loan programs may be just one step ahead of disaster."[84] Senator Sam Nunn was even more blunt. He concluded that the system of student loans was in shambles and that "nothing less than a comprehensive, sustained, and intensive reform effort is needed."[85]

The reasons for such harsh judgments are easy to see. Students were borrowing far more than they had in the first decade of the program and concerns were emerging over the consequences the larger debt burdens now facing graduates. Default rates were high and rising rapidly. The college participation rates of minority students had been sliding downward since the mid-1970s. This trend renewed fears that the prospect of such large debts were discouraging many disadvantaged from entering college.

Yet, as the 1992 reauthorization of the HEA approached, there were also several hopeful signs. The combination of growing public concern about college prices, and the deteriorating performance of the student aid system, seemed to set the stage for the first major overhaul in the student aid programs since 1972. Charles Saunders of the American Council on Education, wrote that the 1992 reauthorization could produce "the broadest changes in student aid in 25 years."[86] Finally, it seemed to many, something was going to be done to get the student aid programs working properly again.

THE 1992 REAUTHORIZATION: HIGH HOPES DASHED

Those entrusted with reworking the Title IV programs in 1992 faced an overwhelming task. Everyone agreed that there were problems, but there was substantial disagreement over which of the many problems were most severe. To some, it was the high costs of the programs, to others it was the inadequate access it provided to lower-income students; some wanted to expand the borrowing power of upper- and middle-income students, and others to reduce loan defaults.

These problems not withstanding, it was with high hopes for reform, and public pressure for action mounting, that Congress began the reauthorization process in mid-1991. The year-long battle which followed was dominated by three principle issues. The first was the desire by some to reverse the cutbacks of the past decade and expand the size and scope of the programs. The second issue was a move to replace the GSLP with a system of direct loans. This plan called for the elimination of banks and financial intermediaries from the program and origination of all loans directly from college campuses. The final issue which shaped the reauthorization debate was concern over federal spending. President Bush, preparing for his approaching reelection bid, was determined to hold the line of federal spending. With Bush unwilling to spend more on the programs, and congressional reformers determined to expand eligibility and increase benefits, the specter of a Bush veto hung heavily over the proceedings and influenced the outcome at several key points.

William Ford and the Guaranteed Pell Grant

In late 1991, House Committee Chair William Ford unveiled his plan for a creating a new student aid system.[87] In addition to increased eligibility for both federal grants and subsidized loans,[88] Ford's plan would require automatic funding of all Pell grants each year. Put another way, he called for making the Pell grant an "entitlement." This would force Congress to appropriate sufficient funds each year to insure that all students would receive the full grant they are eligible to receive. In 1991, for example, Congress authorized a maximum Pell grant of $3,100 a year, but it only appropriated enough to award grants of $2,400.

In developing this plan, Ford followed a strategy of proposing extended aid to the middle- and upper-income in the hope that he could use their political clout to win support for expanded aid to the lower income.[89] This was an expensive and risky strategy. The cost of the entitlement provision alone, estimated at $12 billion, put him on a collision course with President Bush and risked undermining his entire proposal. But buoyed by public concern over college prices, and the failings of the GSL, Ford was confident he could persuade Congress to accept increased spending levels.[90] Sensing that the end of the Cold War presented a unique opportunity to refocus government attention on domestic concerns, Ford announced that he wanted to be first to scoop up a chunk of the coming "peace" dividend.

As Ford struggled to build support for the Pell grant entitlement, a complication arose. The Education Department revealed a $1.4 billion shortfall in the 1992 appropriation for the Pell grant program. That amount had to be paid out of the same pot as the appropriators for Pell grants in 1993.[91] This revelation made crystal-clear that the Congress was unable to fully fund the Pell grant even at its current level. Many members of Congress wondered how, given the budget situation, they would be able to afford larger grants to more students.[92] Clearly, unless they were willing to substantially increase the funding for the program (which would certainly incur a Bush veto), making more students eligible for Pell grants would mean less, not more, money for needy recipients.

This troubling news about the higher than expected cost of the 1992 Pell grant program made it even more difficult for many members of Congress to support a potentially uncontrollable new entitlement. In light of this, Ford concluded that the time was still not right for a guaranteed Pell grant.[93] When President Bush announced in early spring he would veto any new entitlement, Representative Ford announced that he would abandon his plan.

The First Battle over Direct Lending

With the fight for a guaranteed Pell grant now lost, Congress turned its attention to whether to retain the GSLP or replace it with a system of direct lending.[94] Supporters of direct lending argued that it offered several advantages over the GSLP.[95] By cutting out the private lenders and financial intermediaries, the program could save between $160 million and $1 billion dollars. By employing an income-contingent repayment system, the rising default rate could be reduced. And by administering the programs on campuses, institutions would be freed of the red tape now necessary when dealing with dozens of different lenders, guarantee agencies, and secondary markets. The result, it was said, would be a less expensive, more flexible, more user-friendly lending system.[96]

Opponents of direct lending countered that it constituted little more than a dangerous, untested experiment conducted at the public's expense.

They challenged the plan's cost savings, and the ability of campus financial aid offices and the Department of Education to deliver on the promise of improved management. Lawrence Hough, president of the Student Loan Marketing Association, argued that the cost savings from the plan amounted to nothing more than a shifting of costs from banks to colleges and that "any minimal savings that might occur would come at the expense of student's loss of the ability to chose the lenders and the companies with whom they want to deal.[97]

Even as the direct lending plan was gaining congressional support, however, it was raising the threat of a presidential veto. Education Secretary Lamar Alexander announced that the addition of any direct lending plan would "destroy" the bill, and that no such plan was acceptable to the administration.[98] That announcement seemed to signal the end of any major Title IV reform in 1992. Ford's plan for a Pell grant entitlement was dead and the direct loan reform was in deep trouble.

But, in the end, all sides had too much invested in the reform process to come away with nothing. With the 1992 election only four months away, President Bush and congressional leaders agreed on a compromise version of the reauthorization plan. In that compromise, the direct loan plan was designated a "demonstration project" which would include no more than 300 institutions. This allowed all sides to claim victory. A new program had been created, but Congress had not promised to provide any additional funds for college student aid.

The Substance of the 1992 Act

While the 1992 amendments proved to be the largest reform in the federal student aid programs since MISAA in 1978, it failed to produce the kind of comprehensive reform that many had expected and most felt was needed. It did, however, make some important adjustments in both the grant and loan programs and created the framework for a significant reform of the troublesome loan guarantee programs. The act changed the Pell grant program in several ways which broadened eligibility.[99] It also increased the maximum grant to $3,700 in 1993–94, rising progressively to $4,500 in 1997–98.[100]

The 1992 reauthorization also increased eligibility for federally guaranteed loans. It established a new "Unsubsidized Stafford Loan for Middle-Income Borrowers" with the same loan limits and eligibility as the need-based GSLs.[101] This gave more students access to the ever larger sums necessary to cover their rising college costs. But it did nothing to come to terms with the negative consequences resulting from increased borrowing. Loans were now easier to get and easier to repay, but students would be expected to use those loans to finance a larger portion of the costs of their educations.

The Charade of the 1992 Act

Of its face, the 1992 act seemed to provide both lower- and middle-income students with more resources to pay for college. Given the rapidly rising college prices, that should have been an important step. But a closer look reveals that much of those increased benefits were an illusion. The bill promised larger grants to lower-income students, but, without the entitlement provisions, Congress was unlikely to provide the funds to make those larger awards possible.[102]

At the same time, middle-income students continue to be guaranteed access to ever larger loans. The act expanded eligibility for the new loan program so that virtually anyone who is attending an accredited college, and is willing to go into debt, has access to more than $20,000. Those with parents willing to assume further debt, have access to the funds to cover the full cost of college through the PLUS program.

Thus in important ways, the reauthorization of the HEA in 1992 represented a kind of charade. The Congress pretended to provide lower-income students with more resources to attend college, but it failed to provide the money to make those grants available. It pretended to provide middle-income students with more aid, but that aid was really nothing more than access to larger loans which the student will be required to repay with interest. For both groups, then, what had appeared to be much-needed federal help to cover rising college prices, was in reality only the opportunity to take on additional debt and to finance an even greater portion of their educational costs.

THE CLINTON BREAKTHROUGH

Bill Clinton was the first president since LBJ who came to office promising to do something about the problem of college affordability. Time and again during the presidential campaign, Clinton spoke of the fears of families who wondered about how they would pay for their children's educations, of the recent college graduates who were forced to abandon a career in public service in order to repay their college loans, and of the costs to the nation and to the economy of price barriers which keep talented lower-income students out of college.[103]

In his campaign book *Putting People First*, Clinton promised that, if elected, he would scrap the existing student loan system and replace it with a new Nation Service Trust fund.[104] Students would borrow from the trust to cover the cost of college or job training and they would repay their debt either as a percentage of their earnings over ten years or by performing public service work. This proposal allowed Clinton to simultaneously address two seemingly unrelated problems. The first was the short-term problem of rising college prices and the inadequacy of the financial aid system. The second was the president's longer term desire to "change the ethos of the nation" and rebuild a spirit of service and citizenship in the country.[105]

Enacting Direct Lending

After his election, Clinton moved quickly to submit his proposal to reform the student loan program. The central element of that plan was a modified version of the direct lending plan which had been debated in 1992 and was about to be tried as a demonstration project. The new president's plan would abandon the demonstration project and phase in direct lending at all schools right away. Under Clinton's plan, the loan repayment system would also be reformed. Students could either repay their loans over ten years, as they do with the GSLP, or extend the repayments over a longer term and use a graduated repayment system in which borrowers would repay smaller amounts at first, and larger amounts as their incomes increase.

The battlelines in the 1993 fight over direct lending were almost the same as they had been in 1992. But this time the new president was working for the plan and not against it. While this strengthened the supporters of direct lending, they still did not have enough votes to enact an immediate phase-in of direct lending.[106] Several longtime advocates of improving college affordability, including Claiborne Pell, expressed "deep reservations" about switching to direct loans without first testing the system in a demonstration project.[107]

It was Pell, however, who engineered the final compromise.[108] Under this arrangement, the existing GSLP would be left in place while partially phasing in the new program of direct lending. Direct loans would constitute 5 percent of new loan volume in 1994–95, 40 percent the next year, 50 percent for the next two years plus any additional schools who wanted to join, and 60 percent plus any additional schools in 1998–99. Participation by the schools was voluntary, but if many schools volunteered, much more than 50 percent of loan volume be handled through direct loans beginning in the third year of the program.

The final compromise pleased both sides. Supporters were pleased that they had saved the GSLP from elimination. John Dean of the Consumer Bankers Association, who had worked hard to defeat direct lending, said he felt as though the GSLP had "a new lease on life."[109] He went on to suggest that:

> There's a continued belief on the part of the financial side and many on the school side that the actual experience under the direct loan program will make it a much less attractive program than it is as a concept on paper.[110]

On the other side, David Longanecker, Assistant Secretary for Postsecondary Education, and the person responsible for implementing the direct lending plan, hoped to phase out the existing system totally and switch to direct loans. He said the Clinton Administration intends to "provide a program that is so attractive to the institutions and the students that it will become the program of the future."[111]

Thus, the compromise bill created a competition between the Department of Education and the financial industry to sell their programs to the schools. The hope was that this competition would give everyone more time to evaluate their respective performances and to select the program which best serves the needs of students and schools. By the end of the century, the outcome of this competition could lead to anything from a stable co-existence between the two alternate loan approaches, to a voluntary transition to direct lending in which the GSLP slowly disappears as fewer schools choose to participate in the program.

Enacting National Service

The call for national service had been a central part of the Clinton presidential campaign in 1992. Rep. David McCurdy echoed the hopes of many when he said that "the concept of service and citizenship can become the defining element of his administration."[112] But during the campaign, Clinton had always painted his vision of a national service corps with a very broad brush. As he took office, the new president needed to turn that undefined vision into a practical reality.[113]

While past efforts to develop a system of national and community service and efforts to reform the student aid system had remained distinct, Clinton linked the two. In his address at Rutgers University to announce his national service initiative, Clinton made the point that the student loan system was discouraging participation in community service:

> And as we rekindle the spirit of national service, I know it won't disappoint many of the students here to know that we also have to reform the whole system of student loans. . . . Today when students borrow money for an education, the repayment plan they make is based largely on how much they have to repay without regard to what the jobs they take themselves pay. It is a powerful incentive, therefore, for young college graduates to do just the reverse of what we might want them to do: to take a job that pays more, even if it is less rewarding, because that is the job that will make the repayment of the loans possible.[114]

Under the president's proposal, students could receive money for college or a job training program in return for working on community service projects. These participants would also receive student loans and then have a constant percentage of their future income deducted until the loan was paid off. This would enable recent graduates to take low-paying public service jobs without worrying about how to repay their loans. Students could also perform community service projects after college and have $5,000 in loans forgiven (for a maximum of two years) in exchange for work as teachers, police officers, social workers, or other service-oriented employees.[115] Clinton hoped to begin the program with 25,000 participants in 1994 and expand to about 150,000 in four years.[116]

Educational grants were by no means the only costs of the national service program. Each participant would also receive a stipend of up to $7,400 a year. The federal government would pay 85 percent of that stipend. Washington would also provide up to 85 percent of the cost of health and child-care benefits. These cost concerns threatened to undermine enactment of the program. But by further reducing the size and expense of the program, Clinton was able to muster the votes to pass the National and Community Service Trust Act of 1993. The size of the educational award was dropped to $4,750/year and the maximum number of participants was reduced to 100,000.

National Service and College Student Aid

Much of the congressional debate over national service revolved around the impact the creation of the program would have on the Title IV programs. The concern was that, given the on-going budget constraints, any money appropriated to national service would result in reduced funding for need-based student aid. Representative Susan Molinari warned: "It is crystal-clear that we are in a zero-sum game when it comes to funding for education programs."[117] Similarly, Bill Goodling argued that with a limited amount of money available, it was not right for the government to give money to the children of the Rockefellers or Donald Trump, who do not need help.[118]

But supporters made clear that they did not view national service as a student financial aid program at all. They argued that students should not be required to pass a needs test to participate because one of its greatest virtues was that national service brings together participants from all economic and social backgrounds to work for a common purpose.[119] In this view, national service offered many benefits to individuals and communities, and education grants were only a small part of that greater good. Moreover, because the program had no direct budgetary relationship with the Title IV programs, each dollar spent on national service provided a new opportunity for disadvantaged Americans, without reducing those opportunities provided by need-based student aid.

STUDENT AID AND COLLEGE AFFORDABILITY: THE VIEW FROM THE MID-1990S

By the mid-1990s, the legislative stalemate which had frozen efforts to reform or expand the student aid programs had come to an end. President Clinton has broken the deadlock in 1993. But the college affordability problems which had developed during the 1980s continued to accelerate even after the 1993 reforms had been put into place. As college prices were rising, the federal government was unable to respond with sufficient resources, or sufficient political will, to refocus their limited resources and offset these price increases.

Lower-income students suffered the most. In constant dollar terms, the average tuition at a public four-year college increased by 70 percent between 1980 and 1993. The maximum Pell grant increased less than 4 percent. After 1980, repeated federal efforts to increase the size of that grant failed. Efforts to make the grant an entitlement failed. As a direct consequence, needy students experienced declines in the value of their grants, and more were forced to borrow if they hoped to go to college.

Middle-income students fared only slightly better. Efforts to expand eligibility for the Pell grant to middle-income families failed. As a result, rising college prices and stable family incomes have also forced them to borrow ever larger sums to finance their higher education. In 1980, all students had been eligible for federally subsidized and guaranteed student loans. But in 1981 eligibility was slashed and the needs test reinstated for the GSLP. Since that time, loan eligibility has been slowly re-expanded so that today everyone is again eligible to borrow for college. Today, however, those loans are unsubsidized for those students who do not pass a needs test. Such loans do not reduce the cost of college facing borrowers, they delay and increase them. The federal government has thus been responsible for shifting a larger portion of the cost of higher education on to lower-income students and their families.

Two major pieces of federal legislation were passed in 1993 which promised to address the college affordability problem. The enactment of direct lending should reduce the price of student loans to the federal treasury. But those savings may not be passed on to students in the form of larger grants or cheaper loans. The plan will allow some borrowers to repay their loans as a portion of their income. But even this does nothing to reverse the increased reliance of lower- and middle-income students on borrowing. It simply makes it easier for them to repay their larger and more expensive loans.

Students do, now, have the option of participating in the national service program. For those selected to participate in the program, the educational grant or the loan forgiveness will go a long way toward paying their college bills. But the program will only be available to 100,000 people when fully operational. That compares to 4.1 million now receiving Pell grants and almost 7 million borrowing through the various federal student loan programs. Of those, only a portion of participants will be from lower-income families. As such, the national service program provides some new resources to pay for college, but it will do little to make new resources available to those in the most need and hence will have little long-term impact on the problem of declining college affordability.

Thus, from the perspective of the mid-1990s, the federal student-aid programs are working poorly for all concerned. College prices are climbing steadily upward, but the purchasing power of the grant programs is declining. The volume of student loans is increasing, even as the government has attempted to limit borrowing. And while students are experiencing declining federal support, the price-tag of those federal programs to the taxpayers continues to grow at a troubling rate. In 1992, the real cost of the Title IV programs was up 21 percent since 1990 and more than 100 percent since 1980. When the price of the national service initiative is added to the mix, these costs will be even higher. The federal government is thus paying more for these programs which are providing less valuable assistance. In turn, they are expecting students at all income levels to assume a greater burden in the financing of their higher education.

5

The Costs and Consequences of the Transformation in Federal Student-Aid Policy

The transformation in the federal student-aid effort over the past three decades has many dimensions. But without question, the fundamental difference between the student aid programs created in the 1960s and early 1970s and those of the 1990s, is the dramatic increase in the volume, and relative importance, of the various student loan programs. The first federally guaranteed loan program was designed to provide a convenient source of aid to middle-income students at a very low cost to the federal government. However, by the mid-1990s, after numerous modifications, revisions, and amendments, the now multiple federal student loan programs have grown dramatically in both their size and scope.

This expansion translated into important changes in the resources available to lower-income students to pay for college. As far back as 1988, Senator Claiborne Pell lamented that the typical student aid package was intended to be three-quarters grant and one-quarter loan, but now "it is precisely the opposite."[1] This sent a clear message to lower-income students: If you can't afford to pay for college, borrow the money.

Today, almost no one is happy with the balance between grants and loans in federal student-aid policy. Potential students, former students, colleges, and the federal government all have their own concerns over the growing levels of student borrowing. Yet, in spite of these concerns, and repeated efforts at reform, an ever larger number of students borrow through these programs each year while the cost of these programs to the federal government has continued to grow.

In this chapter, I examine the costs and consequences which have resulted from the expansion in the role of student loans in the federal effort to remove college price barriers. After reviewing how the various loan programs work, I look at why the costs of operating them have increased so rapidly since 1980. I then turn to the unintended consequences which have followed the expansion of student borrowing. In particular, I examine concerns that the prospect of substantial post-collegiate debt discourages disadvantaged students from entering college, that it distorts the career choices of those who do attend, and that they saddle borrowers with unreasonably large debts when they leave school. Finally, I explain how the growth of loans has distorted federal policy by shifting subsidies towards middle- and upper-income families and away from lower-income students.

UNDERSTANDING FEDERAL LOAN GUARANTEES

In order to understand how and why the various loan programs have grown so rapidly, it is useful to examine their operation in detail. The principle of these is the large and complex set of federally guaranteed student loan programs which are now referred to under the umbrella title "Federal Family Education Loan (FFEL) program." Unlike Pell grants and the campus-based student-aid programs, the FFEL programs are not direct student aid programs at all. They are complex structures designed to encourage private lenders to make loans that they would not otherwise make. As such, most of the federal expenditures resulting from the program do not go to students at all but rather to banks and financial institutions. While this system has succeeded in making large sums of private monies available to students, it has done so at a very high price to the federal treasury and to many lower-income students.

The Logic of Loan Guarantees

In order to insure that all students have access to the capital they need to attend college, policy-makers face two problems. Potential lenders find student loans too risky and too expensive to offer, and potential borrowers find the loans too risky and too expensive to take. From the lender's perspective, student loans can be prohibitively expensive. They are for a small amount, there is no marketable asset that can provide collateral, and the highly mobile borrowers often have no credit history. As a consequence, prior to 1965 "private education loans were virtually unavailable" unless they were based on the income and financial positions of the student's family.[2]

Potential borrowers also face risks and costs which can make college loans unattractive, even if they can find a willing lender. While the average return for an investment in higher education is high, it is subject to a wide variance. In any individual case the future return from an investment in education can be quite risky. The student-borrower must be willing to assume that risk. Moreover, the high interest rate that a lender would charge to make such an uncollateralized loan made college loans even less attractive to potential student-borrowers.[3]

Government loan guarantees thus serve to increase the supply of, and demand for, private student loans by lowering the costs and the risks to both lenders and borrowers. In addition to the guarantee of full repayment, the federal government pays lenders a variety of subsidies to encourage them to make loans. By holding down interest rates, and by making loans available to all students without collateral or credit checks, the federal government insures that lower-income students are both willing and able to borrow for college.

The Operation of Loan Guarantees

As first enacted in 1965, undergraduates could borrow up to $1,000 a year at a 6 percent interest rate through the GSLP. The federal government guaranteed repayment of all loans and paid the interest on loans to families with incomes of less than $15,000. While these were attractive terms, the price to the federal government remained small. In 1970, about one million students borrowed about $3.5 billion through the program.[4]

From this relatively modest beginning, the FFEL grew at an astounding rate. In 1992, more than $4 billion in guaranteed loans were made to about four million student-borrowers. There are now five separate FFEL programs, more than 8,000 eligible education institutions, 13,000 participating lenders, 35 secondary markets, and 46 state or non-profit guarantee agencies.[5] The costs of the programs to the federal government have also grown. In 1992, the cost to the federal government of the various loan guarantee programs was $6.3 billion.[6]

Figure 5.1 shows the complex flow of funds which occurs whenever an FFEL is made. FFELs are generally provided by the private financial sector, primarily commercial banks, savings and loan institutions, and credit unions.[7] Most students seeking a student loan never need to visit a lending institution. The application process is handled by the financial aid office at the school the student attends. To receive a guaranteed student loan, a student must first complete the Free Application for Federal Student Aid and return it to the Department of Education. Based on the information provided by the student, the federal government calculates the student's Expected Family Contribution (EFC). This is the amount the student's family is judged to be able to afford to cover college costs. Then, the school's financial aid office takes the cost of education at that school and subtracts the EFC to determine the student's financial need. If the price of the school is greater than the amount the family is judged able to contribute, the difference is considered to be the student's need. That need is the amount that the student is eligible to receive in federal financial aid.

Based on the student's need, the financial aid office at the school then puts together a package of Pell grants, campus-based aid, state grants, and institutional aid tailored to the student's individual circumstances. If that aid package does not cover the full cost of the student's education, the student can then borrow the remaining amount, up to the loan limits. Once the financial aid office has determined the student's loan eligibility, that information is then forwarded to the lender. After the student has signed a promissory note agreeing to repay the loan, and has enrolled in a qualified institution of higher education, the loan disbursement check is sent by the lender directly to the school to cover tuition, fees, and room and board (if the student is living in campus housing). Anything that is left over is passed on the student-borrower to cover living expenses. The loan becomes due following a grace period after the student leaves school unless the student applies for a deferment[8] and it must be repaid over a ten-year period and the minimum monthly repayment is $50.

For each loan made, the federal government provides a subsidy payment to the lender as compensation for the lower interest rate charged to the student. This payment is intended to make the return on these student loan's competitive with alternative lending opportunities. The federal government also commits to pay full interest on the loan while the student remains in college. In return, an "origination fee" is deducted

Figure. 5.1
*The Flow of Funds under the Federal Family
Education Loan Programs*

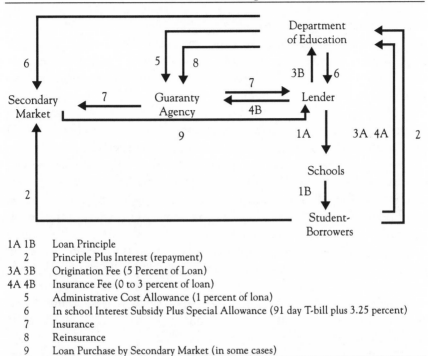

1A 1B	Loan Principle
2	Principle Plus Interest (repayment)
3A 3B	Origination Fee (5 Percent of Loan)
4A 4B	Insurance Fee (0 to 3 percent of loan)
5	Administrative Cost Allowance (1 percent of lona)
6	In school Interest Subsidy Plus Special Allowance (91 day T-bill plus 3.25 percent)
7	Insurance
8	Reinsurance
9	Loan Purchase by Secondary Market (in some cases)

Source: Adapted from General Accounting Office, *Direct Loans Could Save Money and Simplify Program Administration*, September 1992, p. 17.

from the loan principle and paid to the federal government to cover their administrative costs. That fee, which is now between 5 percent and 6.5 percent of the loan, is deducted from each loan disbursement. The lender may also collect an insurance premium of up to 3 percent of the loan principle. This premium is also deducted from each disbursement.

The lender is responsible for the collection of all loans. If the student fails to repay the loan because of death, disability, bankruptcy, or default, the lender must make "due diligence" efforts, such as phone calls and letters to the defaulter, to collect the loan. After 180 days, if collection attempts have failed, the lender passes along the defaulted loan to the state's guarantee agency and receive full reimbursement.

A guaranty agency, which is established in each state, must then try to collect the loan. If they successfully collect the defaulted loan, the guaranty agency can retain 30 percent of the amount collected to reimburse its costs. But if they cannot collect, the agency can apply to the Department of Education for federal reimbursement 270 days after the loan went into default. The state guaranty agency must assume part of the responsibility for defaulted loans. Agencies with 5 percent or fewer of their loans in default are fully reimbursed. Those with higher default rates receive only partial reimbursement.

Many lenders prefer not to be involved in the collection of relatively small loans from very mobile student-borrowers. Such lenders may still participate in the origination of student loans and then sell them in one of the secondary student loan markets before they come due. These secondary markets provide liquidity for participating lenders by purchasing student loans which should, in turn, allow the originating lenders to expand their FFEL portfolios. Secondary markets also encourage the development of organizations which specialize in the collection of outstanding student loans. The largest of these secondary markets is the Student Loan Marketing Association (Sallie Mae) which is a federally chartered stockholder-owned corporation established in 1972 to provide a national secondary market for loans made under the FFEL. In 1991, Sallie Mae's outstanding loan purchases of $15.6 billion constituted approximately one-third of all dollars outstanding in the FFEL.[9]

While Sallie Mae is the largest of the secondary student loan markets, several states have created their own secondary markets to make participation in the FFEL more attractive to local lenders. Today, the New England Educational Loan Marketing Corporation, the Nebraska Higher Education Loan program, and the California Student Loan Financing Corporation are all among the top ten holders of outstanding student loans.[10]

The Proliferation of Loan Guarantee Programs

As the demand for student loans has grown since 1980, the federal government has responded by expanding and subdividing the FFEL to better serve the diverse types of students seeking loans.[11] Today there are five different loan guarantee programs.[12] Each operates by different rules and

Table 5.1

Characteristics of Federal Loan Guarantee Programs

Program	Need-Based Loan?	Yearly & Aggregate Loan Maximums	Interest Rates
Subsidized Stafford	Yes	Year 1-2 = $4,000 Year 3-5 = $5,000 Maximum = $23,000 for undergraduates	3.1% above the 91 day T-bill rate Capped at 9%
Unsubsidized Stafford	No	Cost of education minus financial aid No aggregate maximum	3.1% above the 91 day T-bill rate Capped at 9%
Parent Loan for Undergraduate Students (PLUS)	No	Cost of education minus financial aid No aggregate maximum	3.1% above the 91 day T-bill rate Capped at 10%
Supplemental Loans for Students (SLS)	No	Cost of education minus financial aid No aggregate maximum	3.1% above the 91 day T-bill rate Capped at 11%

serves a different constituency. The differences between these loans are described in table 5.1.

Stafford Loans. By far the largest of the FFELs is the Stafford loan program. In 1991, Stafford loans accounted for about 80 percent of all FFELs made and 78 percent of the dollar volume of all FFEls. There are two types of Stafford loans. Those students from families with demonstrated financial need may receive a federally subsidized Stafford loan to cover that documented need. Under these loans the federal government pays the interest charges on the loan while the student is in school, during the grace period, and during authorized deferments.

Students whose families do not demonstrate financial need, and therefore do not qualify for a subsidized Stafford loan, may borrow through the unsubsidized Stafford loan program. In this program the rules for borrowing are the same except that the interest rate is higher and the student, not the government, must pay the interest which accrues on the loan while the student is in school or has deferred payment.

The interest rate charged on both types of Stafford loans is variable. The rate is adjusted each year and is capped at 9 percent for subsidized and 10 percent for unsubsidized loans. Qualified students may borrow up to $4,000 during their first and second years in college. They can borrow up to $5,000 during their third through fifth year. Undergraduates can borrow no more than $23,000 under the Stafford program. However, if they subsequently go on to graduate or professional school, their loan limit is increased to $73,000.

PLUS Loans. The Education Amendments of 1980 established the Parent Loan for Undergraduate Students (PLUS). This program provides additional funds for parents of dependent undergraduate students. PLUS allows families to borrow more than they can under the Stafford program. In fact, students can borrow the entire cost of their education minus any financial aid they receive. In return for these higher loan limits, the borrower must pay a higher interest rate (variable up to 10 percent) and have no grace period or deferment options. No needs test is required for the PLUS loan. In 1991, PLUS loans accounted for about 8 percent of the total volume of FFEL loans awarded.

SLS Loans. The Higher Education Amendments of 1986 created the Supplemental Loans to Students (SLS) program. It is similar to the PLUS loan except that it is available only to independent students. An independent student must apply for a subsidized Stafford loan first, then for an unsubsidized Stafford, and only then can they apply for an SLS. Like the PLUS, the SLS provides loans which cover the entire cost of the education minus any other financial aid received. The interest rate is variable and capped at 11 percent. SLS loans also allow no grace period or deferred payment options. In 1991, SLS loans accounted for about 14 percent of all FFELs.

Consolidated Loans. The Higher Education Amendments of 1986 also authorized lenders to make consolidation loans. These loans allow students to consolidate multiple Stafford, PLUS, SLS, and even Perkins loans into a single loan. This can only be done when all of the loans are in repayment or grace periods. The interest rate on consolidated loans is the weighted average of the underlying loans or 9 percent, which ever is the greatest. In 1991, consolidated loans accounted for 6 percent of the total volume of federally guaranteed loans.[13]

The Success of Loan Guarantees

This complex system of incentives, subsidies, and guarantees was designed to insure that every student who is enrolled in an approved institution, and who is willing to take the risks inherent in borrowing to pay for a higher education, will have access to the necessary funds. The structure of the programs also guarantees that the lending institution will make a profit on each loan while incurring almost no risk. Given the structure of the program, it is easy to see why so many students are willing to take out these loans and why so many lenders are willing to make them.

Indeed, if the federal student loan programs are to be judged by their original purpose alone, they are nothing short of an overwhelming success. They have made billions of dollars of loans available to an ever larger percentage of students and have induced the creation of a large financial industry which lends huge amounts of private funds to students based on federal loan guarantees. In 1991, more than 13,000 banks, credit unions, and non-profit lenders participated in the origination of FFELs.[14] While some of these lenders made only a few student loans, many others have made student loans a large part of their portfolios. Twenty-two different lenders each originated more than $100 million in FFELs, and another seventeen originated between $50 and $100 million of new student loans. The impressive size, and scope of the FFEL leaves little doubt that the student loans programs have firmly established themselves in the financial community.[15]

THE CREATION OF DIRECT LENDING

In 1993, a system of direct lending was enacted as an alternative to the FFEL. The first direct loans will be made in the 1994–95 academic year and as much as 60 percent of all student loans will be made through direct lending by 1998. Under this plan, schools will have the option of participating in the direct lending programs. Those schools which did not wish to operate their own program would continue to participate in the loan guarantee programs.

Figure 5.2
The Flow of Funds under the Direct Loan Program

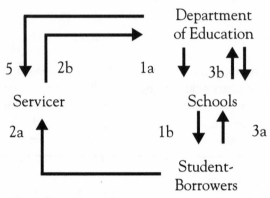

1a 1b	Loan Principle
2a 2b	Principle Plus Interest (repayment)
3a 3b	Origination Fee (five percent of loan)
4	Administrative cost allowance for processing
5	Contract fee

Source: Adapted from General Accounting Office, *Direct Loans Could Save Money and Simplify Program Administration*, September 1992, p. 17.

Figure 5.2 shows how much simpler the flow of funds is under direct lending than it is under the FFEL.[16] Direct lending streamlines the lending process by eliminating private lenders, guarantee agencies, and secondary loan markets. The U.S. Treasury will sell securities to meet the capital requirements of direct lending. Institutions will apply annually to the Department of Education for funding based on the estimated financial needs of their students. On behalf of the government, institutions will determine student eligibility, prepare promissory notes, and distribute loan funds to students following procedures similar to those used in the Perkins loan program.

The Department of Education will operate the servicing aspects of the direct lending program through competitive private contracts. This will relieve the schools of the burden of loan collection and eliminate the need for a secondary market. Direct loans will carry interest rates similar to those charged on Stafford loans. The origination fee and the insurance premiums would be substantially reduced. The result, it is argued, will be lower costs to the schools, to students, and to the federal government.

Disadvantages of Direct Lending

While direct lending has some obvious merit, it also presents some substantial drawbacks.[17] It is not clear that all, or even most, institutions have the capacity, or the desire, to succeed as lending agents. Moreover, if the administrative costs of operating such a program on each campus are large, they could eat up most of the savings resulting from the by-passing of traditional lending agencies.

There is also substantial disagreement over the potential savings which will result from the switch to direct lending. A 1992 study conducted by the GAO estimated that "the federal government could save from $120 million to $1.5 billion annually by using direct rather than guaranteed loans to provide loan assistance to postsecondary students."[18] This estimate was widely cited in the congressional debate over loan reform and may well have been responsible for its eventual enactment.

But a 1993 Congressional Research Service (CRS) study reached a starkly different conclusion. It found that the direct lending reform was likely to produce only small savings to the federal government. This savings would be achieved by reducing needlessly high subsidies to private lenders. The CRS noted, however, that substantial savings could be achieved within the existing framework simply by reducing the subsidies currently paid to banks in the FFEL.[19]

Critics of direct lending also argue that it will not serve students and their families as well as the FFEL. Many wonder why we should expect schools, with no experience in lending, to perform this task better than banks, who are highly skilled at making loans.[20] Further, they wonder why anyone should expect the Department of Education, with little experience in servicing and collecting loans from millions of borrowers, to perform that task better than lenders, Sallie Mae, and the other agencies who have been doing this for years. Indeed, if schools are unable to efficiently originate loans, and/or if the federal government is unable to effectively service and collect loans, direct lending could result in a deterioration in the quality of loan services.

The change to a mixed system of direct and guaranteed loans promises some cost savings to the federal government. It will reduce the large subsidies now paid to financial intermediaries and reduce default rates. But it will have virtually no impact on the college price barriers facing lower-income students. It will not change the amount they must borrow, only the source of their loan. Indeed, even if the entire system of loan guarantees was replaced with direct loans, and nothing else changed, disadvantaged students would face the same discouraging combination of large post-collegiate loans, and the high monthly payments they require. Direct loans streamline the system of student loans, and may reduce the costs of such loans to the government, but it leaves untouched the fundamental problem of more students needing to borrow more money to attend college.

Over the next decade, the number of FFELs should decline steadily and the number of direct loans should increase proportionately. Both systems will operate side by side during the 1990s. In effect, this will constitute an experiment in which the two programs can be compared to each other. Unless Congress chooses to step in to alter the balance, the last half of the 1990s should provide a clear picture of whether direct lending can produce the cost savings and improved service promised by its supporters.

THE HIGH COST OF LOAN GUARANTEES: SUBSIDIES, ALLOWANCES, AND DEFAULTS

As student loans have become an essential resource for families to pay for college, and as they have become an essential element in the portfolios of many financial institutions, they have become more costly to the federal government. For each FFEL made, the federal government incurs several costs. Each of these costs has increased substantially since the late 1970s. Today, the various federally guaranteed student loan programs cost the federal government substantially more than anyone anticipated when they were created.[21] And in spite of determined efforts since 1980 to control the costs of these programs, they have continued to grow, consuming an ever larger percentage of overall federal student aid spending.

Cost #1: Increased Loan Volume

A large part of the increased costs of the loan guarantee programs in the late 1970s and early 1980s was simply due to the fact that a great many more loans were being made. The combination of more students entering college, the loosened loan eligibility requirements, and very attractive interest rates, produced a substantial increase in the volume of student loans.

The fact that the number of loans more than doubled in the 1970s, should not be a surprise since the number of students attending college was growing and the eligibility for the loan programs was expanding rapidly. But the number of loans nearly doubled again in the 1980s when the number of college students was stable and the eligibility for the programs was being reduced. During those two decades, the dollar volume of student loans increased even more rapidly than did the number of student loans. FFEL volume increased an astonishing 200 percent in the 1970s. It then increased another 60 percent in the 1980s. Today, the $15.0 billion awarded in FFEL loans dwarfs the $6.1 billion awarded in Pell grants.[22]

Cost #2: Increased Subsidies and Allowances

There was much more involved in the increases in the costs of the loan guarantee programs than simply an increase in the number of loans being made. Policy changes and economic conditions were making the FFEL more expensive for the federal government at all levels of lending. These factors caused the operating costs of the FFEL to increase even more rapidly than did the volume of student loans.

Each time a student loan is made, the federal government incurs a three-part financial obligation. First, if the loan is a subsidized Stafford loan, it makes payments to the lender on behalf of the borrower for interest that accrues during the in-school, grace, and authorized deferment periods. For unsubsidized Stafford, PLUS, and SLS loans, no interest subsidies are paid. Second, it pays lenders a "special allowance" based on the outstanding principle of all Stafford, PLUS, SLS, and Consolidated loans. This allowance, along with the borrowers interest payment, assures lenders an equitable yield on their loan. The special allowance was developed to insure that banks would be willing to participate in the program.[23] Third, the federal government guarantees lenders that they will be repaid for all loses incurred as a result of borrower death, bankruptcy, or default. While both the lender and the state guarantee agency must make a serious effort to collect defaulted loans, today virtually all default claims by lenders are eventually reimbursed by the Department of Education.

Table 5.2 shows how the total cost of the FFEL has grown since 1980. Even after accounting for inflation, federal expenditures on these programs increased by a troubling 156 percent between 1980 and 1990. In the first half of the decade, each of the major program costs increased

Table 5.2
Federal Expenditures for Student Loan Programs:
1980–1990 (in millions of 1994 dollars)

Federal Expenditure Type	1980	1985	1990
Interest Benefits	$693	$2,093	$1,709
Special Allowances	1,247	1,988	1,610
Reinsurance Default Claims	449	1,352	2,826
Other Expenditures	102	220	238
Total Federal Expenditures	2,491	5,652	6,381

Source: U.S. Department of Educatiom, *FY 1992 Guaranteed Student Loan Data Book*, 1992.

significantly. High interest rates forced the government to pay lenders substantially more in both interest subsidies and special allowances. The increased loan volume also translated into higher default costs. As a consequence, constant-dollar federal expenditures on student loan guarantees increased by 127 percent is just five years.

These cost increases have slowed since 1985, but only slightly. As interest rates began to drop in the late 1980s and early 1990s, the costs to the federal government for interest subsidies and special allowances also dropped. By 1990, these costs were more than $600 million less than they had been in 1985. But the late 1980s also produced a dramatic increase in the costs of loan defaults which more than overshadowed the savings in other areas. The net result was that the overall costs of the FFEL continued to rise, even as lower interest rates were producing substantial reductions in some of the principle costs of the programs.[24]

Cost #3: Increased Default Rates

By the early 1990s, loan defaults constituted the principle cost of the federal loan-guarantee programs. This is not a new problem. As far back as 1975, Congress was holding hearings on what should be done to stem the rapidly rising costs of loan defaults. But while concerns over defaults are long standing, table 5.3 provides an indication of how much worse that problem became since 1980. Even as measured in constant dollars, federal default costs increased 700 percent in the 1980s.

Table 5.3
Federal Expenditures Paid to Lenders to Cover Defaults in the Student Loan Programs: 1970–1990 (in constant 1994 dollars)

Year	Total Default Expenditures (in millions)
1970	$ 25
1975	369
1980	430
1985	1,415
1990	3,028

Source: U.S. Department of Education, FY 1992 Guaranteed Student Loan Data Book, 1992.

In the first years of the program, default costs were relatively small. It was in the early 1980s that the default costs of the FFEL began to increase to alarming levels. Their $1.2 billion cost in 1985 made defaults a major topic of congressional debate during the reauthorization of the Higher Education Act in 1986.[25] That act tightened requirements for both students and institutions to participate in the program and toughened enforcement regulations. But in spite of these efforts, these costs have continued to mount in the 1990s. In 1992, although the rates of loan defaults dropped slightly, the annual costs of defaulted loans was still $3.0 billion.[26]

Why Defaults Increased So Rapidly

There are three principle reasons that default costs have increased so rapidly since 1980. The most obvious is that the number of loan defaults increases as the volume of student loans increases. With the number of students borrowing through the FFEL increasing from 2.3 million in 1980 to 4.5 million in 1990, the number of loan defaults also increased. The Department of Education explains that, although it may take a few years to run its full course:

Invariably, a close relationship exists between annual loan volume and annual default costs. A sudden and sharp increase in loan volume will trigger a substantial increase in dollars entering repayment a few years later and eventually lead to increases in default costs.[27]

Indeed, that is exactly what happened after 1980. As the number of students who had borrowed under the loosened MISAA rules in the late 1970s had their loan become due in the early 1980s, the number of defaults began to increase accordingly.

The second reason that FFEL defaults have increased since 1980 was a change in the character of the students who were borrowing under the FFEL. As net college prices rose after 1980, more lower-income and disadvantaged students began to borrow for college. In a 1990 study, *The Black Undergraduate*, Alexander Astin compared changes in the frequency of borrowing between black and white freshmen between 1978 and 1989.[28] He found that before 1984, white students were more likely to take out a student loan. But since 1984, black students have been more likely to take such loans. Astin goes on to conclude that:

> Changes in the federal financial aid policies during the past decade have had a substantial impact on the black freshmen's financial aid package: Fewer black freshmen have access to federal grants and more must now rely on federal loans.[29]

Using a similar approach, Thomas Mortenson examined the link between family income and borrowing for college. He found that during the 1980s, "While loans have become more widely used by all freshmen to finance their higher education, not all income groups have shared in this expanded use of loans."[30] He concluded the use of loans increased the most rapidly among freshmen with family incomes between 100 and 200 percent of the poverty line, followed by those students whose family income was below the poverty line. The portion of students with family incomes more than 200 percent of the poverty line reporting loan use declined.[31]

The fact that more lower-income and disadvantaged students were borrowing created more costs to the federal government because these students were the most likely to default on their student loans. Students who failed to pay back their loans were disproportionately from disadvantaged backgrounds, program drop-outs or graduates of programs offering narrow vocational training, and were unemployed or earning a low wage when the loan became due. In short, defaulters were usually not wealthy deadbeats using their loans to buy new cars or stereos. Instead, the typical defaulters were, in the words of a task force of experts convened by Congress in 1988 to recommend changes in the FFEL, "individuals with very

Table 5.4

Default Rates Among Stafford Loan Borrowers by Institutional Type

Type of Institution	Default Rates
4-Year Public	14%
4-Year Private	15
2-Year Public	29
2-Year Private	20
Proprietary	50
Total All Borrowers	29

Source: Data for 1987 undergraduate students drawn from the *Student Aid and the Cost of Postsecondary Education*, Washington D.C.: Congressional Budget Office, 1991.

limited resources and academic preparation . . . [who] are taking out loans, enrolling in an educational program, failing to complete that program, and subsequently finding themselves unemployed."[32] As a result, the task force concluded that "a significant portion" of the default costs are simply "uncontrollable." They are just the costs inherent in making college loans to high-risk students.[33]

But the fact that providing loans to disadvantaged students brings high risks, and hence high costs, is not to imply that the government should reduce lending to disadvantaged students in order to save money. Indeed, it is precisely these students who have the most difficult time securing a loan without the guarantee and who gain the most from participation in higher education. As the net price of college rises, these students have no choice but to borrow if they are to go to college.

The final cause of the increasing rates of student loan defaults is a change in the types of schools that borrowers are attending. Table 5.4 shows the default rates for students at various types of institutions. It makes clear that while less than 15 percent of all borrowers who attend four-year colleges eventually default on their loans, nearly half of the students from proprietary schools default.

Cost #4: The Rise of Proprietary Schools

The alarmingly high default rates among students attending proprietary schools is exacerbated by another important shift in the character of the federal loan-guarantee programs.[34] The portion of guaranteed loans which go to students attending proprietary or for-profit educational institutions, has increased dramatically since 1980.[35]

In 1970, nearly 90 percent of all guaranteed loans went to students attending four-year colleges. Less than 6 percent of loans went to students at proprietary schools. During the 1970s, that distribution shifted only slightly. But the distribution of student loans among the various types of institutions changed fundamentally after 1980. The percent of loans recipients going to four-year colleges dropped to only 62 percent while the percent at proprietary schools jumped to 27 percent. Throughout the 1980s, more than one-in-four of all FFELs went to students at proprietary schools.

This was all part of the long chain of events which led to higher costs of the FFEL for the federal government. More loans were being made to students attending proprietary schools, and students at proprietary schools have higher default rates. This drove the default rate up for the entire FFEL. As the default rate increased, so too did the government's costs.

DIFFICULTY OF CONTROLLING FFEL GROWTH

The logic of loan guarantees is that they can be used by the federal government to leverage large amounts of lending from private institutions at a very low cost to the federal government. But today when the interest subsidies, special allowances, default reimbursements and administrative costs are combined, the total cost of these programs are substantial. In 1991, for example, total federal expenditures on the FFEL was $6.1 billion. The program generated $1.3 billion in revenues from origination fees and other reimbursements, but this still left the federal treasury with a price-tag of $5.6 billion for student loan guarantees.[36]

Looked at in one way, this price-tag looks like a bargain. The $5.6 billion of FFEL spending in 1991 generated $14.2 billion in privately originated loans. As such, each $1.00 of federal spending on the FFEL produced about $2.50 in new loans to students. This value notwithstanding, the FFEL presents some significant concerns beyond the rising price of subsidies and defaults. The structure of the program makes it difficult for policy-makers to control the growth of the dollar volume of student loans. The rapid expansion of the FFEL since 1980 did not follow an explicit policy decision to spend more on student loans. Indeed, it happened in spite of efforts by policy-makers to control and limit spending.[37]

The federal loan-guarantee programs are funded as an entitlement. Francis Keppel, U.S. Commissioner of Education between 1962 and 1965, explains that "[t]he budget process required that costs of loan eligibility be joined with annual appropriations for the Title IV program in calculating the total appropriation for student aid."[38] As such, Congress is obligated to appropriate all funds necessary to cover the costs of the programs each year. This type of spending is often described as "uncontrollable" because Congress does not directly determine how much will be spent on these programs. The federal appropriation is determined by the volume of loans, the rate of default, money market conditions, borrower death, and many other factors beyond the direct control of the federal government.

Of course, the Congress can always limit eligibility for the programs or reduce the size of available awards in order to reduce the programs costs. For Pell grants, and most other programs, such a reduction in eligibility or award size translates into cost savings in the next year's budget. Because fewer students will be eligible, and/or the awards will be smaller, a smaller appropriations is necessary to operate the program. However, reducing eligibility for the loan-guarantee programs, or reducing the size of loans, produces very little immediate budgetary savings. Because of its funding structure, the costs of loan guarantees are largely fixed in the short term. This is because most of the costs to the federal government for loan guarantees go to pay for obligations incurred by loans made many years before. Each year interest subsidies, special allowances, and defaults must still be paid on all outstanding student loans. Accordingly, even if the FFEL was eliminated entirely, it would still incur costs to the federal treasury, albeit at a declining rate, for at least the next decade.

The Danger of Rapid Cost Increases

Unlike the other student aid programs, the costs of the loan guarantee programs can change suddenly even when there are no changes in the program's structures or rules. This is because both the interest payments and the special allowance payments are linked to 91-day Treasury bill rates, which are extremely sensitive to changes in the economy, particularly to concerns over inflation. If short-term Treasury rates move rapidly upward, the costs of the FFEL follow directly and immediately. Robert Reischauer estimates that a every one-percent increase in the T-bill interest rate equates to at least a $500 million increase in federal payments to lenders.

When interest rates are low, as they were in the early 1990s, the costs of the FFEL should also be fairly low. But because default rates increased so rapidly in the late 1980s and early 1990s, aggregate FFEL costs continued to rise even when interest rates were at record lows. When interest rates began to rise in 1994, federal government experienced an increase in the costs of the programs with no increase in the number of loans available or in the dollar volume of those loans.[39] These increased costs are then likely to ripple through the federal budget for years to come, further reducing the funds available for other student aid programs.

THE UNINTENDED CONSEQUENCES OF THE TRANSFORMATION IN FEDERAL STUDENT-AID POLICY

Quite apart from the increased costs of student loans in the past decade, the growth has had a number of negative consequences for students and their families. As the volume of loans continued to grow, these unintended consequences threatened to undermine its earlier successes.

Chief among these negative consequences is that the increased reliance on loans by disadvantaged families may discourage potential students from low-income families from continuing their educations, and that increased borrowing may cause students to leave college with a large debt which distorts their career- and life-choices. The growth of the loan programs also distorted overall federal student-aid effort in ways which made it less useful to lower-income and disadvantaged students.

Discouraging Disadvantaged Students

Table 5.5 provides an estimate of how much some typical subsidized Stafford loan borrowers would need to pay back at the point the loan comes due. These amounts are estimates based on a 9 percent interest rate (the maximum allowed) and a ten-year repayment period (the maximum allowed). It is important to remember that the total amount repaid will be lower if the interest rate is less or the loan is repaid early.

This amount makes clear that both the size of the monthly payment and/or the total amount of post-collegiate debt, might dissuade a student

Table 5.5
Typical Repayment Schedule for Different Levels of Subsidized Stafford Loans Based on 9 Percent Interest Rates and 10 Year Repayment Period

Total Loan Amount	Monthly Payment	Total Amount Repaid
$4,000	$ 50.67	$ 6,080.44
$10,000	$ 126.68	$15,201.09
$18,000	$ 228.02	$27,361.97

from a disadvantaged background from borrowing for money necessary to attend college. Take the case of the first-year student who borrows $4,000 to attend college but drops out of school late in the year or chooses not to return to school the next year. This is a common circumstance among students who begin college without the skills or the maturity necessary to succeed. Even though that student received no degree or perhaps even no academic credit, he or she would face a $50 monthly payment for the next ten years.

Even students who complete their academic programs can face daunting post-graduation debts. The student who borrows the maximum Stafford loan amount for each of his or her four years of college will have borrowed $18,000 when they graduate. Six months after they have left school, that student will begin monthly payments of $228 which will continue for ten years. When the loan is finally paid off, he or she will have repaid more than $27,000.[40]

There is widespread concern that the prospect of such debts, and the monthly payments that follow, has discouraged disadvantaged students from participating in higher education. When viewed from the perspective of a lower-income student, it is easy to see how this could happen. The pre-college family income of college students is strongly correlated with the eventual success of students in college. As a consequence, low-income students are much less likely to finish college and those who finish are less likely to do well. This higher risk of failure serves to discourage disadvantaged students from borrowing the large sums necessary to enroll in higher education.[41]

But the differential impact goes beyond its chilling effect on the propensity of potential students to enroll in school. Students from traditionally disadvantaged groups may be just as willing to borrow as other students, but they may subsequently become more dependent upon loans because they are likely to have lower post-graduation earnings. This is because of the vast disparities in income between white males on the one hand and women and minorities on the other, even after adjusting for differences in education and work experience. These differences mean that borrowers from disadvantaged backgrounds are likely to find themselves making larger monthly payments out of a lower income than advantaged students with similar educations working in similar jobs.

Another differential impact that loans have on low-income students is that, unlike grants, loans must be repaid with interest. The student that borrows $18,000 in subsidized Stafford loans will pay more than $9,000 in interest charges. This does not include the 5 percent origination fee and the 3 percent insurance premium, a total of $1,440, which are deducted from the loan disbursement.

For a low-income student, the prospect of such large debt reinserts the cost barriers to higher education which the federal financial aid programs were designed to remove. A disadvantaged student, or a student from a lower-income family, might reasonably decide that the risks associated with such large debts are too great to take a chance on borrowing for college. But as the price of college rises, and the value of Pell grants declines, the choice not to borrow may also be the choice not to go to college at all.

The Dependence of Disadvantaged Students on Loans

While the prospect of large debts may discourage many lower-income or disadvantaged students from going to college, more of those who do enroll are taking out loans. As a consequence, even as concerns are emerging that loans were holding down the enrollments of disadvantaged students, a separate concern emerged that such students were becoming dependent on federal loans.

Table 5.6 shows the differences in the sources of college funds used by white and African-American freshmen. African-Americans rely much more on various types of government support while whites rely more on private family resources in order to meet college costs. This difference is especially evident in Pell grants, where African-Americans are twice as likely as whites to receive an award. But African-Americans are also more likely than whites to take out a student loan.[42]

The fact that African-Americans are more likely to receive government aid is no surprise. Since most aid is need-based, it is awarded dispro-

Table 5.6

*Sources of College Funds Used by African-American and
White Freshman College Students: Fall 1989*

Source of College Funds	Percent of Freshmen		Difference
	African-Americans	Whites	
Pell Grant	41%	20%	+21
Stafford Loan	28	23	+ 5
State Scholarship	17	15	+ 2
Personal Savings	19	32	− 13
Parents or Family	71	83	− 12

Source: A. Astin *The Black Undergraduate* (Los Angeles: Higher Education Research Institute, University of California, Los Angeles, 1990), p. 10.

portionately to disadvantaged students. But this distribution has important implications for future federal student-aid policy. Reductions or alterations in any of the major federal aid programs are likely to have a differential impact on African-American students.

If the continued growth in the loan guarantee programs forces policy-makers to reduce further limit the size of the maximum Pell grant, the impact will be felt disproportionately by African-American students. It is perhaps ironic that as these programs make progress toward the goal of assisting disadvantaged students in paying for college, they raise concerns that these students would be unable to get by without continued government assistance.

The Specter of Post-Collegiate Debt

Rapidly rising college costs, coupled with the increase in student borrowing, have raised concerns that federal policy was creating what Senator Pell has called "a new class of indentured servants" whose career choices and personal lives are distorted by the significant debt they have acquired to get an education.[43] It is easy to imagine how the prospect of such debt could affect a student's career choice. Allan Ostar, worries that large post-collegiate debt, and the resulting financial squeeze, may well constrict a former student's occupational decisions. He argues that because of this debt:

low salary professional positions such as teaching or journalism, for example, will prove far less appealing than the higher salaried positions in business or engineering to someone who graduates from college owing $10,000 or more.[44]

John Heileman puts the problem in more blunt terms:

Having taken the money to pay for a degree, students are frequently forced to make a bitter compromise: They must, after college, give up doing socially useful but ill-paid work, like teaching or public interest law, and settle for more uninspiring jobs that bring in enough to cover hefty monthly loan payments. For others (usually the less well-off) the fear of Student Loan Prison has them thinking twice about going to college at all.[45]

Robert Reischauer expresses the slightly different concern that students who depend heavily on loans to finance their education may begin to view college as narrow vocational training. As such, the broader liberal arts education which can be so valuable to students in the long run may be sacrificed as students choose courses based on the degree to which they increase future job prospects rather than the intellectual value of the subject matter.[46]

There is little systematic evidence to link the impact of post-collegiate debt to the career or life choices of students.[47] But the concerns listed above, coupled with a large amount of anecdotal evidence from students, parents, and college financial aid officers, strongly suggests that such a link may exist. If it does, the growth of student borrowing may alter the behavior and limit the opportunities of students in ways that were unintended and even unrecognized by the program's creators.

Distorting Federal Policy

At the other end of the economic spectrum, the growth of the federal loan programs raises concerns that more and more student-aid funds are going to families that have the least need for federal support. This is because the broad availability of federally guaranteed loans may encourage upper- and middle-income students to substitute those loans for parental support and student savings.

If the federal government is going to insure that below-market-rate loans are widely available, many upper-income families will find these loans attractive. In order to insure that subsidized loans go only to the most needy students, eligibility for a subsidized Stafford loan is determined by a needs test. That test examines the financial status of the student's family each year that a loan is requested and relates that status to the cost of attending college.

But even with a needs test, many families with higher incomes qualify for subsidized loans. Students attending public colleges can qualify for a Stafford loan if their family income is less than $33,000. The income limit for a student attending a private college is about $50,000. But a cutoff of well over $100,000 is possible if a student attends a high-priced college, has few family assets, or has another child in college.[48]

This current method of determining loan eligibility also allows, even encourages, upper-income students to participate in the program. The cost of each loan to the government is based largely on how much each student chooses to borrow and how long he or she remains in school. Among eligible students, those who attend more expensive colleges tend to borrow more money and stay in college longer. Therefore, they receive the greatest benefits from the FFEL. But, as Robert Reischauer points out, "students at higher priced schools also tend to come from families with the greatest resources and to be the borrowers who are most likely to have the highest lifetime earnings."[49]

There is a similar concern that the growth of the loan programs is being funded largely at the expense of the grant programs. In a zero-sum spending environment, every dollar awarded to middle-income students in the form of loans is a dollar which cannot go to need-based grants.[50]

The federal government now spends more than $13 billion on the major student aid programs. That amount has grown steadily throughout the 1970s. Aggregate federal spending on student aid continued to increase during the 1980s and into the 1990s. But student aid spending as a percent of total federal outlays reached a peak in 1980 and had held steady at about 0.8 percent. The efforts of the Reagan and Bush administrations thus stopped the overall growth of federal student-aid spending, but they were unable to make progress towards their goal of reducing it.

Table 5.7 shows how the balance between grant and loan aid has changed since 1970. It is here that the dramatic growth of the student loan programs is most visible. In 1980, grant aid constituted half of all federal student aid and loans less than one-third. Since that time, MISAA and the subsequent efforts to control federal spending on student aid has caused a larger portion of federal outlays to shift to loans.

Table 5.7

Types of Student Aid Awarded As a Percentage of Generally Available
Federal Student Aid Selected Years, 1970–1990

Year	Grants[a]	Loans[b]	Other
1970	8%	78%	14%
1975	36	54	10
1980	26	66	8
1985	28	68	4
1990	27	69	4
1992	29	68	3

[a] Grants = Pell + SEOG
[b] Guaranteed Loans = All FFELs + Perkins Loans

The increasing concentration of federal student-aid spending in the loan-guarantee programs tends to skew federal subsidies away from the most disadvantaged students and toward middle- and upper-income students. This shift erodes the traditional federal emphasis on equity and equal opportunity. As more of the federal money goes to the FFEL, if a large portion of the money is going to upper-income students, the clear losers are the disadvantaged and lower-income students whom the programs were intended to help.

CONCLUSION: COSTS AND CONSEQUENCES OF INCREASED STUDENT BORROWING

Since 1980, the federal government has helped to make more than $100 billion in new loans available to college students. But that growth has also produced a larger than anticipated price-tag, the danger of rapidly rising future costs, and a variety of negative consequences for lower-income and disadvantaged students. As federal spending on student loans increased, it has commanded a much larger portion of overall federal student-aid spending. This, in turn, has constrained the growth of the other federal student-aid programs and distorted the national effort to improve college affordability. The result is that federal policy-makers now find that they are spending more each year on student aid, but having less to spend on those programs which aid disadvantaged students.

These developments also have had important consequences for lower-income and disadvantaged students. Rising net college prices have forced increasing numbers of students to either borrow for college or not to go at all. But loans carry special risks and costs for disadvantaged students. Because they are often less prepared for college, are less likely to complete their academic program, and those who do graduate are likely to earn less, disadvantaged students are more hesitant to borrow. Those who do borrow, may have their career- or life-choices altered by the large debt they have incurred.

As federal student-aid spending shifted from grants to loans, it brought about a corresponding shift in the types of students who could receive federal aid. No longer was it just lower-income students who were receiving financial aid, but now middle- and even upper-income students were now eligible. This further reduced the value of federal aid to the lower-income and disadvantaged students as they were left to divide a smaller share of the limited amount of federal subsidies.

Perhaps most fundamental, increased borrowing for college is antithetical to the goal of removing college price barriers. Loans do not reduce college prices at all. They simply postpone their payment. When fees are deducted and interest payments added, the price that a disadvantaged student-borrower must pay to go to college is far greater than the amount paid by the student who has substantial family resources. This higher cost is further exacerbated by the fact that their post-collegiate income is likely to be much lower. The result is that even as federal student-aid spending is increasing, disadvantaged students are finding that federal aid is less and less helpful in paying the rapidly rising college prices. The growth of student loans thus has not served to open the door to college for disadvantaged students but has reinserted, and even extended, the price barriers that the federal student-aid programs were designed to eliminate.

6

THE STATES AND COLLEGE AFFORDABILITY

(with Kevin Mohr)

State governments are the principle source of revenue for public colleges and universities.[1] When viewed in aggregate, the $65 billion that the states spent on higher education in 1994 dwarfed the federal effort. States provide most of these dollars directly to public colleges and universities as instructional subsidies, which colleges, in turn, use to keep their tuitions considerably below their cost of providing a higher education. Another portion of those state dollars, at least $2 billion, is allocated for need-based grants which are awarded directly to lower-family-income students. These grants are given with the express purpose of removing college price barriers. State governments are thus major players in the effort to provide affordable higher education to all Americans.

During the 1970s, most states were able to effectively improve the affordability of higher education for their residents, both by increasing appropriations for higher education and stimulating larger college enrollments. With the support of new federal programs, the states also rapidly increased the availability of need-based state grants. As a consequence, public college affordability in most states improved somewhat during the 1970s. Yet, like college affordability more generally, these trends reversed after 1980.

But like students, families, and colleges, state governments have been whipsawed between rising costs and stagnant revenues since 1980. To make matters worse, because their fiscal and economic problems have

139

mirrored those faced by the federal government, most states were poorly positioned to take the lead in removing college price barriers. However, with the gap between the price of higher education and the financial resources of lower-income families widening, no one else remained to take up where the federal government had left off. To put it simply, if the states were unable, or unwilling, to fill that gap, government efforts to remove price barriers to college would certainly fail.

Since 1980, facing mounting budget pressures and a declining number of traditional college-age residents, states slowed down their increases in appropriations to higher education, which drove public college tuitions up. Simultaneously, the states reduced the rapid growth in spending on need-based grants experienced in the previous decade. Because grant spending was growing more slowly than tuition increases, the purchasing power of those grants was declining.

While declining college affordability was evident in almost every state after 1980, there were substantial differences among the states in public college prices and the availability of state financial aid. This translated into substantial variation in the net price of higher education for residents of different states. These differences were directly related to the commitment of state policy-makers to allocate state resources to higher education and strategic decisions about how state funds would be allocated among various higher-education activities.

This chapter reviews the recent efforts of the states to maintain and enhance college affordability. Without going into detail about specific legislative or budgetary actions in each state, we examine the role of state government in higher-education finance. Then, we turn to an examination of how much money the states spent, how those monies were allocated, and the impact of state spending on public-college affordability. Finally, we consider the various strategies pursued by the states to keep higher education affordable, and evaluate which of the strategies produced the best results.

THE GROWTH OF PUBLIC HIGHER EDUCATION

Public higher education has grown substantially since 1950. David Henry observed that while this enrollment growth was often described as a tidal wave, the "connotation of disaster was hardly appropriate."[2] Enrollment growth fueled an unprecedented expansion in both the size and scope of

Table 6.1
Enrollments at Public Colleges: Selected Years, 1971–1991

Year	Total Enrollment at Public Institutions	FTE Enrollment at Public Institutions
1971	6,804,309	5,344,356
1976	8,653,477	6,349,903
1981	9,647,032	6,781,300
1986	9,713,893	6,778,045
1991	11,310,000	7,863,000
20 Year Change	4,505,691	2,518,644

public higher education. By 1995, there were more than 1,500 public institutions of higher education enrolling more than 10 million students, and awarding almost 1.5 million associate's or bachelor's degrees annually.[3]

The diversity of these institutions is striking. They range from very large research universities to very small technical colleges. They offer programs and courses from extremely specialized postdoctoral seminars to remedial instruction for students lacking the skills to do college-level work. Students at these public colleges range from the traditional 18-year-old studying American literature, to the working single mother taking business courses at night, to the curious senior citizen tracing his or her genealogy, to the advanced graduate student working on a cure for bone cancer. With such fundamentally different purposes, structures, and student bodies, these institutions have little in common other than that they use public funds to provide some form of postsecondary education.

Table 6.1 shows the enrollment growth in public higher education since 1970. As baby-boomers entered college in unprecedented numbers during the 1970s, enrollments at public colleges increased by 47 percent. That growth, exceeding more than 9.4 million students by 1980, precipitated a corresponding expansion in the number of public colleges, the programs those colleges offered, the faculty and staff they employed, and the physical plants they occupied.

By 1980, however, the number of traditional college-age Americans had began to decline. As a consequence, many experts predicted that the resulting decline in the number of college students would produce an oversupply of higher education, a "college enrollment crisis." But that enrollment crisis never materialized.[4] Because of increasing college participation rates of high school graduates, the increasing college retention rates of all students, and the expanding number of non-traditional students going to school, public college enrollments actually increased by 14 percent between 1980 and 1990. This growth rate, while unexpectedly rapid, was considerably slower than that of previous decades. This slow growth forestalled the predicted problems of oversupply, but it brought to a close the rapid expansion of higher education which had spanned the previous three decades.

THE STATE ROLE IN FUNDING HIGHER EDUCATION

The relationship between state governments and public institutions of higher education is complex and multifaceted. State governments provide more than half of the revenues currently used to operate public institutions of higher education. Nonetheless, public colleges retain substantial autonomy in their administrative and financial operations. In most cases, it is the colleges themselves, acting through boards of trustees, who determine the tuitions they will charge. Of course, states, acting through their legislatures, can mandate changes or limits in those tuition levels.

At public colleges, the determination of the tuition level charged each year is the product of countervailing pressures. Long traditions of institutional autonomy from direct government control mandate that campuses retain control over expenditure and pricing decisions. But growing public pressures for accountability in the use of public funds demand that state governments act to control or limit price increases. Whether or not those public pressures are manifested in explicit governmental action, campus decision-makers are certainly aware that rapidly rising tuitions make them the target of increased scrutiny by governors and state legislatures. As such, public colleges must establish their own price levels within the context of limited state appropriations and the need to be responsive to broad public and political pressures.

The critical role the states play in determining college affordability for their residents is illustrated by the wide disparities in the price of public colleges from state to state. In 1992, one year's tuition at a public four-year college in California cost about $1,000. In Vermont, that price was more than $3,600. The differences between states were even more evident in the provision of state grants to lower-income students. New York, for example, provided more than $1,000 of need-based student aid for each full-time equivalent (FTE) undergraduate student enrolled in the state's public colleges. North Carolina, on the other hand, provided just $13 of need-based aid per undergraduate FTE. As a result of these wide differences in college prices and grant funding, the net price facing any lower-income students is largely a function of the state in which he or she happens to live.

States and Campuses: Diverging Viewpoints

Historically, state governments and public colleges have shared a common interest in keeping public tuitions low.[5] States benefitted from the economic and social development which accrued from increased participation in higher education, and states saw low tuitions as the most direct way to increase the levels of participation in public higher education. Moreover, because colleges are attended disproportionately by higher-income residents, a low-tuition policy was an easy way to distribute public benefits to well-to-do residents.

Public colleges also saw low tuitions as advantageous. Low tuitions gave them an advantage in the competition with private schools for the best students, and also allowed them to attract large numbers of first-generation college students who might otherwise not have attended college. The resulting increase in college participation, in turn, fueled economic development and generated new revenues for state governments.[6] More recently, however, the budgets of both state governments and public colleges have been squeezed by rising costs and falling revenues.[7] As that happened, the interests of state governments and public colleges began to diverge. Their different views of how best to respond to this fiscal stress are the natural result of the different constituencies that each serve.

Governors and state legislators focus their attention on the big picture of state finance.[8] They must generate sufficient revenue to provide the services demanded by their constituencies and still keep the state's operating budget in balance. But the dual pressures to expand public services and limit tax increases makes balancing state budgets a political minefield. In particular, the costs of prison construction, medical care, and worker's compensation are all growing faster than state revenues.[9] In order to meet those costs, states have few options. They can either raise taxes, cut state spend-

Table 6.2

State and Local Appropriations per FTE to Higher Education by State: Selected Years, 1981–1991 (in constant 1994 dollars)

Rank	State	1981	1986	1991	10 Year Change
1	Alaska	$13,002	$15,029	$10,709	$– 2,293
2	Hawaii	6,409	8,366	8,777	2,368
3	Wyoming	8,066	8,656	6,372	– 1,694
4	Connecticut	4,575	5,896	6,311	1,736
5	New Jersey	4,139	5,727	5,562	1,423
6	North Carolina	4,229	5,632	5,427	1,198
7	New York	5,136	6,256	5,407	270
8	New Mexico	4,976	5,490	5,352	376
9	Florida	4,089	5,261	5,322	1,223
10	Idaho	5,192	5,375	5,285	93
11	Washington	3,925	4,572	5,229	1,304
12	Iowa	4,487	4,426	5,001	514
13	California	4,157	4,766	4,972	815
14	Maine	3,494	4,421	4,913	1,419
15	Wisconsin	4,399	4,539	4,876	477
16	Nevada	4,211	4,972	4,871	660
17	Minnesota	4,162	4,776	4,693	531
18	Georgia	4,228	4,873	4,641	413
19	Delaware	4,250	5,352	4,640	390
20	Pennsylvania	4,199	4,782	4,606	407
21	South Carolina	4,143	4,445	4,552	409
22	Oklahoma	3,803	5,065	4,511	708
23	Massachusetts	4,149	5,612	4,508	359
24	Oregon	3,362	4,432	4,493	1,131
25	Indiana	3,931	4,310	4,467	536
26	Illinois	3,716	4,344	4,413	697

ing in other areas, increase the efficiency of service delivery, or develop alternative revenue sources. From the perspective of the governor's mansion and the statehouse, higher education looked like a good place to cut. State appropriations to higher education had grown rapidly during the 1970s, and enrollment growth was beginning to slow in the 1980s. In response to these forces, elected officials in many states began to reduce the rates of growth in their appropriations to higher education.

Table 6.2 (continued)

Rank	State	1981	1986	1991	10 Year Change
27	Michigan	3,483	4,693	4,402	919
28	Utah	4,461	5,149	4,400	− 61
29	Maryland	3,978	4,253	4,338	360
30	Arizona	3,773	4,733	4,236	463
31	Rhode Island	4,396	5,056	4,217	− 179
32	Kansas	4,226	4,514	4,150	− 76
33	Tennessee	3,417	4,776	4,114	697
34	Nebraska	3,845	3,550	4,085	240
35	Virginia	3,661	4,304	3,985	324
36	Kentucky	3,845	4,607	3,948	103
37	North Dakota	3,914	3,920	3,927	13
38	Texas	3,661	4,007	3,924	263
39	Missouri	3,931	4,344	3,917	− 14
40	Montana	3,529	4,409	3,888	359
41	Ohio	3,261	3,878	3,828	567
42	Arkansas	3,552	4,697	3,735	183
43	South Dakota	3,367	3,752	3,480	113
44	Alabama	3,122	5,030	3,450	328
45	Louisiana	4,225	4,017	3,207	− 1,018
46	Mississippi	3,517	3,266	3,192	− 325
47	Colorado	2,658	3,333	3,145	487
48	West Virginia	3,261	3,738	2,940	− 321
49	New Hampshire	2,604	2,965	2,826	222
50	Vermont	2,296	2,543	2,530	234
	National Aggregate	4,003	4,729	4,558	555

Source: K. Halstead, State Profiles: Financing Public Higher Education 1978–1992 (Research Associates: Washington D.C., 1992).

Declining State Appropriations

Table 6.2 shows that most states increased their appropriations to public higher education between 1981 and 1991.[10] In constant dollars, forty-two states appropriated more money (per FTE) to public higher education in 1991 than in 1981. In fact, eight states increased the value of their appropriation per FTE undergraduate by more than $1,000 during the ten-year period.

Most of this growth, however, occurred prior to 1986. As state budgets deteriorated during the late 1980s, state appropriations began to decline. Thirty-five states decreased the real value of their appropriations to public higher education between 1986 and 1991. Although for most states the decline in spending was not enough to erase the rapid growth of the early 1980s, it did offset many of the gains they had made.

The Revenue Squeeze at Public Colleges

During those same years, public colleges were struggling to pay the increasing costs of operating their programs and facilities. When state governments cut appropriations for higher education, which translated into revenue reductions for campuses, the budget crunch felt by colleges was magnified. To make matters worse, because the costs of providing higher education are relatively inelastic, slowing rates of enrollment growth do not necessarily produce decreases in the costs of operating a public college. Buildings must still be maintained. Many of the programs are protected from cuts by entrenched supporters on campus and in the capitol. Faculty are often tenured or essential to provide promised programs. There are few places for campus leaders to cut which will produce substantial savings in the short term. From the perspective of the campus, state budget cuts left colleges with no choice but to raise tuitions and face the consequences of declining college affordability.[11]

Public college leaders saw the slowing of state appropriations for higher education as shortsighted and misguided efforts of state governments to shift the responsibility for funding higher education to students and their families. On campus, this raised concerns that a disastrous chain of events was being set in motion. Rising college costs would lead to lower college-participation rates, which would lead to declining economic growth in the state, which would lead to reduced state revenues, which would require further cuts in all types of state services. In the end, students, colleges, and states, would all end up in worse economic condition.

The 1980s and early 1990s were thus a time of on-going budgetary conflict between states and public colleges. Both sides argued, often correctly, that the other did not understand the fundamental problem. But the differences of opinion were not simple misunderstandings. The college affordability problem, and the appropriate response to the problem, look quite different on the green at a public college than in the deliberations of a state appropriations committee.[12]

THE MANY ROADS TO PUBLIC COLLEGE AFFORDABILITY: COMPARING THE STATES

The fact that a state spends more money on higher education does not necessarily translate into wider access to higher education for the residents of that state. State and public college leaders may choose to use those increased funds for some other purpose than low prices, such as improved facilities, increased research capacity, or higher salaries for faculty and staff. Such spending has little or no direct impact on college affordability; in fact, it may make college more expensive. Indeed, if college spending rises more rapidly than appropriations, college prices will increase even as a state spends more on higher education. Determining changes in public college affordability thus requires a careful examination of the components that determine net college price—tuition and grants.

There are several ways that states can, directly or indirectly, improve the affordability of public higher education for their residents. Most directly, they can influence the price of public higher education by adjusting the subsidy they provide to public colleges and universities. In addition, states can give subsidies directly to students in the form of grants. Traditionally, most states have directed the bulk of their funding into tuition subsidies, but in recent years, many states have dramatically increased their spending on grants.

Different states have produced significantly different mixtures of low tuitions and need-based grants in their efforts to keep public colleges affordable. Some states, North Carolina and Texas in particular, pursued a strategy of keeping public college tuitions low. Vermont and Pennsylvania, among others, chose to allow public college tuitions to rise, and then relied on generous grant programs to mitigate the impact of high tuition on lower-income students. Most other states fell somewhere inbetween these two extremes, each striking a different balance between subsidies to all students through lower tuitions and subsidies targeted to lower-income students through grants.

But which of these state spending strategies was the most effective? The following section evaluates the various state efforts to remove college price barriers. Our objective is to determine the extent to which each

Table 6.3

Average Tuition and Required Fees at Four-Year Public Colleges and
Universities by State: Selected Years, 1981–1991 (in constant 1994 dollars)

Rank	State	1981	1986	1991	10 Year Change
1	California	$365	$874	$981	$616
2	Texas	645	965	1,057	412
3	New Mexico	702	894	1,071	369
4	North Carolina	929	986	1,143	214
5	Wyoming	969	937	1,212	243
6	Oklahoma	522	775	1,265	494
7	Idaho	776	1,362	1,301	525
8	Hawaii	786	1,226	1,401	615
9	Montana	872	1,178	1,407	532
10	Arkansas	982	1,075	1,418	436
11	Florida	1,160	1,006	1,419	259
12	Kentucky	949	1,239	1,429	480
13	Alaska	806	1,418	1,442	636
14	Nevada	1,178	1,402	1,457	279
15	Utah	1,035	1,234	1,476	441
16	West Virginia	616	1,120	1,487	871
17	Tennessee	871	1,207	1,494	627
18	Nebraska	1,103	1,337	1,501	398
19	Missouri	687	1,244	1,505	818
20	Kansas	1,089	1,484	1,532	443
21	New York	1,634	1,912	1,578	− 56
22	Colorado	1,143	1,443	1,594	451
23	Georgia	1,066	1,497	1,596	530
24	Alabama	1,140	1,445	1,622	482
25	Arizona	982	1,286	1,626	644
26	Washington	$994	$1,474	$1,701	$707
27	North Dakota	970	1,339	1,752	782

state was able to maintain public college affordability in the face of the
severe fiscal pressures which have developed since 1980.[13]

Comparing Tuitions at Public Colleges

As shown in table 6.3, tuitions at public colleges and universities increased in every state after 1980. But the magnitude of the increase varied

Table 6.3 (*continued*)

Rank	State	1981	1986	1991	10 Year Change
28	South Dakota	1,357	1,720	1,780	423
29	Louisiana	955	1,379	1,794	839
30	South Carolina	1,105	1,325	1,901	796
31	Connecticut	1,205	1,490	1,903	698
32	Mississippi	1,252	1,532	1,911	659
33	Wisconsin	1,440	1,694	1,931	491
34	Oregon	1,527	1,893	1,953	426
35	Rhode Island	1,280	1,603	1,954	674
36	Minnesota	1,169	1,973	1,995	826
37	Iowa	1,267	1,614	2,006	739
38	Maine	1,577	1,887	2,131	554
39	Indiana	1,596	2,010	2,225	629
40	Maryland	1,550	2,030	2,239	689
41	Michigan	1,654	1,919	2,294	649
42	Illinois	1,321	1,850	2,341	1,021
43	Massachusetts	1,261	1,636	2,624	1,363
44	Ohio	1,770	2,281	2,665	894
45	New Hampshire	1,771	2,372	2,700	929
46	Pennsylvania	1,991	2,328	2,713	722
47	New Jersey	1,598	2,102	2,722	1,124
48	Virginia	1,652	2,438	2,790	1,138
49	Vermont	1,964	2,811	3,247	1,283
50	Delaware	1,634	2,728	3,301	1,667
	National Average	1,191	1,561	1,831	640
	Low Tuition/				
	Low Aid Average	930	1,204	1,377	470
	High Tuition/				
	High Aid Average	1,627	2,146	2,730	1,103

Source: State of Washington, 1992 Report of the Higher Education Coordinating Board.

greatly. New York was the only state to hold tuition increases below the 6.3 percent average annual increase in the CPI. At the other extreme, tuitions at public colleges in California increased more than 31 percent per year between 1981 and 1991.

Although tuitions went up everywhere, those states with low tuitions in 1981, such as California, Texas, and New Mexico, generally remained among the least expensive in 1991. Those states which were among the most expensive in 1981, such as Pennsylvania, Vermont, Ohio, and New Hampshire, remained among the most expensive in 1991. There were, however, a few important changes in the tuitions charged in some states during the decade. North Carolina, Wyoming, and Florida held tuition increases down, and in turn, moved from among the more costly states to among the least costly. On the other hand, Massachusetts, Illinois, and Iowa experienced large tuition increases, which moved them from among the least expensive to among the more expensive states.

Comparing the State Grant Programs

The 1970s were a period of unparalleled growth in state student aid. The principle stimulus for that expansion was the creation of the State Student Incentive Grants (SSIG) program in the Education Amendments of 1972.[14] This program provides federal funds to states for the expansion of grants to undergraduate students. The resulting growth in state programs led to a corresponding growth in the number of students receiving state grants. In 1971, fewer than 500,000 students were receiving state grants. A decade later, that number had increased to 1.3 million.[15]

There are many ways of measuring the size of the state need-based grant programs. Our analysis compares the number of need-based grant dollars per FTE enrollment in public higher education in each state. Using grant dollars per FTE enrollment, we compare need-based grant programs in states of vastly different size, as well as over time.[16] In table 6.4 the states are ranked according to grant dollars per FTE in 1991, from highest to lowest. In addition, it shows aggregate expenditures per FTE for all fifty states.

Most states expanded their average need-based grant during the decade. Indeed, thirty-three states increased their grant spending per FTE faster than the CPI over those years. Only seven states spent fewer current dollars per FTE in 1991 than they had in 1981. Several states, such as Washington, Oklahoma, and New Mexico, increased their grant spending tremendously, moving them from among the lowest spenders to among the highest. Massachusetts, Minnesota, New Jersey and Illinois, which operated large programs in 1981, were able to expand those programs at relatively rapid rates and continued to operate large programs in 1991.

The seven states which experienced current-dollar declines in grant spending per FTE during the decade all operated very small programs in 1981. As such, many of the states which committed few resources to their grant programs at the beginning of the decade, maintained that low level of support throughout the decade. Except for Pennsylvania, all of the states which operated large grant programs in 1981 increased their real spending on grants during the decade.

A TYPOLOGY OF STATE AFFORDABILITY STRATEGIES

Since 1980, every state has developed, either explicitly or implicitly, a strategy for coping with the public college affordability problem. While each state chose a unique mix of tuition subsidies and grants, when the two factors are placed along the axis of a two-by-two table, four distinct affordability strategies emerge.[17] The four cells in table 6.6 represent the major types of strategies employed by the states. The table also shows some of the states which followed each strategy.

The classifications used in table 6.6 are based on the 1991 data presented in tables 6.3 and 6.4. As used here low tuition is considered to be any state where the average public college tuition is less than $1,500. High tuition is more than $2,100. States are considered to be high aid if they spend more than $300 per undergraduate FTE on need-based grants. Low aid is defined as less than $75 per undergraduate FTE. While such distinctions are artificial, they illustrate the different mixes of the two factors in various states.

The High Expenditure Strategy

The most aggressive, and certainly the most expensive, approach a state can take to remove college price barriers is to keep public college tuitions low *and* to provide generous grants to lower-income students. This strategy combines the advantages of both features. Low tuitions insure that the price of attending college is within the reach of middle-income families. At the same time, need-based grants insure that lower-income students will be able to meet those costs.

Table 6.4

Need-Based Grant Dollars Per FTE Public Undergraduate Enrollment by State: Selected Years, 1981–1991 (in constant 1994 dollars)

Rank	State	1981	1986	1991	10 Year Change
1	New York	$930	$1,142	$1,031	$101
2	Vermont	565	690	683	118
3	Pennsylvania	529	501	525	– 4
4	New Jersey	414	531	525	111
5	Illinois	375	454	526	151
6	Minnesota	272	378	439	167
7	Massachusetts	209	457	399	190
8	Iowa	281	306	373	92
9	Rhode Island	284	395	367	82
10	Connecticut	195	246	343	148
11	Indiana	248	227	288	40
12	Wisconsin	190	189	238	48
13	Michigan	138	247	216	78
14	Kentucky	115	131	183	68
15	South Carolina	183	199	180	– 3
16	Ohio	148	190	168	20
17	Washington	45	77	144	99
18	Maine	71	38	143	72
19	California	115	130	134	19
20	Tennessee	86	103	125	39
21	Oregon	109	137	122	52
22	Oklahoma	33	106	118	85
23	New Mexico	23	35	109	86
24	Maryland	70	61	99	29
25	West Virginia	73	129	97	24
26	Colorado	$90	$108	91	1
27	Florida	82	88	78	– 4

In practice, few states were willing to devote the substantial resources necessary to improve affordability in this way. In 1991, only New York offered its residents very low tuitions and operated a very large grant program. New York was able to sustain this high expenditure strategy throughout the post-1980 period by limiting tuition increases while maintaining one of the nation's most generous grant program.

Table 6.4 (continued)

Rank	State	1981	1986	1991	10 Year Change
28	Missouri	124	99	77	– 47
29	Kansas	93	80	65	– 28
30	Arkansas	61	98	63	2
31	Delaware	35	46	46	11
32	North Dakota	34	34	43	9
33	Texas	44	47	41	– 3
34	Virginia	35	32	36	1
35	Nebraska	33	23	35	2
36	Alaska	43	23	33	– 10
37	Louisiana	16	21	32	16
38	New Hampshire	52	41	31	– 21
39	Georgia	38	37	30	– 8
40	South Dakota	36	44	24	– 12
41	Arizona	22	26	23	1
42	Hawaii	27	27	21	– 6
43	Alabama	16	21	18	2
44	Utah	49	27	16	– 33
45	Montana	21	20	15	– 6
46	Mississippi	25	18	13	– 12
47	North Carolina	35	30	12	– 22
48	Nevada	22	25	11	– 13
49	Idaho	30	23	11	– 19
50	Wyoming	6	15	11	5
	National Aggregate	188	223	216	28
	Low Tuition/Low Aid Aggregate	58	55	46	–12
	High Tuition/High Aid Aggregate	485	459	509	106

Source: Annual Report of the National Association of State Scholarship and Grant Programs.

The Low-Tuition/Low-Aid Strategy

The traditional, and most frequently employed, approach by states to college affordability is to provide large instructional subsidies that keep public college tuitions low. Many states (California, Texas, and North Carolina in particular), have made substantial commitments to keeping public college

Table 6.5
Net Price of Public Colleges and Universities by State:
Selected Years, 1981–1991 (in constant 1994 dollars)

Rank	State	1981	1986	1991	10 Year Change
1	New York	$703	$771	$547	$– 156
2	California	249	744	847	598
3	New Mexico	679	860	962	283
4	Texas	601	918	1,016	415
5	North Carolina	895	957	1,131	236
6	Oklahoma	710	678	1,147	437
7	Wyoming	993	922	1,202	239
8	Kentucky	834	1,109	1,246	412
9	Idaho	747	1,339	1,290	543
10	Florida	1,078	919	1,341	263
11	Arkansas	921	978	1,355	434
12	Tennessee	787	1,103	1,370	583
13	Hawaii	758	1,154	1,380	622
14	West Virginia	543	992	1,391	848
15	Montana	851	1,206	1,392	541
16	Alaska	761	1,395	1,410	649
17	Missouri	564	1,145	1,428	864
18	Nevada	1,156	1,377	1,447	291
19	Utah	987	1,208	1,460	473
20	Nebraska	1,070	1,314	1,466	396
21	Kansas	997	1,402	1,467	490
22	Colorado	1,053	1,335	1,503	450
23	Minnesota	897	1,595	1,555	658
24	Washington	966	1,497	1,558	592
25	Connecticut	1,010	1,244	1,560	550
26	Georgia	1,027	1,460	1,566	539
27	Rhode Island	956	1,208	1,586	630

prices affordable. While these states all experienced fiscal pressures after 1980, they were still able to keep their public college tuitions low.

Unlike New York, however, the states which followed the low-tuition/low-aid strategy did not take the additional step of developing large student grant programs. In fact, North Carolina, Wyoming, and Idaho, among others, spent only token amounts on state aid programs. California, on the other hand, substantially expanded its need-based

Table 6.5 (continued)

Rank	State	1981	1986	1991	10 Year Change
28	Arizona	960	1,260	1,603	643
29	Alabama	1,125	1,423	1,604	479
30	Iowa	986	1,307	1,634	648
31	Wisconsin	1,250	1,504	1,694	444
32	North Dakota	937	1,305	1,709	772
33	South Carolina	832	1,127	1,721	889
34	South Dakota	1,321	1,675	1,756	435
35	Louisiana	939	1,358	1,762	823
36	Illinois	945	1,395	1,824	879
37	Oregon	1,419	1,757	1,830	411
38	Mississippi	1,189	1,514	1,899	710
39	Indiana	1,347	1,784	1,937	590
40	Maine	1,505	1,849	1,988	483
41	Michigan	1,514	1,672	2,077	563
42	Maryland	1,481	1,968	2,139	658
43	Pennsylvania	1,460	1,828	2,186	726
44	New Jersey	1,184	1,572	2,198	1,014
45	Massachusetts	1,051	1,178	2,225	1,174
46	Ohio	1,622	2,091	2,497	875
47	Vermont	1,399	2,122	2,564	1,165
48	New Hampshire	1,719	2,331	2,670	951
49	Virginia	1,617	2,406	2,754	1,137
50	Delaware	1,599	2,680	3,255	1,656
	National Average	1,003	1,336	1,613	610
	Low Tuition/ Low Aid Average	872	1,149	1,331	459
	High Tuition/ High Aid Average	1,221	1,661	2,220	997

Source: Calculated from Tables 6.3 and 6.4.

grant program after 1980 and, as a consequence, by 1991 it could no longer be classified as a low-tuition/low-aid state.

While keeping public tuitions low is expensive, especially when the costs of providing higher education are rising, it is a politically safe strategy for state policy-makers. Low tuitions are generally supported by all economic groups. Moreover, because it directs state subsidies disproportionately to middle- and upper-income families, who have higher college-participation rates, elected officials may gain support from a politically active constituency by supporting a low-tuition/low-aid strategy.

But relying on a strategy of low tuitions may not be sufficient to remove price barriers to college for lower-income students. Without the availability of grants to cover the substantial non-tuition costs of college, many residents may still find college too costly even if the price is very low. This possibility becomes ever more real when the value of federal Pell grants is declining, as it has been since 1980.

The High-Tuition/High-Aid Strategy

The high-tuition/high-aid strategy involves the decision to take state funds away from institutional subsidies and direct then instead towards need-based grants.[18] This is the most cost-effective way for a state to remove price barriers for lower-income residents. If properly administered, each dollar spent on student aid results in a dollar increase in college affordability for a lower-income student.

Economic efficiency notwithstanding, the high-tuition/high-aid strategy demands a great deal of political courage and determination. State policy-makers must require upper- and middle-income families to pay a larger portion of their college costs while they discount those costs for needy students. In other words, states must redistribute public subsidies away from powerful and politically active groups, and toward unorganized and less powerful constituents. Such actions bring high political costs in return for little political benefit.

Since 1980 many states expanded their grant programs to some degree, while still struggling to limit tuition increases. Only Vermont, Pennsylvania, New Jersey, Illinois, and Massachusetts seemed to fully embrace the logic of the high-tuition/high-aid strategy. After 1980, each of these states experienced substantial increases in public college tuitions, as well as substantial growth in funding for need-based aid. Although Minnesota, Iowa, Rhode Island, and Connecticut all provided substantial funds for student aid, these states were able to hold tuitions below the amount necessary to be labeled a high-tuition/high-aid state.

The Low Expenditure Strategy

The combination of high public college tuitions and low state student aid can hardly be called an affordability strategy at all. Particularly in light of what has happened to family incomes and Pell grants since 1980, this approach amounts to little more than an implicit repudiation of the goal of equal access to higher education. In their defense, many of these states were hit hard by the recession of the late 1980s. But by following the low-expenditure strategy, Delaware, New Hampshire, and Virginia risked turning a short-term economic downturn into a long-term economic decline. By pricing higher education beyond the reach of many of their citizens, these states denied themselves the educated work-force necessary to compete for high-wage jobs in the next decades.

Moreover, the low-expenditure strategy risked precipitating a "brain drain" of migration from the state. If tuitions rise to the point that in-state students are paying close to what they would pay to attend school in another state or at a private college, the best students may find less incentive to attend an in-state public school. These future business and political leaders may never return, leaving their home states without an essential element of economic development.

THE NET PRICE OF PUBLIC COLLEGES AND UNIVERSITIES

Which of these various state strategies had the greatest impact on college affordability since 1980? This question can be answered by comparing the net price of college across the states. This measure considers both the price of public colleges and universities in a state as well as the need-based grants provided by that state to help lower-family-income students to pay those costs. As used here, net college price is calculated by depreciating the average tuition charged at a state's public colleges and universities by the number of grant dollars per FTE that state provides.[19]

In table 6.5 the states are ranked according to their net price in 1991, from lowest to highest. At the beginning of the decade, California offered its residents a year of public undergraduate higher education at a far lower price than any other state. By 1991, while still among the lowest net price states, California's net price had more than tripled. To a lesser extent, this trend occurred in virtually every state. In Delaware, Massachusetts, Vermont, and Virginia, the real net price of a year of public higher education increased by more than $1,000 in ten years.

New York, on the other hand, actually decreased its real net price between 1981 and 1991. New York began the decade with the sixth lowest net price. But with a combination of low tuition increases and signifi-

Table 6.6
A Typology of State Affordability Strategies

State Spending on Need-Based Grants	Tuitions at Public Colleges	
	Low (below $1,500)	High (above $2,500)
HIGH (above $300/FTE)	HIGH EXPENDITURE STRATEGY New York	HIGH AID STRATEGY Illinois Massachusetts New Jersey Pennsylvania Vermont
LOW (below $75/FTE)	LOW TUITION STRATEGY Arkansas Alaska Florida Hawaii Idaho Kansas Missouri Montana Nebraska Nevada North Carolina Texas Utah Wyoming	LOW EXPENDITURE STRATEGY Delaware New Hampshire Virginia

cant increases in need-based grant spending, New York ended the decade with a net price less than that in any other state. New Mexico, Florida, North Carolina, Wyoming, Nevada, and Oregon also experienced small growth in real net price (less than $300), which moved them from among the least affordable states to among the most affordable.

There are several possible explanations for the dramatic increase in net public college prices. The most obvious is the high rate of tuition inflation experienced in most states. Few states were able to increase grant spending enough to compensate for rapidly rising tuitions. In California, for example, to hold real net price constant over the decade, the state would have had to have spent almost $900 million on need-based grants in 1991 (447 percent more than it actually spent). West Virginia, Missouri, and Massachusetts were in much the same predicament, because tuitions in those states increased much more rapidly than grants available to students.

Changes in the amount of grant funding were less of a factor than tuitions in determining the change in the state's net college price. This occurred, at least in part, because those states which had generous grant programs in 1981 maintained them, while states which gave little grant support in 1981 continued to provide little grant support throughout the decade. A few states, however, were able to effectively mitigate the overall impact of their tuition inflation on net college price by rapidly expanding their grant programs. New Mexico and Kentucky, for example, experienced relatively slow increases in net college price, in large part, because they significantly increased their level of grant spending.

While this high-tuition/high-aid approach may be effective, it was not the only way states could reduce the net public-college price facing their residents. Some states reduced their grant spending in order to channel their scarce resources into tuition subsidies, which maintained relatively low rates of tuition inflation. Using the low-tuition/low-aid strategy, North Carolina and Nevada ranked among those states with the very lowest increases in net college price since 1980, in spite of decreases in their need-based grant programs.

A final possible explanation for the decline in the real level of grant spending since 1980 is a change in state priorities. In Missouri, for example, grant spending declined by 37 percent during the decade. At the same time, public tuitions increased by 119 percent. These simultaneous funding decreases indicate that policy-makers in Missouri chose to shift state funding away from higher education and into other areas.

Net College Price: Comparing the Strategies

By comparing the net price of the states using each affordability strategy, we can see which strategies had the greatest impact on net price during the decade. Not surprisingly, New York, the only high-expenditure state, had the lowest net price of any state. And as one would expect, the three states which followed the low-expenditure strategy had the three highest net prices in 1991.

The most revealing aspect of this comparison is the net price of the states following the low-tuition/low-aid and high-tuition/high-aid strategies. The fourteen states pursuing the low-tuition/low-aid strategy all had a relatively low net price. The five high-tuition/high-aid states, on the other hand, all had very high net price. Inasmuch as net price shows the price each state expects a student to pay for college, public colleges in the low-tuition/low-aid states are clearly more affordable.

This pattern is hardly surprising. Whether by design or by accident, state governments in the high-tuition/high-aid states shifted to that strategy precisely because it called for less spending. Those states chose to spend less money on tuition subsidies, and to direct some of the savings into larger grant programs. However, since instructional subsidies and student aid are often determined separately in state expenditure decisions, there is no necessary correlation between spending on the two items. A one-dollar decrease in direct subsidies to colleges may not produce a one-dollar increase in grant aid.

Moreover, instructional subsidies comprise a much greater portion of state spending on higher education than do need-based grants (more than twenty times as much in 1991). Since changes in appropriations tend to be incremental, grant programs tend to receive smaller dollar increases from year to year than instructional subsidies. Few legislatures will double the size of their state grant program in one year, even though the value of the increase may be less than the value of a 5 percent decrease in tuition subsidies. As a result, when state governments decrease direct subsidies to colleges, as many did in the late 1980s, a comparable percentage increase in grant spending will not produce a comparable decrease in net price.[20]

Net price shows what each state expects its students to pay for college. It is a more complete method than comparing tuitions alone to look at what happened to college affordability among the states, and between each affordability strategy. However, net price says little about why a state chose to fund higher education at a particular level, or with a particular strategy.

STATE AFFORDABILITY EFFORT

It is difficult to compare the fifty states in a way that fully explains their resource allocation decisions. Population, wealth, economic and social needs, and political culture vary so much between states, and over time, that an accurate comparison of states must control for many different factors. In this section, we attempt to control for the size of each state's population, as well as its tax wealth, so that we can compare the resources states devote to reducing the price of higher education. We term this a state's "Affordability Effort."

The model of state Affordability Effort used in this chapter cannot isolate every factor that influences a state's effort to fund higher education. A complete model would have to include a huge number of variables, some of which can not be measured. Demographics, economic and political forces, and even the personalities of individual lawmakers all affect a state's policy of higher-education finance. This analysis is intended to show what happened to state Affordability Effort since 1980, and to identify some possible relationships between Affordability Effort and the factors that influence it.

The model we use here is a variation of one developed by Kent Halstead, who presented state-funding effort as the ratio of state appropriations for higher education to tax revenues per capita. Here, we substitute tax capacity for tax revenue. Tax capacity is a measure presented by Halstead which shows the revenue-raising potential of each state. This is the per capita tax revenue that each state would raise if it applied a national average tax rate to its tax capacity. By using tax capacity instead of tax revenue, we can compare states' willingness to tax itself, as well as its willingness to spend tax revenues on higher education.[21]

This model is certainly not perfect. Each state has a unique set of resources at its disposal, and each state faces a different set of demands on those resources. The Affordability Effort of a state with an unusually large tax base may appear low, even if much of its tax wealth must be devoted to other needs such as health care or prison maintenance. Likewise, the Affordability Effort of a fairly poor state may appear high, even if it faces relatively few demands on its resources. The model used here, however, provides a good approximation of each state's effort to reduce the price of public higher education.

To illustrate this model, consider the state of Minnesota, which had a typical Affordability Effort since 1980. In 1991, Minnesota appropriated $4,444 to higher education per undergraduate FTE, and spent $416 per FTE on need-based grants. Minnesota had a tax capacity in 1991 of $2,085. Thus, Minnesota's total spending on higher education per FTE ($4,860) was 2.33 times its tax capacity, giving Minnesota an Affordability effort of 2.33.

Table 6.7 shows each state's Affordability Effort as well as change in Affordability Effort between 1981 and 1991. The states are ranked according to their Affordability Effort in 1991, from highest to lowest. Since Affordability Effort is an index, it allows us to compare various states and across time.

While Affordability Effort does not correlate exactly with net price, there is a strong inverse relationship between the two measurements. As one would expect, states with high Affordability Effort tend to have a low net price, and states with low Affordability Effort tend to have a high net price. There are a few notable exceptions to the trend. California, West Virginia, and Nevada each maintain a low net price, with low Affordability Effort. Two factors help to explain this discrepancy. First, states that operate an extremely efficient or low-cost public higher-education system can maintain a low net price without a large Affordability Effort. Second, states with great tax wealth can operate an averaged priced system without a large Affordability Effort. The inverse is also true. Pennsylvania has high Affordability Effort, but still has a high net price. Nonetheless, most states' position on the Affordability Effort table varies only slightly from their position on the net price table.

The most obvious conclusion to be drawn from table 6.7 is that state effort to keep higher education affordable dropped precipitously since 1980. With the exception of eight states, Affordability Effort dropped across the country between 1981 and 1991. For most states, the drop was severe. In addition, most of the decline occurred in the latter half of the decade. Twenty-six states were able to maintain or increase their Affordability Effort during the early half of the 1980s, and the national aggregate actually increased between 1981 and 1986.

These trends are hardly surprising. Most states encountered severe fiscal stress after 1980, and many of the budgetary problems grew worse after 1986. With growing demands on limited resources, most states directed fewer resources each year toward higher education. However, Affordability Effort dropped in some states much more than in others.

Affordability Effort: Comparing the States

States which had very high Affordability Effort in 1981 tended to suffer large declines during the decade. The ten states that began the decade with the highest Affordability Effort suffered an average decline of 24 percent. On the other hand, states which had low Affordability Effort tended to suffer small declines. The ten states with the lowest Affordability Effort in 1981 suffered an average decline of less than 7 percent.

These patterns make clear that different states responded to their fiscal stress in different ways. There is no evidence that budgetary problems affected high Affordability Effort states more than low Affordability Effort states. However, it is reasonable to conclude that states beginning the decade with high Affordability Effort levels suffered the greatest decline simply because they had the greatest distance to fall. Under fiscal stress, those states could drastically reduce their funding of higher education without causing a proportional reduction in the quality of their public college systems. On the other hand, a state that was already making a low Affordability Effort in 1981 could scarcely afford to cut much from its higher education budget. Public demand for a quality higher-education system, the danger of causing long-term harm through short-term underfunding, the fixed costs of providing a higher education, and public resistance to tuition increases all imposed a floor on how low a state's Affordability Effort could drop. As a result, by 1991 nearly all states made a smaller effort to fund higher education than in 1981, but fewer states made an Affordability Effort that varied greatly from the national aggregate level.

Another noticeable trend is the positive relationship between state Affordability Effort and state tax revenues. A state's tax revenue is determined by the size of its tax base, and its rates of taxation. Thus, a state can have high tax revenues because of a wealthy tax base, high tax rates, or both. In general, states with high per-capita tax revenues have high Affordability Effort, and states with low per-capita tax revenues have low Affordability Effort. Some slight variation in this trend occurs in states that tax themselves very heavily or very lightly, because their available tax revenue is disproportionate to their tax capacity.

However, some states do not follow this pattern. Several large, industrialized, states, such as California, New Jersey, and Ohio, have Affordability Efforts significantly below what their tax revenues suggest is possible. On the other hand, several small, mostly rural states, such as Arkansas, Utah, and Idaho have Affordability Efforts well above what their tax revenues would suggest. One explanation of these exceptions is that large urban states must spend more of their tax revenue to address problems that do not exist (or need less attention) in smaller, more rural states. Without cause to believe that small states are simply more dedicated to higher education than large states, this size distribution pattern

Table 6.7

Affordability Effort by State: Selected Years, 1981–1991

Rank	State	1981	1986	1991	10 Year Change
1	Hawaii	3.89	4.40	3.68	− 0.21
2	Alaska	3.24	3.18	3.66	0.41
3	Idaho	3.84	3.77	3.32	− 0.52
4	New Mexico	3.01	3.06	3.22	0.21
5	Iowa	2.91	3.07	3.13	0.21
6	South Carolina	3.70	3.30	2.82	− 0.88
7	North Carolina	3.46	3.60	2.82	− 0.64
8	New York	4.32	4.00	2.75	− 1.57
9	Utah	3.39	3.51	2.74	− 0.66
10	Wisconsin	3.13	2.92	2.68	− 0.45
11	Washington	2.49	2.52	2.62	0.13
12	Indiana	2.91	2.85	2.61	− 0.31
13	Wyoming	2.66	2.81	2.54	− 0.12
14	Oklahoma	2.12	2.70	2.54	0.42
15	Pennsylvania	3.28	3.24	2.52	− 0.76
16	Florida	2.69	2.83	2.45	− 0.24
17	Arkansas	2.95	3.55	2.45	− 0.51
18	Oregon	2.17	2.64	2.45	0.28
19	Maine	2.86	2.74	2.41	− 0.45
20	Tennessee	2.85	3.21	2.38	− 0.48
21	Kentucky	3.07	3.32	2.37	− 0.69
22	Illinois	2.45	2.72	2.35	− 0.10
23	Georgia	3.35	2.97	2.34	− 1.01
24	Minnesota	2.79	2.78	2.33	− 0.46
25	Mississippi	3.28	2.60	2.32	− 0.97
26	Michigan	2.40	2.87	2.28	− 0.12
27	Kansas	2.55	2.55	2.26	− 0.30
28	North Dakota	2.35	2.13	2.25	− 0.09
29	New Jersey	2.79	2.93	2.25	− 0.54
30	Montana	2.03	2.68	2.24	0.21
31	Nebraska	2.58	2.09	2.21	− 0.37
32	Rhode Island	3.59	3.39	2.16	− 1.43

Table 6.7 (*continued*)

Rank	State	1981	1986	1991	10 Year Change
33	Alabama	2.67	3.68	2.15	− 0.52
34	Connecticut	2.75	2.65	2.14	− 0.61
35	South Dakota	2.42	2.53	2.14	− 0.28
36	Missouri	2.79	2.69	2.14	− 0.65
37	California	2.36	2.23	2.09	− 0.26
38	Arizona	2.76	2.63	2.05	− 0.71
39	Ohio	2.26	2.45	2.00	− 0.26
40	Texas	1.94	2.00	1.98	0.04
41	Maryland	2.63	2.26	1.92	− 0.70
42	Louisiana	2.50	2.29	1.91	− 0.60
43	Virginia	2.51	2.42	1.83	− 0.69
44	West Virginia	2.29	2.74	1.82	− 0.47
45	Delaware	2.47	2.40	1.77	− 0.70
46	Nevada	1.78	1.87	1.76	− 0.01
47	Massachusetts	2.91	2.94	1.73	− 1.18
48	Colorado	1.57	1.59	1.47	− 0.11
49	Vermont	2.18	1.82	1.45	− 0.73
50	New Hampshire	1.77	1.47	1.06	− 0.71
	National Aggregate	2.70	2.71	2.25	− 0.45
	High Expenditure Aggregate	4.32	4.00	2.75	− 1.57
	LowT uition/Low Aid Aggregate	2.50	2.58	2.37	− 0.14
	High Tuition/High Aid Aggregate	2.54	2.63	2.00	− 0.54
	Low Expenditure Aggregate	2.42	2.30	1.70	− 0.72

Source: K. Halstead, *State Profiles: Financing Public Higher Education 1978–1992* (Research Associates: Washington D.C., 1992).
[a] Affordability effort measures are rounded to two decimal places. Two or more states that to have the same effort in 1991 are ranked according to difference beyond the second decimal place.
[b] Aggregate represents the affordability effort of a group of states calculated as if they are one state.

lends support to the conclusion that in state expenditure decisions, higher education usually takes a backseat to social needs like crime control and health care.

These patterns provide further evidence that state governments find it difficult to fund higher education at a high level during times of fiscal stress. Public and political pressures demand that scarce resources be spent to address other social and economic problems. However, it is also clear that public higher education receives some support from public and political interests. From the perspective of the state legislator who wants to support higher education, what can a state government do to maximize that support? The next section compares the Affordability Effort of states employing the various affordability strategies, to suggest that strategy may play some part in a state's ability to maintain high Affordability Effort.

Affordability Effort: Comparing the Strategies

Table 6.7 also shows the aggregate Affordability Effort of states using each affordability strategy, and where each strategy would rank among the states. As one would expect, the states using the low-expenditure strategy tend to have a very low Affordability Effort. Even though these states have very wealthy tax bases, they each tax themselves very lightly and devote little tax revenue toward higher-education appropriations or financial aid. On the other hand, New York taxes itself very heavily, and directs much of its tax revenues to higher education. As a result, New York maintains its high-expenditure strategy through a fairly large Affordability Effort.

However, most states have neither the resources to pursue a high-expenditure strategy, nor the desire to adopt a low-expenditure strategy. For the majority of state governments, who want to give higher education as much funding as possible but have limited resources, the only real choice is between the low-tuition/low-aid and high-tuition/high-aid strategies. As shown in table 6.7, the aggregate Affordability Effort of the fourteen states in the low-tuition/low-aid category would rank 21st among the states in 1991. The mean Affordability Effort of the five states in the high-tuition/high-aid category would rank 39th. Although we should be careful not to overstate the importance of this discrepancy, it is clear that states which held tuition low can and do direct more resources to higher education than states that strive to keep financial aid high.

Several factors help to explain this discrepancy. First, the low-tuition/low-aid states usually operate much smaller public higher education systems than the high-tuition/high-aid states. Nine out of fourteen low-tuition/low-aid states had FTE enrollment below 100,000 in 1991, whereas four out of five high-tuition/high-aid states operated systems with more than 100,000 FTE students. Since the fixed costs are spread over a smaller area, a small public system requires more spending per student than a large system.

Second, the high-tuition/high-aid states may have made conscious policy decisions to allow their Affordability Efforts to decrease. Located primarily in the Northeast, most of the high-tuition/high-aid states contain an extensive and prestigious private system of colleges and universities. On the other hand, the low-tuition/low-aid states, located primarily in the South and West, must rely on public institutions to provide higher education to their residents. Private institutions and private college students benefit from need-based grants much more than from low public college tuitions. To satisfy this constituency, the high-tuition/high-aid states may have intentionally allowed tuition to rise so that they could direct more money into grants. And since need-based grants increase affordability much more efficiently than instructional subsidies, the high-tuition/high-aid states could let their total Affordability Effort drop without raising price barriers.

Finally, the low-tuition/low-aid states may produce greater public and political support for higher-education spending. Since low tuitions benefit all students and their families, while need-based grants disproportionately benefit low-income students, spending to keep tuition low receives support from many of the more vocal and organized groups in society. When states experienced the fiscal stress since 1980, policymakers may have encountered strong resistance to cuts in appropriations, but little resistance to a reduction in grant programs. As a result, low-tuition/low-aid states were able to maintain or increase their total spending on higher education, while the high-tuition/high-aid states found it difficult to maintain or increase grant spending.

This potential inability to maintain political support for grant spending is a common criticism of the high-tuition/high-aid approach. Careful analysis of the data indicates that this criticism may have some validity. Figure 6.1 shows how aggregate Affordability Effort, average tuition, and aggregate grant size of the high-tuition/high-aid states changed during after 1980 relative to the national aggregate baseline.

Table 6.8

Affordability Effort, Tuition, and State Spending for Need Based Grants: National and High Aid Aggregates

	Affordability Effort		
	1981	*1986*	*1991*
National Aggregate	2.70	2.71	2.25
High Tuition- High Aid Aggregate	2.54	2.63	2.00

	Public College Tuitions		
	1981	*1986*	*1991*
National Aggregate	$930	$1,204	$1,377
High Tuition- High Aid Aggregate	$1,627	$2,146	$2,730

	State Spending on Need-Based Grants Per FTE		
	1981	*1986*	*1991*
National Aggregate	$188	$223	$216
High Tuition- High Aid Aggregate	$485	$459	$509

Table 6.8 shows that during the early 1980s, tuitions in the high-tuition/high-aid states increased at nearly the same rate as tuitions in the rest of the nation. At the same time, grants in those five states rose much faster than the national aggregate. Consequently, although still below the national aggregate, Affordability Effort in the high-tuition/high-aid states rose slightly faster than in the rest of the country. In the late 1980s, however, these trends reversed. Tuitions rose much faster in the high-tuition/high-aid states than in the rest of the country, while grants grew at just slightly above the national rate. As such, aggregate Affordability Effort of the high-tuition/high-aid states slipped against the national baseline.

This evidence indicates that in the early 1980s, when state budgets were fairly good, the high-tuition/high-aid states were able to hold tuition increases low while making large increases in grant spending. Then, when fiscal troubles arose in the latter half of the decade, those states slowed down their grant increases while they let tuitions rise rapidly. Whether because of conscious choice or scarce resources, the High Tuition/High Aid states halted the rapid growth of their grant programs when budgets became tight. However, there is no evidence that these states were unable to maintain their high levels of need-based aid. To the contrary, real grant dollars per FTE went up or remained fairly constant after 1980 for every high-tuition/high-aid state except Massachusetts. So while they did not continue to increase grant spending at a rate well above the national aggregate, the high-tuition/high-aid states were able to maintain the high spending levels that they had achieved.

This analysis of Affordability Effort does not suggest that one strategy is "superior" to another. Many of the advantages and disadvantages of both strategies cannot be measured empirically. Nonetheless, if states continue to face tight budgets and rising demands on their resources, more states will consider adopting the more efficient high-tuition/high-aid strategy. If so, the evidence here, as well as common sense, suggests that they might encounter severe political resistance to raising tuitions. In addition, this analysis suggests that it may be hard to increase grant spending when budgets are tight. However, once a state has implemented a high-tuition/high-aid strategy, there is little evidence that it will be unable to maintain the high level of grant funding.

HOW DID THE STATES DO? AN OVERALL PERSPECTIVE

States help to make public higher education affordable to low-income students primarily through some combination of tuition subsidies and need-based grants. Although new programs were developed in many states and the amount of need-based grant spending increased after 1980, state Affordability Efforts to aid low-income students did not fare well. Tuitions increased so rapidly across the country that only New York was able to hold increases in the net price of college below inflation in the CPI. Thus since 1980, students in every other state saw their public colleges becoming more and more expensive.

Economic conditions were, certainly, an important determinant of how effectively states maintained public college affordability. During the first half of the decade, when the economy was plagued by high levels of inflation and unemployment, net college prices increased markedly. But even as economic conditions improved during the latter half of the decade, many states were unable to reverse the trend of rapidly declining affordability. Although the economy improved, many of the demands on state budgets remained, and even worsened. This helps to explain why Affordability Effort dropped so precipitously after 1986: although tax capacity increased due to the healthy economy, many states found it difficult to translate that increased capacity into increased revenue, or to direct the increased revenue to higher education. As a result, college affordability eroded consistently during the decade.

NEW DEVELOPMENTS IN STATE FUNDING

With the exception of funds for capital projects, the vast majority of state dollars which are appropriated for higher education are given to public colleges in the form of state subsidies or to students in the form of need-based financial aid. But as public pressures to improve college affordability increased more rapidly than state dollars to fund these programs, state policy-makers began to look for alternative ways to address affordability problems.

Foremost among the innovations which have received attention are merit-based aid and assured-access programs. These two approaches seek to channel state aid carefully to particular target groups. Such channeling holds the prospect of producing a greater impact on the target groups' access to college for fewer dollars than the more traditional approaches. While these state innovations are too new to fully evaluate, it is worthwhile to review their purpose and promise.

The Growth of Merit-Based Aid

Prior to the early 1960s, a large percentage of all student financial aid was awarded on the basis of merit. Colleges competed for the best students by offering them academic scholarships without regard for student need. The expansion of need-based aid by the federal government throughout the 1970s and by state governments in the 1980s and 1990s, shifted the focus of financial aid programs.

Since the mid-1980s, however, academic scholarships have experienced a resurgence.[22] Between 1986 and 1991, merit-based aid programs grew much more rapidly than the need-based grant programs.[23] This growth has taken several forms. Some state programs were designed to lower the cost to a student attending a private school, others to encourage good students to study in their home state, and others to encourage good students to enter a profession deemed important by the state. But all had in common a selection process based on academic merit, or special skills, rather than financial need.

When compared to the development and funding of need-based programs, the shift to merit-based aid programs seems to be a nationwide trend. As recently as 1986, only seventeen states awarded merit-based scholarships for a total of $44.6 million (constant 1994 dollars). By 1991, twenty-three states were awarding $89.4 million in such aid. This is an average annual increase of more the 16 percent per year. During that same time, need-based aid increased by only 6 percent per year. While the majority of the growth in merit aid occurred in two states, Missouri and Florida, the total was still impressive.

Hauptman argues that the growth in merit aid is due, in part, to the declining number of traditional college-age Americans, which has set off a competition among educational institutions for students.[24] The growth of merit aid may also be a reaction against concerns about declines in educational quality. Schools may be awarding merit aid as a way of attracting more qualified students. This might indicate a kind of bidding war among some states to attract top-quality undergraduates.

The increase in the percent of dollars devoted to merit aid is an interesting trend, but it must be viewed with considerable caution. Such aid amounts to only 4 percent of all state grant aid and less than one percent of state appropriations on higher education. As such, while merit aid may play an increasing part in the efforts of families to pay for college, its total amount is still extremely small when compared to the funding levels of established need-based grant programs. Academic scholarships thus remain only a small part of the overall college finance picture.

The Promise of Assured Access

Another recent trend is the development of programs that guarantee low-income elementary and secondary students that their college tuition will be paid by the state. These programs are modeled on Eugene Lange's widely acclaimed "I Have A Dream Foundation," which seems to have been successful at increasing student performance and college hopes for a sixth-grade class in East Harlem.[25] For each student in the class, Lange agreed to pay for the difference between the amount of government grant aid the students could receive and the costs of the college of their choice. Lange's program also supplied tutoring and other support services to make sure the students were prepared for college.

Variations of this assured-access approach became popular since 1980. Rhode Island and Florida developed programs which identify at-risk students in grade school and then offer the students a tuition guarantee if the students meet certain conditions and standards during their secondary school careers. New York's Liberty Scholarship Program (which was approved by the New York legislature but not funded) provides, along with other financial aid, a guarantee that the full non-tuition cost of attending college in New York state will be covered.[26]

Hauptman argues that the success of these programs points to the "glaring shortcomings" of the current college finance system.[27] The experience of assured-access programs is that providing student aid without sufficient support services is a strategy doomed to failure. Nevertheless, few reforms pay sufficient attention to the critical role played by tutoring and counseling services in improving the college success rates of low-income students. Most of the debates over how to improve college access revolve around how to remove financial barriers, but these barriers may be only a small part of the problem.

While these developments are promising, they are as yet too small and new to have had much of an impact on college affordability. It is possible that these new approaches may eventually produce important new resources for lower-income families to help pay for college. But today they amount to little more than minor trends and promising pilot programs.

DOES DECLINING AFFORDABILITY MEAN THAT COLLEGE IS BECOMING UNAFFORDABLE?

This evaluation was not intended to determine the precise extent to which public higher education has moved beyond the financial reach of American families. Instead, it examined the trends in college affordability and compared those trends across the states. On this score, the evidence is overwhelming. With the sole exception of New York, public higher education became less affordable in every state since 1980 regardless of the funding strategy. In many states that decline was so dramatic that it called into question whether policy-makers continued to support the goal of equal access to higher education.

While the declines in college affordability were evident almost everywhere, these findings must be viewed with some caution. Public higher education remains highly subsidized, even in states with relatively high tuitions. Students pay far less than the actual cost of providing the education they receive. Moreover, the evidence presented in chapter 1 suggests that the economic returns associated with a college education are substantial and continue throughout a person's life. Thus, even as public higher education is becoming less affordable across the country, it may still be a good value and a wise investment.

The increasing value of higher education notwithstanding, the recent rapid decline in public college and university affordability evidenced here provide reason for concern. Increases in the price of public higher education, declines in the purchasing power of state grants, and the corresponding rapid increases in the net price of public higher education seem unlikely to change in the near term. The forces which are driving these trends, declining federal support, state budget difficulties, decreasing numbers of college-age students, and increasing costs of providing instruction, seem certain to continue for many years to come.

While some states, due to fortunate circumstances or effective management, may be able to limit increases in the net price of public higher education, they have been unable to make further progress in removing college price barriers. Indeed, the evidence seems to be that the states may not have the resources to maintain the initiatives that now exist, let alone develop new or expand old programs.

7

HELPING FAMILIES TO SAVE
FOR COLLEGE

(with Jeremy Anderson)

The analysis presented so far makes clear that during the last decade in particular, the federal and state governments have been shifting an ever larger portion of the costs of higher education to students and their families. Higher tuitions and smaller grants have forced those students who can afford it to pick up more of their own college tab. Those students who cannot afford it now are expected to finance more of those costs and repay them later with interest.

As students and families marshall their private financial resources to pay those rising prices, they make use of both their current income and their past savings.[1] Changes in the availability of private savings thus constitute a final resource which must be considered in any comprehensive evaluation of college affordability. But families do not make savings decisions in a financial vacuum. Governments have several tools they can use to encourage families to save. By adjusting interest rates, tax policies, and by creating special savings incentive plans, governments can increase the benefits which accrue to families if they increase their savings for college.

In this chapter we consider government efforts to encourage families to save for college. First, we examine the recent trends in national and family savings rates. Second, we consider the various mechanisms developed by governments to encourage family savings. Here we look at how these different programs work, and evaluate their potential for reducing college price barriers.

175

THE DECLINE IN NATIONAL SAVINGS

Throughout the 1970s, the personal savings rate of Americans remained at about 7.5 percent of disposable personal income. While from an international perspective this rate was not particularly high,[2] it supplied the nation with a base for private investment and provided families with a cushion against hardships or unexpected expenses. It also provided many families with an essential resource to help pay college costs. Since real tuition inflation was low in the 1970s, and rates of return on many forms of investment were relatively high, this made the rewards for college savings especially great. Even relatively small savings levels, if invested early and wisely, would allow families to build a nest egg sufficient to cover a significant portion of the price of their children's education.

But in the early 1980s, the U.S. savings rate began to slip.[3] That decline continued throughout the decade. By the early 1990s, personal savings as a percent of disposable income had dropped to its lowest level in recent history.[4] Making matters worse, unusually low interest rates in the early 1990s reduced the return for savings and forced even the most conscientious savers to wonder how they could make their investment keep pace with college prices which were reaching all-time highs.

While it is difficult to know with certainty, many economists worry that the decline in U.S. savings rates represents a fundamental change in the way American's view the need to save.[5] In outlining the magnitude of the problem, economist Lawrence Summers makes the point that today most U.S. families engage in virtually no financial savings. As evidence of this, Summers notes that less than 40 percent of U.S. households reported interest and dividend income of $100 or more in six consecutive years during the 1980s. A remarkable 33 percent *never* had $100 in gross interest and dividend income during any year in the 1980s.[6]

Perhaps even more troubling than the low rates of savings is the seemingly widespread public view that savings is unnecessary or even harmful. In a national survey of U.S. attitudes toward savings, Jim Immerwahr, of the California Center for Higher Education Policy, found that "many respondents expressed deep ambivalence about the moral value of saving" while others "insisted that increased savings would hurt the economy.[7]" This combination of public ambivalence toward savings and the easier availability of credit seems to have played a role in the recent decrease in savings.

The declining rate of national savings presents serious problems for the U.S. economy. Lack of national savings means that there is less capital for economic investment, banks must pay higher interest rates in order to attract capital, and families have smaller financial cushions so that a short-term economic crisis is more likely to lead to bankruptcy or long-term economic hardship.[8] Elderly citizens must rely more on Social Security to finance their retirements because they do not have savings to serve as a supplement. The seriously ill or infirm must rely on public support if they have little personal savings. Of particular interest here, however, is the concern that reduced national savings will exacerbate the college affordability problem. Governments are shifting the burden of college financing to families at precisely the same time families are reducing how much they are saving to accommodate these larger obligations. This may eventually produce even larger college price barriers as more families have little or no savings to help pay for their rapidly rising tuitions.

LIMITS OF GOVERNMENT'S ABILITY
TO ENCOURAGE SAVINGS

In light of the significant national and individual benefits which would flow from increased rates of savings, both the federal and state governments have taken action to encourage individuals to save more. Most of these efforts are not linked directly to concerns over college affordability. But if the government can improve individual savings rates for any reason, it will, over time, provide families with important additional resources to meet college costs and reduce their need to rely on government-provided student aid.

The most frequently used mechanism by governments to encourage savings is to alter tax rates in order to reward savings and/or to discourage consumption or borrowing. Programs which allow consumers to place income in tax-deferred savings accounts, such as Independent Retirement Accounts or 401K plans, are the most widely used of these incentive plans. Similarly, through the sale of tax-free bonds, governments can encourage savings as well as raise money to finance current expenditures. Governments can also adjust the tax deductibility of certain types of interest payments to encourage or discourage borrowing for a particular purpose.[9] For example, allowing those who borrow for college to deduct the interest on those loans from post-college income will lower the price of borrowing and encourage families to borrow. On the other hand, allowing families to defer taxation on income saved for college will encourage families to begin saving.

Many economists, however, question the effectiveness of such government efforts.[10] Indeed, the experience of the 1980s seems to indicate that simply the creation of savings incentives is insufficient to change the behavior of most families. In spite of unprecedented levels of return on stock and bond investments, and the very high interest rates on savings accounts, the national savings rate plummeted in the 1980s.[11] This is, at least in part, because most Americans are poorly informed about the tax code and the rates of return on the investment options available to them. Consequently, if it is to effectively influence savings behavior, a government program must also undertake extensive publicity and marketing campaigns.[12]

Even with such aggressive marketing campaigns, some economists doubt how that public policy can have much impact on private savings rates. Lawrence Summers, for example, argues that savings rates are "difficult to influence with the tools that government has at its disposal" and, as a result, personal savings rates are "almost immutable."[13] While this immutability may be evident in the short term, public policies which change public attitudes about savings can be successful over the long term. Only if families begin to recognize the value of savings will they be willing to forego today's consumption for greater benefits in the future.

GOVERNMENT EFFORTS TO ENCOURAGE COLLEGE SAVINGS

In spite of these limitations, many state governments have taken the initiative to develop programs to encourage families to save for their children's education. Using targeted marketing campaigns, tax incentives, and prepayment programs, these states sought to raise public consciousness about the need to save for college and provide citizens with a structured, and often tax-advantaged, means to increase their savings.

New York was the first state government to enact a program with the explicit intent of helping families to save for college. Under the parents and students savings program (PASS), state residents were allowed to deduct up to $750 every year from their taxable income for funds placed in a college savings account.[14] More recently, Missouri developed a plan to allow the deductibility of contributions to college savings accounts from state taxes.[15]

Many states have gone beyond these simple incentive devices to develop full-scale college savings programs. These programs fall into two categories: college prepayment programs and college savings bond programs. Tuition prepayment programs allow people to purchase contracts that are guaranteed to cover a percentage of the future costs of attending college. Parents, relatives, and family friends can pay now for a future student's education. College savings bond programs use public relations campaigns and financial incentives to encourage families to save for college by investing in tax-exempt government bonds. While neither type of program has much impact on college affordability in the short term, they are designed to change family savings patterns in the long term and make it possible for parents to re-assume a greater responsibility for the college costs of their children.

Both types of college savings programs have proliferated since the mid-1980s, at least in part, because they gave state policy-makers politically and economically acceptable alternatives to costly increases in subsidies or need-based grant programs. By creating college savings programs, policy-makers could respond to public concerns that college was becoming unaffordable without having to appropriate large amounts of new spending in the current year. Further, if they are successful, such programs have the potential to provide families with an additional set of resources to pay for college without corresponding increases in direct government subsidies.

TUITION PREPAYMENT PROGRAMS

The first prepaid tuition program was implemented on a single school basis at Duquesne University in 1985. Called the Alumni Tuition Plan, the program allowed parents to buy four guaranteed future years of tuition at a highly discounted price.

In 1985, for example, an alumnus could purchase four years of prepaid tuition for a child who would enroll in the year 2004, for a total of only $4,450. The assumptions behind the plan were that Duquesne would invest the funds in U.S. Treasury zero-coupon bonds carrying an 11 percent interest. This, along with the restrictions on the use of the benefits was intended to make the program self-supporting.[16]

While Duquesne's program received national publicity and spurred broad public interest, it also drew substantial criticism. Potential buyers were critical of the restrictive nature of the program. Students were restricted to Duquesne for at least a year, whether or not the school suited them. Program managers worried that the program was not financially viable. The bond market yields were lower than anticipated and the price of the credits rose rapidly. Such concerns caused participation to drop further. As a consequence, in 1988, after attracting only 622 participants, Duquesne suspended the program.[17]

But the Duquesne experiment caught the attention of policy-makers in Michigan, who proposed a similar prepaid tuition program to cover all state institutions. In 1986, Michigan became the first state to approve legislation creating a tuition prepayment program. Within two months of its enactment in Michigan, and before its implementation, prepaid tuition plans were being discussed in forty states and thirty states were considering actual bills.[18] In 1987, Wyoming, acting more quickly than Michigan, became the first state to implement its program. It seemed as if prepaid tuition was an idea whose time had come.

But problems with the Michigan program began almost as soon as it was enacted.[19] Prior to beginning operation, the Michigan Educational Trust (MET) was required by its authorizing legislation to obtain an IRS ruling clarifying the tax status of the prepayment contracts. After a long delay, the IRS issued a private letter ruling (which was not necessarily binding on other states) that the MET would be liable for trust taxes, and that trust beneficiaries would be taxed on the earnings of the contract in the year that it was redeemed.[20]

Michigan considered the ruling to be favorable enough to proceed with the program in 1988. But in 1990 it filed suit against the IRS, claiming that the fund was "an integral part of state government" and exempt from federal taxation.[21] Michigan lost that appeal in 1992, when a federal court ruled that the MET does not qualify as a tax-exempt organization and was hence liable for trust taxes. Trust beneficiaries were also found to be liable for taxes in the year the credits are redeemed.[22]

Table 7.1 shows the states which have enacted or implemented prepaid tuition programs. It also shows that the great majority of them did so between 1989 and 1991. Since that time, largely as a result of the tax problems faced by the MET, the momentum of the prepaid-tuition idea had slowed. Additionally, many states either repealed or suspended the operation of their programs. Others passed them, but have never put them into

Table 7.1
State Tuition Prepayment Plans

State Program	Year Enacted	Current Status
Alabama	1991	Active
Alaska	1991	Active
Florida	1989	Active
Indiana	1991	Inactive
Kentucky	1991	Inactive
Louisiana	1989	Not Yet Operational
Maine	1990	Repealed
Michigan	1988	Active
Missouri	1991	Not Yet Operational
Ohio	1990	Active
Oklahoma	1989	Not Yet Operational
Pennsylvania	1992	Active
Tennessee	1989	Repealed
West Virginia	1988	Not Yet Operational
Wyoming	1991	Active

operation. As a consequence, while sixteen states had enacted some form of tuition prepayment plan, only seven (Alabama, Alaska, Florida, Michigan, Ohio, Pennsylvania, and Wyoming) are actively selling contracts.

The Logic and Operation of Prepayment Plans

Participants in tuition prepayment plans buy state trust-fund contracts that are guaranteed to cover the cost of tuition at a public in-state college when the beneficiary attends school. In essence, families are allowed to pay in advance a child's education at rates much less than they might expect to pay when that child was ready to enter school. In doing so, participants buy peace of mind by transferring the risk of continued increases in the real cost of tuition to the state trust fund.[23]

It is possible for the state trust funds to offer families such an attractive arrangement because, through pooled risk and resources, trust managers can presumably achieve higher rates of return than individual investors. In doing this, state trust funds are designed to be self-sustaining and, unlike most individual investors, have enough resources to spread out losses and gains over all phases of cyclical market variations.[24] But these programs have limits which can discourage some families from participating. Investments in prepayment programs are largely non-liquid and carry restrictions which severely limit access to the cash value of the contract. Normally, investors cannot redeem the contract until the beneficiary has graduated from high school, even if better investment opportunities appear or a family emergency requires the money.

In order to participate in a program, investors must accept some restrictions on the refundability and transferability of their tuition contracts. All states with prepaid tuition programs, except Florida and Wyoming, allow beneficiaries attending out of state colleges and universities to redeem their contracts for the equivalent of average tuition at public in-state colleges. All states, except Wyoming, allow such portability to in-state private schools. Some states allow contracts to be transferred within a family, but all states prohibit the sale of prepayment contracts.[25]

Criticisms of Tuition Prepayment Plans

These benefits notwithstanding, there are a number of concerns which face tuition prepayment plans.[26] When investors accept the programs restrictions and begin making payments to a prepaid tuition program, they accept several risks. Parents who purchase contracts cannot be sure that in the future their children will want to attend an in-state public college. Furthermore, the investors, whether they be parents, grandparents, family friends, or the students themselves, will have severely limited access to the cash value of the contract until the beneficiary has graduated from high school. Because the costs of these restrictions are hard to predict, it is difficult for an investor to estimate the value of a tuition prepayment plan and compare it with other investments.

From the perspective of the state trust-fund managers, the concerns are much different. Those who manage these programs must insure that the contract prices they charge will adequately account for future financial conditions and tuition levels. Financial markets fluctuate and so do the factors involved in setting tuition. But when state prepayment trust authorities set the price of their prepayment contracts, they must project financial conditions and tuition levels up to fifteen years in the future. If they set the price too low, they will threaten the self-sustaining design of their prepayment trust fund. If they set the price too high, they will outprice many of the people who are most in need of a college savings program.

Critics also worry that the trust funds will not be able to achieve an investment return high enough to meet their financial commitments. The two pioneers in this area, Duquesne University and the Michigan Educational Trust, were both forced to suspend their prepaid tuition program after the investment and tuition projections used to set the contract prices proved to be too optimistic.[27] But even in states which have not explicitly accepted legal responsibility for maintaining the integrity of the fund, there would be strong political pressures to bail out the trust fund if it became necessary. Such a bailout would certainly affect the rest of the state's education budget. It would also cause a direct transfer of wealth from taxpayers to program beneficiaries who are disproportionately drawn from upper-income groups.[28] Thus, ultimately taxpayers and future students, not program participants, bear the risk of future tuition increases.

COLLEGE SAVINGS BOND PROGRAMS

A second way for governments to encourage families to save for college is through the sale of bonds. Illinois was the first state to use federally tax-exempt bonds as a college savings mechanism. Beginning in 1987, Illinois allowed families to purchase zero-coupon general obligation bonds for the purpose of college savings.[29] If the family held the bond for at least five years, and then used the proceeds to pay for higher education, the state agreed to pay a substantially higher interest rate on that bond.

After Illinois, and then North Carolina, enacted bond programs in 1987, twelve states enacted college savings bond legislation in 1988 and ten more followed in 1989.[30] As shown in table 7.2, twenty-seven states have now enacted some form of college saving bond program and twenty-four of those were actively selling bonds. In explaining the broad popularity of these bond programs, as opposed to prepaid tuition plans, Hauptman argues:

> Most of these states seem persuaded by the simplicity of the Illinois approach, its use of an already existing financial instrument that provides federal tax benefits, and its decision not to burden the state with an unknowable and unpredictable contingent liability, such as the kind tuitions guarantees may carry.[31]

Table 7.2
State Savings Bond Programs

State	Status	State	Status
Arkansas	Active	Missouri	Active
California	Active	New Hampshire	Active
Connecticut	Active	North Carolina	Active
Delaware	Active	North Dakota	Active
Hawaii	Active	Ohio	Active
Illinois	Active	Oregon	Active
Indiana	Active	Rhode Island	Active
Indiana	Active	South Dakota	Active
Iowa	Active	Tennessee	Active
Kentucky	Active	Texas	Active
Louisiana	Active	Virginia	Active
Maine	Inactive	Washington	Active
Michigan	Inactive	Wisconsin	Active
Minnesota	Inactive		

Compared to prepaid tuition programs, college savings bond programs provide a simple and risk-free way for states to encourage savings for college. Indeed, the tax rules for such programs are firmly established and there is very little delay between the state's adoption of a program and its implementation.

Different states issue college savings bonds through different mechanisms, but bond programs still have many similar characteristics. Typically, states designate general obligation or revenue bonds as college savings bonds. These bonds are then sold as zero-coupon bonds, which pay interest and principle at maturity. They are typically sold at denominations ranging from $1,000 to $5,000. Returns on college savings bonds may be lower than more aggressive investments, but because interest earned on the bonds is exempt from state and federal taxes, the investment is still attractive to many families wishing to save for college.

Although restrictions vary from state to state, bond purchasers do not need to use their investments for educational purposes. Bond holders can cash them in and use the return in any way they choose, although they may loose some of the tax advantages. But college savings bond programs are almost always preceded by advertising campaigns that encourage families to use them as a means for saving for college. The most visible campaign of this type is in Connecticut, which operates an 800-number phone line and sixty outlets across the state to purchase bonds. The Connecticut market campaign sends information about savings bonds to every child and licensed motorist in the state.[32]

Limitation of College Savings Bonds

College savings programs have few potential drawbacks for the states authorizing them. The cost of the program is very predictable, and unlike tuition prepayment programs, the state's financial liability is always known. States are also able to use the revenue obtained through the sale of bonds to finance a wide variety of projects. States, however, risk the loss of revenues when they encourage investors to move their assets from taxable accounts to tax-exempt bonds. As a consequence, states must weigh the costs of lost tax revenues against the educational and political benefits of beginning or continuing a bond program.

FEDERAL COLLEGE SAVINGS BONDS

In 1988, the federal government passed legislation exempting interest earned on series EE U.S. Savings Bonds from taxation if the bonds are used for college. Under this plan, a $100 savings bond, which was purchased for $50 can be redeemed and used to pay for education expenses of $100 without incurring income tax on the $50 gain. But the benefits of this program do not apply to everyone. To insure that the wealthy were not given an unneeded tax break, the interest income exclusion is phased out for taxpayers who's adjusted gross income exceeds $60,000 ($40,000 for a single person). As such, the beneficial tax treatment is available only to families earning below that level.[33]

The enactment of this federal legislation, which went into effect in 1990, may have contributed to the slowing of state interest in developing their own bond programs. The new federal program may also limit the number of bond sales in states with existing programs. Minnesota, for example, decided against developing a new college savings bond program as a result of the federal program. Instead, the state legislature appropriated money to develop a public relations campaign that encourages families to save for college.[34]

CONSTRUCTING AN EFFECTIVE COLLEGE
SAVINGS PROGRAM

Given that the first of these prepaid tuition and college bond programs was only put into place until the mid-1980s, it is still too early to make a fair evaluation of their impact. Yet there is powerful theoretical and anecdotal evidence that a soundly designed and broadly accessible program to encourage college savings can be a useful part of a comprehensive government effort to improve college affordability. Specifically, it can provide middle- and upper-income families with additional public resources to cover their college costs and hence lessens the need for them to borrow later. This reduces the cost of the loan program to the federal government and reduces the debt burden facing graduates. It may also allow policy-makers to shift the savings resulting from lower loan costs to provide larger grants to disadvantaged students.

But creation of such savings plans can also present some dangers to a state's broad efforts to improve college affordability. In order to be effective, any state savings program must incorporate three principle elements. First, the plan must effectively stimulate new savings for college and not simply shift the location of existing savings. Second, the program must be structured so that it is widely available to middle- and even lower-income families. Finally, policy-makers must be certain that the costs of their savings plan are not paid out of funds which might be better used for need-based grants and instructional subsidies. If they are, the net effect will be to wastefully shift public subsidies away from those who need them and toward those who don't.

Stimulating New Savings

College prepayment and savings bond programs can only be effective if they increase new savings. On its face, it seems obvious that they do. Florida alone has sold more than 200,000 prepaid tuition contracts.[35] Ohio has sold nearly 40,000.[36] Given the widespread concern over college costs, and the desire of policy-makers to increase savings rates, these numbers are certain to grow rapidly.

Still, very little is known about whether the funds being invested in these programs come from families new to saving for college or whether the funds were invested prior to the inception of the savings programs. But by making saving for college an attractive option for families who are not saving, states also encourage those who are already saving to transfer their outside investments into college savings programs. Savings plans must thus include incentives which encourage truly new savings, and not simply increase the wealth of those who are already saving for college.[37]

Polling data indicate that most parents are not interested in tax deductions.[38] They want peace of mind and risk management through a mechanism that makes paying for college easy and manageable. Most families do not need or want a tax subsidy.[39] In this light, such tax deductions can cost a state a great deal in foregone revenues, while providing little that meets the needs of states, colleges, or families. Programs would thus be more effective if they replace such tax subsidies with other benefits that are targeted at groups who are less financially able, and psychologically willing, to save.

Attracting Broad Participation

There is as yet no comprehensive analysis of who buys tuition credits. Preliminary studies, however, suggest that participation in state savings programs may be limited to upper-income families.[40] However, if such programs serve only the wealthy, they are unlikely to have much direct impact on college affordability. This is because most of these families were probably already saving for college before states instituted their savings programs.

There is also the danger that if state savings programs cater exclusively to the needs of upper-income families, they may serve to divert scarce state dollars away from the most needy students. Especially in difficult budget times, when government spending is zero-sum, any state dollar going to a prepaid tuition program is a dollar less that can be used for need-based grants or to keep tuitions low. Also, if participation in savings programs is weighted heavily toward upper-income families, it risks directing scarce financial and political resources to those who least need the state's help in affording college.

In order to avoid providing benefits only to those who have the least need for them, a savings program might be designed to be more broadly accessible to middle- and lower-income families. States might, for example, offer to match payments by families below a certain income level or they might offer tax incentives to employers who match employee contributions. If state policy-makers hope to offer benefits to those with lower- and middle-incomes, they must at least keep entry costs low and provide installment-payment schedules with affordable interest rates. In this light, the real issue is finding a way to structure a savings bond plan that can be modified so that lower-income families will be able to gain access to the program.[41] This has proven a very difficult task for any government savings program.[42]

Complementing Need-Based Student Aid

It is not entirely fair to criticize college savings programs for not serving the disadvantaged. That was never their purpose. Tuition prepayment and college bond programs were designed to entice middle- and upper-income families to save for college. Supporters of these programs assume that the needs of lower-income students will be met through either federal or state aid programs. At best, they should be a complement to, and not a substitute for, need-based grants and instructional subsidies in a comprehensive state effort to keep college affordable.

Still, college savings programs may not be as benign as they seem. As a result of the budget pressures experienced by the states since the early 1980s, state policy-makers did not have the resources available, or were unwilling to generate the resources necessary to respond to public pressure to keep public higher education affordable by containing tuition increases at their state colleges or by increasing grant spending at rates comparable to tuition inflation. Instead, many created college savings programs. If the development of a state savings program mutes public cries for lower tuitions, or expanded state grants, it can indirectly exacerbate the college affordability problem.

By creating college savings programs, state officials diverted public attention away both from the plight of needy students and from other solutions to the college affordability problem. Policy-makers were able to create the impression that they were working hard to solve the problems of the citizenry, when they really had neither the financial resources nor political will to reverse the underlying problems of college affordability.

SAVINGS PLANS AND THE DISADVANTAGED

Tuition prepayment or college savings bond programs are certainly not the answer to the college affordability problems facing lower-income students. Indeed, most potential students from disadvantaged families have little direct use for such plans. Their families simply have too few resources to participate. Even many of those who are beginning to save for college will find the non-liquid character of most such programs to be an inappropriate instrument to begin saving for college.

Government savings plans provide most of their direct benefits to middle- and upper-income students. But they also can provide important indirect benefits to disadvantaged students. If prepayment and college bond programs can encourage increased savings rates among higher-income families, they can reduce the need for those families to later borrow for college. They can also reinstall the ethos that parents bear the primary responsibility to pay for the education of their children. By reducing the need to provide financial aid to ever larger numbers of students, policy-makers might find it easier to target their limited resources to those with the greatest need. As such, savings programs can play an important role in complementing larger state efforts to improve college affordability.

8

FROM PRICE TO PARTICIPATION

Assessing the Impact of the College-Affordability Programs

Up to this point, I have focused my analysis on the increasing price of college and on the government programs designed to eliminate college price barriers. But the purpose of those programs was not just to lower the net price of college, or even to make a higher education affordable to everyone. College affordability was a means to an end. That end was to insure that children from disadvantaged families would have an equal chance to go to college.

Of course, government programs alone could never achieve the larger goal of equal college opportunity. Even the most ardent supporter of the federal and state student-aid programs would not argue that they, by themselves, have the capacity to close the huge gap between the college participation rates of students from lower-income families and those from upper-income families. That gap is held open by a vast network of long-standing and reinforcing barriers. The wide-ranging impacts of cultural norms, opportunity structures, differences in the quality of pre-collegiate educations, and racist and sexist attitudes in the country are not going to be eliminated or reduced by simply keeping tuitions down or giving grants to disadvantaged students. Still, for these programs to be judged a success, they must ultimately have a positive impact on the college-participation rates of their target populations.

In this chapter I examine whether changes in college affordability have translated into changes in the college-going behavior of the groups

191

who were the principle targets of the government programs. My purpose is to determine the extent to which these programs have achieved their original objective. In doing so, I do not undertake a complete evaluation of each of the many federal and state programs or attempt to disentangle the discrete impacts of each on college participation. Instead, I look broadly at the aggregate impact of these multiple government initiatives over time. From this I hope to show how the college affordability programs have altered the broad landscape of college participation.

THE DIFFICULTIES OF STUDYING THE DECISION TO GO TO COLLEGE

People decide to go to college for many reasons. Others decide not to go, or to leave college, for just as many reasons. Economic, social, and psychological factors all can play a role in these decisions. But such important personal choices are rarely made as economists might diagram an investment decision, where potential students act as rational decision-makers weighing the costs and benefits of several carefully selected options and then choosing the one which produces the greatest return at the lowest price. In reality, the process is much more personal, reflecting the dreams, fears, and individual histories of each potential student and his or her family.[1] Going to college is not just an investment decision, it is a choice about how and where a young adult will spend an important part of his or her life and one which will determine, to a large degree, the style and character of the rest of that life. It is a statement about how a young person sees him or herself and about the ambitions and expectations they have for the future.

Accordingly, the decision of any individual regarding whether or not to go to college is a difficult one to study. Often it is impossible to locate the time or place that the decision is made. For many young people, it is really never made. Some always believe that they will go to college and never seriously consider not going. For them the only real choice was which school to attend or which major to choose. Others see college as beyond their academic, social, or financial reach. Their lives are lived and their employment decisions are made without any attention to the possibilities offered by higher education. These individuals would be hard pressed to explain how or why they chose not to pursue a higher education. They were simply on a road that did not lead them to college.

Similarly, for many students the decision to attend college is not made at a single point in time. It emerges from a succession of smaller, seemingly unrelated, choices about such things as whether to try a foreign language in middle school, whether to take a geometry course in high school, or whether their parents decided to open a college savings account when they were young. Individually, these choices are rarely the deciding factor in anyone's decision to attend college. But in combination, these, and countless other, small choices alter and condition the chances that a student will attend college.[2]

COLLEGE PRICE AND COLLEGE PARTICIPATION

It is almost never the case that price is the single factor that prevents an otherwise interested and qualified student from entering college. Certainly, if a family does not have the money to pay the tuition on the day that the bill is due, affordability will be the deciding factor. Yet even here the determination of what a family can afford is very subjective. One lower-income family may make enormous sacrifices to cover the price of a high-priced college, while a more wealthy family may judge that same school to be unaffordable.

The fact that families each determine college affordability in their own way does not mean that college price is unimportant. There is compelling evidence that price plays an important role in the decision to attend college.[3] While the individual decision to go to college may not be made according to a cost-benefit calculus, college price and college participation rates behave in ways much like the price and sales volume of other commodities in the market. All else being equal, as price goes up, participation goes down and as college prices go down, participation rates go up.

Previous Research on Price and Access

Economists and educational researchers have devoted a great deal of attention to the link between net college price and college participation. In general, these studies have found that rising college prices have a negative impact on college participation at several different points in the process of making a decision to go to college.[4] Higher prices discourage some students from applying to college, they discourage some who have applied and been accepted from enrolling, and they deter some who have already enrolled from continuing. While the impact of price is very difficult to specify precisely, these studies provide compelling evidence that price changes are directly and causally linked to changes in college participation.

Perhaps the best known of the studies examining the link between price and participation was conducted by Charles Manski and David Wise.[5] Working with a sample of students who graduated from high school in 1972, they estimate the impact of the newly created Pell grant program on the patterns of college enrollment. Based on a statistical simulation of college choice, Manski and Wise conclude that overall college enrollments increased by 21 percent as a result of the Pell grant program. These enrollment increases were heavily concentrated in two-year colleges and among students from lower-income families. They estimate that the Pell grant program increased the participation of lower-income students by 59 percent. Middle-income participation increased by 12 percent. Upper-income enrollment increased only 3 percent.

Manski and Wise also estimated the number of those who received financial aid who would have gone to college even if they had not received the aid. They found that among lower-income students, 41 percent of Pell grant recipients would have gone to college without the grant. But 83 and 95 percent of middle- and upper-income recipients would have gone anyway. This is powerful evidence that a disproportionately large portion of the benefits of the Pell grant program go to the most needy.[6]

The Manski and Wise study set off a wave of research on the relationship between college prices and college enrollment. These "student demand" studies generally confirmed the view that as prices rise, college participation, particularly among lower-income and disadvantaged groups, declines. In a meta-analysis of twenty-five such studies, Leslie and Brinkman conclude than each $100 increase in net college prices produces between 1.8 and 2.4 percent reductions in enrollment. Based on this estimate, they calculate that within four years, 200,000 to 250,000 fewer enrollments occur as a result of every $100 price increase.[7] These enrollment decreases occur disproportionately at community colleges and low-priced public colleges.

Most of these estimates of the impact of rising prices on college participation rates are based on studies of those students who applied and were accepted to college and then failed to enroll. But this technique may actually underestimate the dampening impact of price increases on the enrollment decisions of potential students from disadvantaged families. Elizabeth Savoca used a variation of the Manski-Wise model to analyze the decision to *apply for admission* to college rather than on the decision to *attend* college.[8] She found that rising net college prices "cause a substantial shift in the composition of the applicant pool away from low-income students."[9] This means that college price increases have a double impact on participation rates. Disadvantaged students are less likely to apply to college, and those who do are less likely to enroll.

While the many student demand studies differ over precisely how much participation is reduced when college prices increase, and whether tuition increases or student-aid reductions have a greater impact, almost all agree that price and participation are inversely related. This conclusion simply supports the conventional economic hypothesis, as well as the commonsense conclusion, that as college becomes more expensive, fewer students will chose to enroll. Seen more positively, however, they provide compelling evidence that monetary subsidies are powerful mechanisms to advance the cause of equal educational opportunity and help secure the wide-ranging benefits which accrue to more educated individuals and communities.

Previous Research on Price and Choice

Net price is not only related to whether students will go to school, it is related to where they will go. As net prices rise, the enrollment of lower-income students tends to shift to less expensive colleges. One of the best studies of this link, by Michael Tierney, examined the college choices made by Pennsylvania students who were admitted to schools with substantially different costs.[10] He compared their enrollment decisions, looking at both their academic records and their family income levels. Tierney found that, as tuitions at private schools rose relative to public schools, the probability that students would enroll in the public schools increased. In a more recent study, Michael McPherson and Morton Schapiro also find that rising net college prices are negatively related to lower-income enrollment in private colleges.[11] In explaining this trend, Gary Orfield observes that:

Students often consider only those schools they think they can afford, applying on the basis of their expectations of financial aid. Because the maximum Pell grant is substantially less than one-fifth the cost of an elite university, and other forms of aid are poorly publicized or packaged, low-income students may in effect be steered to low-cost institutions.[12]

A similar pattern exists between two- and four-year colleges. As the prices of four-year colleges rise, lower-income students are more likely to choose to enroll in a two-year college. One major study of Illinois found that low-income students receiving state grant support were disproportionately enrolled in two-year colleges.[13] Nationally, as college prices have increased since 1980, the distribution of students from low-income families has shifted from universities to four-year colleges and from four-year colleges to two-year colleges.[14]

The fact that rising net college prices may be forcing students into less expensive two-year colleges is a particular concern. Students who enroll in two-year colleges are substantially less likely to earn a degree, and those who do take considerably longer to complete their degree requirements. Moreover, those who earn only an associate's degree have substantially lower earnings than those who complete a bachelor's degree. As such, pricing lower-income students out of four-year colleges and into local community colleges may be reducing their life chances and not simply limiting their choice of colleges.

THE COLLEGE PARTICIPATION OF THE DISADVANTAGED

Children from lower-income families are much less likely to attend college than are their more advantaged counterparts. Price barriers at the time of enrollment are only a part of the reason for this. The dampening impact of low family income on college participation can be seen in three critical places. First, disadvantaged potential students are less likely to aspire to attend college. Second, they are less likely to take the courses necessary to succeed in college. Third, even those who aspire to college, and who have taken the proper courses, seem to overestimate the real price of attendance. These forces, working together, serve to exaggerate the impact of price barriers for those students who already have the lowest participation rates.

Table 8.1

College Aspirations and College Participation

Percentage of 1982 High School Sophomores Who Attended College Within Four Years of Graduation By Race, Hispanic Origin, and College Aspirations

	Race or Hispanic Origin		
College Aspirations	*White*	*African-American*	*Hispanic*
No BA/BS	42%	36%	32%
At Least BA/BS	88	74	77
All Students	58	47	45

Source: U.S. Department of Education, *High School and Beyond* adapted from Pelavin and Kane *Changing the Odds* Table 5.13, p. 55.

The College Aspirations of the Disadvantaged

High School and Beyond is a massive longitudinal study of 58,000 students from 1,100 high schools which was begun in 1980 by the National Center for Educational Statistics.[15] These data provide information about the attitudes and behaviors of these young people at a number of different points in time. The data collected cover the students' test scores, grades, demographic data, and their attitudes and values concerning a number of important subjects. This study provides valuable insights into the factors affecting a student's decision to enter college.

Perhaps the most interesting finding of the study is that one of the best predictors of whether a student will eventually attend college is whether that student aspires to attend college when he or she is a sophomore in high school.[16] In fact, more than 85 percent of all students who, as a sophomore, expected to earn at least a bachelor's degree, had enrolled in college within four years of high school graduation. But only about 40 percent of the sophomores who did not expect to earn a B.A. were enrolled in college four years after graduation.

As table 8.1 shows, the impact of college aspirations is evident across all races and ethnic groups. While white students have a slightly higher college-participation rate, the fact that three out of four of the African-American and Hispanic students who expected to go to college as a high school sophomore had enrolled in college within four years after graduation shows the powerful impact of aspirations on college participation.

High School Course Selection and the Disadvantaged

The impact of educational aspirations on college-participation rates is reinforced by the course-taking behavior of high school students. Those students who expect to go to college, take the courses that will prepare them to go. Those who don't expect to go, do not take those courses. Sol Pelavin and Michael Kane, in a study using the *High School and Beyond* data, found that courses in geometry, laboratory sciences, and foreign languages, are especially important.[17] These are, of course, a large part of the college-bound curriculum at most high schools. After controlling for race, ethnic origin, income, and gender, students who took these course were more likely to go to college. And students who aspired to go to college as a sophomore, were more likely to take these courses.

This impact of high school course-taking on college attendance results in a significant time lag between any change in the net price of college and the corresponding change in college-participation rates. In an uncertain economy, or in times of rapidly rising college prices, disadvantaged children or their families may judge college to be beyond their financial reach many years before they can possibly know the tuition levels or financial aid resources that will be available to them. Such students then self-select a non-college curriculum in high school or drop out entirely. As such, even vast immediate reductions in net college prices facing disadvantaged families are unlikely to have much impact on their college participation. However, over the long term, reductions in net price may increase the percentage of students who see college as an affordable option. This, in turn, encourages them to select the right courses in high school, and increases college participation in the future.

Price Misperceptions by the Disadvantaged

The more than 1.3 million people who live in the rural Appalachian region of southern Ohio have faced decades of economic isolation and social problems.[18] Reductions in the coal-mining industries which have been occurring since the 1950s, have recently been accelerated by the shifts away from high-sulfur coal mandated in the Clean Air Act of 1990. As these forces have caused high-paying mining jobs to be eliminated, many of the ancillary business, stores, and services closed down as well. In the 1990s, there are fewer jobs and fewer opportunities in the region than there had been a decade before. In 1980 there were fewer jobs and opportunities than there had been in 1970. It is a downward spiral which is unlikely to be reversed soon.

In this environment of economic decline, it is little surprise that the college-participation rates of high school graduates from this region are far lower than they are for any other region of Ohio. In 1991, the Ohio Board of Regents commissioned a survey of the high school seniors and their parents about the choices they had made for the future and the reasons underlying those choices. Their findings shed some light on how these students made their college choices and the role that price played in that process.

Appalachian students and their parents clearly recognize the economic value of a college education. More than 60 percent of these students felt that going to college was necessary to attain financial security. More than 75 percent of the parents thought college was an economic necessity. An even larger portion of these students expressed a desire to attend college. When asked whether they wanted to attend college, 80 percent of the high school seniors said yes. Of the parents, 84 percent said that they wanted their children to attend college.[19]

Even in light of the recognized economic benefits of college and their personal and family desires to attend, local school district officials in Appalachian Ohio estimate that only about 40 percent of area high school graduates attend some form of higher education. Many local experts, however, believe that this figure overestimates actual participation by as much as 12 percent. If this lower figure is correct, college participation in Appalachian Ohio may be among the lowest in the nation.[20]

So how can this gap between the hopes of high school seniors and their parents by squared with the realities of their post-graduation behaviors? The combination of low family income, low parental educational attainment, poor self-esteem, lack of information about higher education, and lack of encouragement from family and school personnel all play a role. So do the underfunded and antiquated conditions of the area's elementary and secondary schools. But, at least as viewed by the high school seniors and their parents, the rapidly rising price of higher education also plays an important role. More than two-thirds of Appalachian high school seniors and their parents said that they could not afford, or were unsure whether they could afford, college.[21]

These families have legitimate reasons to be concerned over college prices. But their concerns are magnified by misinformation about the actual price of going to college. Table 8.2 shows how much each group thought it would cost to attend college for one year. More than 50 percent of the seniors and more than 60 percent of their parents thought that a year at a four-year college would cost more than $10,000. Similarly, more than 50 percent of parents thought that a year at a two-year college would cost more than $5,000.

These estimates reveal a startling overestimate of the actual price of local colleges. In 1992, for example, the full price of attending a state university in Ohio ranged from $5,000 to $6,000, including room and board. The price of attending a local community college was less than $3,000. For students who lived at home, the annual price might be as low as $2,000 for a full-time student. By overestimating the actual price by so much, many Appalachian families may have based their decisions on an incorrect impression that college was beyond their financial reach. In a region where going to college provides many young people with their only real opportunity to achieve their dreams, and where improved college-participation rates are the best hope for an economic revitalization, this is especially troubling.

Appalachian high school seniors and their families face substantial barriers to college participation. But by operating with unrealistic estimates of the price of college, these families are erecting for themselves even larger price barrier than they actually face. If these same misperceptions about price are widespread among lower-income families, they may negate any changes in net price produced by the college-affordability programs and hold participation rates unnecessarily low.

Low Aspirations, Poor Choices, and Price Misperceptions

In the complex decision about whether on not to go to college, disadvantaged families are disproportionately discouraged from choosing college at several points. They begin with fewer financial resources. When their wages are stable and college prices are going up, these families naturally develop serious concerns about how they will pay the bills if their children decide to go to college. Media accounts about the college affordability "crisis" extend and deepen these fears.

While some of their college affordability concerns are certainly real, fears about college price barriers can also be unnecessarily discouraging

Table 8.2
*Estimates of College Price by High School Seniors and Their Parents
from Appalachian Ohio*

Estimated Annual Price of a Four Year Colleges		
Estimated Annual College Price	Appalachian H.S. Seniors	Parents of H.S. Seniors
Less than $1,000	1%	–
$1,000 to $4,999	12	6
$5,000 to $9,999	39	34
$10,000 to $14,999	28	22
$15,000 to $29,999	13	8
More than $20,000	8	30

Estimated Annual Price of a Two Year Colleges		
Estimated Annual College Price	Appalachian H.S. Seniors	Parents of H.S. Seniors
Less than $1,000	12%	5%
$1,000 to $4,999	55	45
$5,000 to $9,999	19	10
More than $10,000	14	40

Source: *Appalachian Access for Success* a report to the Ohio Board of Regents prepared by Institute for Local Government Administration and Rural Development at Ohio University, Athens OH.

for lower-income families. This is especially true if they make their decisions based on exaggerated estimates of college price and far before they can know the types of student aid available to them. Such groundless fears about affordability can cause potential students from disadvantaged families to perceive college as an unrealistic goal. This may begin to happen as early as middle school. As these disadvantaged students lower their educational expectations, they change their high school course selections. As a consequence, many may find themselves off of the road to college even before they are old enough to make reasonable decisions about their futures. Rising college prices may play an important role in this chain of events, but the subtle nature of that role may make it nearly impossible to fully detect with surveys or interviews.

EVALUATING THE IMPACT OF THE
AFFORDABILITY PROGRAMS

The wide range of previous studies discussed here provide evidence that changes in the net price of college should produce changes in the college-participation rates of lower-income students. But it remains to be shown that the various college affordability programs developed and implemented since the early 1970s are, themselves, associated with changes in the college-participation rates of the target groups. In the following section I trace the changes which have occurred in the college participation of various target groups in light of the changes in the college-affordability programs since 1970.

Deciding What and How to Compare

Accurately charting the course of changing patterns of college participation is more difficult than it might seem. The difficulty revolves around the selection of the proper definitions and the appropriate measures. The first decision is determining what will constitute participation in college. In collecting data on educational attainment, the Census Bureau employs three mutually exclusive categories. They are: currently enrolled in college, no longer enrolled in college after having completed one to three years of college, and no longer enrolled having completed four or more years of college.

While some advantage may be gained by examining these categories separately, I have chosen to combine them into the comprehensive category "college participation". In this way, anyone who is currently enrolled in college, or who has completed at least one year of college, is considered to have participated in college. This broad definition of participation tells us nothing about persistence in college. Groups with equal participation rates, of course, may have different completion rates.[22] But defining participation in this way provides a complete picture of who has attended college and shows how that picture has changed over time.

The next issue which must be decided is who should be included in the analysis. Because I am interested in how changing affordability levels changed the college participation behavior of young adults, I have focused the analysis on 18–24-year-old unmarried high school graduates. I have thus narrowed the universe of potential college students in three separate ways. Each limitation was made to insure the most accurate comparisons between the behaviors of the target populations and the behaviors of otherwise similar non-target populations.

The decision to focus on young adults, 18–24 years old, was made because traditional college-age students are the primary target group of the programs. When the programs were enacted in 1965 and 1972, they were intended to encourage these young adults to attend college. While the programs have subsequently been expanded to include non-traditional students, those 18–24 years old remain the primary clients of the federal programs. In spite of the growing numbers of non-traditional students now in college, the 18–24-year-old population still constitutes the vast majority of undergraduate students today. In 1993, these young adults constitute 62 percent of all college students and 82 percent of all full-time students.

The decision to consider only unmarried young adults was made to insure that the income comparisons are fair. It is the parents' income, and not the married young adults' income, that is the primary basis of the federal and state need-based student assistance programs. Because the Census Bureau gathers data about family income, and not spouse's income, many married students have an additional, and unmeasured, resource which might influence their college participation. By limiting the analysis to the unmarried, it is most likely that the comparisons based on family income will accurately reflect the real financial resources available to potential students at the time they make their college decision.

On its face, the decision to limit the field to high school graduates seems obvious. Since most colleges require a high school degree to enroll, the college participation rates of non–high school graduates is quite low. But including only graduates in the analysis skews the results in some important ways. Lower income and disadvantaged students are much more likely to drop out of high school. As a consequence, including only the college participation rates of graduates significantly overstates the college participation of lower-income and disadvantaged groups. If policy-makers are interested in equalizing the college participation between advantaged and disadvantaged groups, the problem they face is far greater than that discussed here.

THE CHANGING PATTERNS OF COLLEGE PARTICIPATION

The trends in college participation rates between 1970 and 1990 seem to run counter to the efforts of the government to remove price barriers. As

Table 8.3

College Participation Rates of Unmarried 18–24 Year Old High School Graduates Selected Years, 1970–1990

Year	Participation Rate
1970	61%
1975	60
1980	57
1985	59
1990	63
1992	69

Source: Author's calculations from T. Mortenson and Z. Wu, *High School Graduation and College Participation of Young Adults by Family Income Backgrounds* (Iowa City: ACT Student Financial Aid Research Report Series, September 1990).

shown in table 8.3, during the 1970s, when the federal government was marshalling ever larger sums to reduce the net price of college, the overall participation rates of unmarried 18–24-year-old high school graduates actually declined from 61 percent to 57 percent. But then, paradoxically, as those government efforts were diminished in the 1980s, participation rates began to increase. By 1992, as college affordability was reaching an all-time low, college-participation rates were reaching all-time highs.

This counter-intuitive pattern has caused many observers to conclude that changes in net college price are not related to changes in the college-participation rates of disadvantaged and low-income students. Robert Zemsky concluded that after "nearly two decades of massive investment in student aid programs . . . college participation rates have not substantially changed."[23] Such evidence would seem to be a clear indication of the failure of the student aid programs.

But a closer look at the data reveals that the impact does exist but is hidden by changes in other trends occurring at the same time. Orfield observes that:

> studies showing the relatively small impact of financial aid mean, in good measure, that there are other factors, such as high school grades and family background, that are better predictors of college attendance than the financial aid policies in effect when the data were collected.[24]

With so many independent variables driving college-participation rates, it is not surprising that, when viewed in the aggregate, these trends do not closely mirror changes in college prices.

One way to sort out the impact of changes caused by social and economic conditions from the impact of changes caused by the student-aid programs and college prices, is to look at the gap between the college-participation rates of low-family-income students and middle- and high-family-income students. By assuming that social trends are affecting all students equally, these higher-income groups serve as a kind of control group. The lower-income group, who are receiving financial aid to reduce their costs serve as the experimental group. If the gap between lower- and upper-income students is closing, the programs can be said to be having the desired effect. If the gap widens or remains stable, the programs are not working.

Family Income and College Participation

Using data published by in the *Current Population Survey*, Thomas Mortenson regularly charts the relationship between family income and college participation.[25] Based on family income, he divides all unmarried 18–24-year-old high school graduates into quartiles. The income levels associated with the quartiles used in a recent analysis are shown in table 8.4.[26]

Table 8.5 shows the link between family income and college participation over twenty years. It is a link which is both powerful and enduring. In each year, the greater the family income the higher the college-participation rate. But the income–participation relationship is also complex. While the behavior of the various income groups generally move in the same directions over time, they move at different speeds.

In the 1970s, college-participation rates dropped across all income quartiles. But it was among the highest-income groups that the decline was the most rapid. The two lower quartiles dropped much more slowly. Then, after 1980, as the economic returns to higher education were increasing, the resulting increase in participation rates were also uneven. The highest quartile experienced the most rapid increase, while the bottom two quartiles continued to fall in the first half of the decade and then increased only slowly in the second half of the decade. Perhaps most remarkable, and most discouraging, is that in spite of all the government's efforts, the college-participation rates of the four income quartiles stand at almost exactly the same place in 1990 that they did in 1970. The early

Table 8.4

Family Income Quartiles for Unmarried 18–24 Year Old High School Graduates in 1992

Lowest Quartile	Less than $21,606
Second Quartile	$21,606 to $38,820
Third Quartile	$38,820 to $63,567
Fourth Quartile	More than $63,567

Source: These figures are from Mortenson *Postsecondary Education Opportunity* (September 1993). Using data from the Census Bureau, Mortenson reports the family incomes for the population of unmarried 18–24 year old high school graduates. In 1992, there were 12.8 million persons in this group, 92 percent of whom were dependent family members. Since 1970, there has been substantial redistribution in family income in the United States. As a consequence, the threshold for the bottom two income quartiles has fallen steadily while the threshold for the upper two quartiles has risen.

Table 8.5

College Participation Rates of Unmarried 18–24 Year-Old High School Graduates by Family Income Quartiles: Selected Years, 1970–1992

Year	Lowest Quartile	Second Quartile	Third Quartile	Highest Quartile
1970	46%	56%	64%	79%
1975	47	54	63	75
1980	42	53	63	69
1985	41	53	67	76
1990	44	59	69	79
1992	52	64	75	86

Source: Author's calculations from T. Mortenson and Z. Wu, *High School Graduation and College Participation of Young Adults by Family Income Backgrounds* (Iowa City: ACT Student Financial Aid Research Report Series, September 1990); and Mortenson *Postsecondary Education Opportunity* (September 1993).

1990s brought a renewed growth in college-participation rates, but family income remained a critical determinant of college participation.

Another way of looking at changes in the college-going behavior of lower-income students is to examine the gap between their participation rates and the rates of the highest-income families. It is this gap which the federal programs were designed and implemented to help close.

Table 8.6 shows the difference between the college participation rates of the highest-income quartile and the other three. Here the impact of the various college-affordability programs can be most clearly seen.

Table 8.6

College Participation Gap Between Different Income Quartiles of Unmarried 18–24 Year-Old High School Graduates: Selected Years, 1970–1990

Year	Gap Between Lowest & Highest Quartiles	Gap Between Second & Highest Quartiles	Gap Between Third & Highest Quartiles
1970	– 33%	– 23%	– 15%
1975	– 29	– 22	– 12
1980	– 27	– 15	– 5
1985	– 35	– 23	– 9
1990	– 34	– 22	– 11
1992	– 34	– 22	– 11

Source: Author's calculations from T. Mortenson and Z. Wu, *High School Graduation and College Participation of Young Adults by Family Income Backgrounds* (Iowa City: ACT Student Financial Aid Research Report Series, September 1990); and Mortenson *Postsecondary Education Opportunity* (September 1993).

While the gap between the lowest and highest income groups remained high during the entire twenty-year period, it moved in ways which correspond directly to the changes in college affordability.

Indeed, all of the lower income quartiles seemed to gain ground on the highest in the 1970s. The college-participation gap was reduced by between 7 and 10 percentage points during the decade. While much of this was due to reductions in the college participation of the highest income group, it was still a significant achievement. The forces driving down those rates for upper-income families were, almost certainly, felt by middle- and lower-income families as well. But given the increased resources made available to them through the various government programs, their participation did not decline by as large an amount.

In the 1980s, trends in college participation also closely followed changes in college affordability. As the net price of college increased, the gap between the highest and the other income quartiles opened up again. Nearly all of that change occurred in the first half of the 1980s when the increases in net price were the greatest. After 1985, however, that gap seemed to stabilize at a very high level.

By examining the college-participation rates of the various income groups in the 1970s, it is clear that the government programs were having the desired effect. While the participation gap between the top and bottom quartiles remained high, it was reduced by almost 25 percent in the 1970s. For the middle two quartiles, which benefitted from the wider availability of Pell grants and the vast expansion of Stafford loan eligibility, the reduction was even greater. This was far from a complete success. But it did constitute the type of steady progress against a very difficult problem that should have encouraged policy-makers to continue or even expand their efforts.

But that, of course, did not happen. The various federal and state college-affordability programs were transformed after 1980 from targeting subsidies to the lowest-income students to spreading that aid out to more and more students. As a consequence, the participation gap widened again. What is particularly troubling about this pattern is that the reopening of the gap occurred much more rapidly than it had closed. While price barriers in the mid-1990s are certainly higher than they were in 1980, they are not as high as they had been in 1970 before the creation of the major federal programs. Still, by the early 1990s, the college-participation gap between the highest- and lowest-income families was greater than it had been in 1970.

Race, Ethnic Origin, and College Participation

The goal of universal college affordability has always been closely associated with the broader goal of building an equal opportunity society. Beginning in 1965, the federal and state governments began a thirty-year effort to knock down college price barriers as part of a fight for racial and social justice. Supporters of the college-affordability programs argued that by creating a climate in which a college education was brought into the legitimate financial reach of all Americans, disadvantaged racial and ethnic groups would experience disproportionate benefits. Equalizing access to college was an essential first step to equalizing outcomes in a whole host of other areas. Over time, increased access to college would open the full range of possibilities following from a higher education.

Table 8.7 shows the changing rates of college participation for African-Americans, Hispanics, and whites between 1970 and 1990. The picture here is slightly different than that seen when looking at income levels. Unlike almost all other groups, the college-participation rates of African-Americans increased in the first half of the 1970s. In spite of the decline of economic returns, their rate increased from 45 percent to 52

Table 8.7

*College Participation Rates of Unmarried 18–24 Year-Old High School
Graduates by Race and Hispanic Origin, 1970–1990*

Year	African-Americans	Hispanic Origin	White
1970	45%	N.A.[1]	63%
1975	52	60	61
1980	48	54	58
1985	44	53	61
1990	50	49	64

Source: Author's calculations from T. Mortenson and Z. Wu, *High School Graduation
and College Participation of Young Adults by Family Income Backgrounds* (Iowa City: ACT
Student Financial Aid Research Report Series, September 1990).
[1] The Census Department did not begin collecting data under the classification
"Hispanic Origin" until 1972.

percent between 1970 and 1975. Whites and Hispanics experienced declining college-participation rates during those years.

In the 1980s, the college participation of African-Americans and
whites dipped slightly in the first half of the decade and gained some ground
in the last half. But the college-participation rate for Hispanics continued
to fall precipitously. When coupled with the fact that Hispanics are the
least likely to graduate from high school, the fact that those who graduate
are now the least likely to go to college is especially alarming.

Again, the best way to see the impact that changing levels of college
affordability had on college-participation rates is to look at the differences between whites and African-Americans and between whites and
Hispanics. This is done in table 8.8.

There are many possible explanations for the dramatic reduction in
the college-participation gap between whites and African-Americans in
the early 1970s. The fact that the gap was reduced by nearly 50 percent
between 1970 and 1975 probably had little to do with the federal student-
aid programs. The powerful impacts of the civil rights movement, school
desegregation, and the emergence of affirmative-action programs on campus are more likely causes. So too were changes in the opportunity structure which opened doors to a more African-Americans.

But paradoxically, that progress came to an abrupt stop in 1975 just
as the Pell grant was being put into place. Then, as the other Title IV
programs were being expanded in the late 1970s, the gap between the
college-participation rates of African Americans began to slip further

Table 8.8
*College Participation Gap Between Races and Hispanic Origin of Unmarried
18–24 Year-Old High School Graduates: Selected Years, 1970–1990*

Year	Difference Between Participation Rates of Whites and African Americans	Difference Between Participation Rates of Whites and Hispanics
1970	– 18	N.A.
1975	– 9	0
1980	– 10	– 4
1985	– 18	– 9
1990	– 14	– 15

Source: Author's calculations from T. Mortenson and Z. Wu, *High School Graduation and College Participation of Young Adults by Family Income Backgrounds* (Iowa City: ACT Student Financial Aid Research Report Series, September 1990).

behind white participation rates. The increased spending on college-affordability programs seemed to have little positive impact on the behavior of young African-Americans. By 1985, when the decline stopped, the gap was as wide as it had been in 1970.

After 1985, the college participation of African-Americans began to increase again. The participation gap with whites also closed. While this is an encouraging trend, the situation today remains worse than it was in 1980 when the student-aid programs were expanding and college prices were stable.

The progress of Hispanics toward equal college opportunity is even more problematic. In 1975, Census Department figures show that Hispanic college-participation rates were nearly identical to those of whites. But since that time there has been a continual decline. By 1990, the picture was bleak. Hispanics had the lowest college participation of any group, and the gap between their college participation and that of whites was growing rapidly. In spite of increasing student-aid spending, Hispanics were enrolling in college in ever smaller numbers.

Gender and College Participation

Without question, the rapid increases in the college-participation rates of women constitute the most consistent and enduring change which oc-

Table 8.9
College Participation Rates of Unmarried 18–24 Year Old High School Graduates by Gender: Selected Years, 1970–1990

Year	Male	Female
1970	66%	57%
1975	60	60
1980	55	59
1985	57	61
1990	59	65

Source: Author's calculations from T. Mortenson and Z. Wu, *High School Graduation and College Participation of Young Adults by Family Income Backgrounds* (Iowa City: ACT Student Financial Aid Research Report Series, September 1990).

curred in the twenty years examined in this chapter. Table 8.9 shows that in 1970, the college-participation rates of 18–24-year-old female high school graduates were significantly lower than they were for male. By 1980 that gap had completely disappeared and, in fact, women were now more likely to participate in college than men. This is a remarkable achievement in light of the many disadvantages women have faced, and continue to face, in American society.

Table 8.10 shows the gap between the college-participation rates of women and men. It shows how, after 1980, the gender gap continued to increase, albeit at a slower rate. By 1990, young women participated in college at a rate 6 percentage points greater than men.

The increasing college participation of women is driven by broad social trends and the on-going struggles of the women's movement. It is still noteworthy that much of this increase came after 1980 when the affordability of higher education was declining. While women presumably face the same, or even larger, price barriers than men, their rates of college participation continue to grow even as college affordability is declining.

ASSESSING THE LINK

Government efforts to remove price barriers to college are predicated on the assumption that price has a significant and direct impact on rates of college participation. When states hold tuitions down, or when the fed-

Table 8.10

College Participation Gap Between Male and Female Unmarried 18–24
Year-Old High School Graduates: Selected Years, 1970–1990

Year	Difference Between Male and Female College Participation Rates
1970	– 9
1975	0
1980	4
1985	4
1990	6

Source: Author's calculations from T. Mortenson and Z. Wu, *High School Graduation and College Participation of Young Adults by Family Income Backgrounds* (Iowa City: ACT Student Financial Aid Research Report Series, September 1990).

eral governments gives grants, policy-makers are lowering the net price of college in order to stimulate participation. This chapter has shown that while students decide to attend college for many reasons, price plays an important role in that decision. This confirms the commonsense view that higher prices produce lower rates of college participation and lower prices produce increases in college-participation rates. Moreover, the impact of changes in net price is felt disproportionately by lower-income and disadvantaged students.

Further, the college-participation rates of 18–24-year-old high school graduates between 1970 and 1990 show that the behavior of disadvantaged students closely followed the trends in college affordability. During the 1970s, the gap between the college participation of lower- and upper-income students began to close. Then, after 1980, that gap began to open again. By 1990, the college-participation gap between low- and high-income families stood at about the same level it had in 1970. All of the progress that had been made during the 1970s was lost after 1980.

There were a few noteworthy exceptions to this general trend. For African-Americans and Hispanics, the decline in relative college-participation rates began sooner and was more severe. For African-Americans, college participation peaked in 1975, and has moved steadily downward since that time. Similarly, the college-participation rates of Hispanics have dropped steadily since 1975. This is especially troubling since these declines in participation began at the same time that the Pell grant program was funded at its highest level.

The other exception to the link between price and participation is found among women. Women continued to increase their college-participation rates throughout the two decades. In each year after 1975, they were more likely to go to college than men. The gap remained high even as college affordability was declining in the 1980s.

THE BIGGER PICTURE

It is certainly discouraging that, in spite of substantial government efforts over nearly thirty years, college-participation rates for disadvantaged groups are now in the same position as they were before those programs was created. But, seen another way, the evidence presented here is quite encouraging. It shows that college-participation rates respond to changes in net college price. When governments were able to reduce net college prices, as they did in the 1970s, many more young adults from lower-income and disadvantaged families went to college. This empirical evidence confirms the premise on which the affordability programs were based: the government can effectively stimulate college participation among target groups.

But by focusing on relatively small changes in a few variables, and by looking at only a portion of the problem, this analysis may exaggerate the progress that was made, or perhaps that can be made. The federal and state student-aid programs seem to have had the desired effect on the target populations. But, even when they were expanding rapidly in the early 1970s, the gap between the educational opportunity available to the advantaged and disadvantaged remained enormous.

Today, several facts remain unchanged after nearly thirty years of on-again off-again government efforts. Students from lower-income families are less likely to complete high school; if they go to college, they are more likely to enroll in a two-year institution; they are more likely to drop out of college; and they are less likely to graduate from college. The cumulative effect of these factors can be seen in table 8.11. These figures represent the estimated chances that a young adult will earn a bachelor's degree by the age of 24. Not only are these differences enormous at each point, they have widened. In 1990, young people from the highest income quartile were almost eight times as likely to complete a degree program than those from the lowest income quartile. They are almost three times as likely to complete a degree as students from the third quartile.

Table 8.11

*Percentage of Population Earning a B.A./B.S. Degree by Age 24
by Family Income Quartile*

Year	Lowest Quartile	Second Quartile	Third Quartile	Highest Quartile
1970	7%	10%	15%	40%
1975	6	8	18	41
1980	7	10	19	29
1985	7	12	21	59
1990	8	12	22	60

Source: Author's calculations from T. Mortenson and Z. Wu, *High School Graduation
and College Participation of Young Adults by Family Income Backgrounds* (Iowa City: ACT
Student Financial Aid Research Report Series, September 1990).

These discouraging figures make clear that, while improving college
affordability is important, the college graduation gap is held open by far
more than just high net prices. Unless the other causes of this gap are
successfully addressed, even the most effective college-affordability programs will make only modest progress in providing an equal educational
opportunity for disadvantaged Americans.

9

WHAT WENT WRONG AND WHY

Reviewing the Causes of Declining Affordability

It is important not to overstate the failings of the college affordability programs.[1] The many and varied government efforts to improve access to higher education over the past three decades have accomplished a great deal. Today, more than four million students received a government grant to go to college, the number of Americans enrolled in college was at an all-time high, and the percent of U.S. citizens who graduate from college is higher than it is in any other nation.[2] Something in the system of financing higher education is certainly working.

Still, the signs of a breakdown are unmistakable. Since the early 1980s, the net price of a college education has increased rapidly, the participation gap between upper- and lower-income students has expanded, and the focus of government subsidies has shifted from the most needy students to middle- and upper-income students. As a consequence, the goal of universal access to higher education is further away in the mid-1990s than it has been in more than a decade.

This chapter reviews why these important and well-intentioned programs have produced such discouraging results. Based on the evidence presented previously, I draw together the causes of the transformation in the government effort to keep college affordable. I examine how the rising costs of providing a higher education, limited government resources, and political barriers to program reform, combined to alter the higher-education finance system in ways which increased and reinforced price barriers rather than reducing or eliminating them.

215

AN INEFFICIENT ALLOCATION SYSTEM

Put simply, the programs to improve college affordability proceed in a highly inefficient manner. Each dollar spent on the programs produces far less than a dollar reduction in the net price of higher education facing a lower-income student. This is because only a fraction of the money appropriated for the programs goes to the type of need-based aid which is targeted to lower-income students. A large portion of these subsidies are, instead, allocated to either upper- and middle-income students or directly to institutions.[3]

There are inefficiencies at all levels. The federal government provides interest subsidies to private lenders to encourage them to make loans. It guarantees the loans of almost all student-borrowers. It provides loans so that middle- and even upper-income students can attend very expensive colleges. It subsidizes a vast network of guaranty agencies and a secondary market in which student loans are bought and sold. In contrast, the Pell grant is a much more efficient way to target aid to the students with the greatest financial need. Yet many of the lowest-income students still have insufficient resources to attend their college of choice.

States are even more inefficient in their efforts to make college affordable to everyone. By using funding formulas which encourage public colleges to keep their tuitions low, states often subsidize all public college students at an equal amount regardless of that student's private resources. Public colleges receive the same state funds for their lowest- and for their highest-income students. These colleges, in turn, charge rich and poor students an equal amount to attend. As such, states are providing large subsidies to students who can afford college without those public dollars.

Every state also operates its own system of need-based grants. Like Pell grants, these programs are a much more efficient way to target state dollars to the most needy students. Each dollar spent on these grants produces close to a dollar reduction in the net price of higher education facing lower-income students. But their recent growth notwithstanding, spending for need-based grants accounts for only a small portion of state spending for higher education. And a portion of that total is being shifted to merit aid, which is awarded disproportionately to more wealthy students.

Federal and state efforts to encourage savings for college also raise important questions about whether they are an efficient use of scarce public funds. Since lower-income families have little money to save, it is difficult for them to take advantage of such programs. For upper-income families who are already saving for college, these programs may do little other than to encourage them to change their savings instruments. Accordingly, government-operated savings programs may have little short-term impact on rates of personal savings. In the long term, these programs may reduce the pressures to provide grants to higher-income students. But, today, the dollars awarded as tax subsidies go exclusively to those families who can already afford to save for college.

These inefficiencies in the major college-affordability programs are no accident. They are the result of a strategy followed by these program's creators to generate the maximum level of political support.[4] If the various college-affordability programs targeted their aid to the most needy, they might attract the support of only the disadvantaged. But by spreading that aid broadly among more middle- and upper-income students, the programs have a much wider, and more powerful, base of clients. They benefit from the active support of middle- and upper-income students, lenders and financial intermediaries, and expensive private institutions who would have little interest in a grant program exclusively for the most disadvantaged students. Such broad support serves to protect the programs from political and budgetary pressures to alter or reduce them.

The fact that these programs are inefficient does not necessarily mean that they are ineffective. Indeed, after the federal government made the removal of college price barriers a explicit objective in 1965, the combination of state instructional subsidies, direct federal and state grants, and federal loan guarantees proved to be reasonably effective. From 1970 to 1980, real college tuitions remained stable, the Pell grant program was created and expanded, twenty-eight states developed new grant programs, the volume of state grant-spending increased, and private savings (as a percent of disposable income) increased. As a consequence, the college-affordability programs left lower income families with the pleasant task of paying stable college prices with a growing set of financial resources.

This reduction in the net price of college fueled an increase in the college-participation rates among lower-income students and the college-participation gap between the children of lower- and upper-income families began to close. Thus, at least until 1980, the government's attack on college price barriers seemed to be producing the desired effect. Despite their inefficiencies, the programs were lowering price barriers and more people were making it into college.

WHAT WENT WRONG

The good news about college affordability ended in 1980. Since that time, net college prices have increased at a rapid rate. Three factors account for this troubling turnaround. First, the cost of providing higher education began to increase substantially. Second, while the government resources directed to the multiple college-affordability programs increased, they did not grow fast enough to compensate for the rising cost of providing that education. Finally, when faced with the growing gap between college prices and family resources, federal and state policy-makers made a series of decisions which aggravated rather than relieved the problem. In the following section I review how these educational, economic, and political factors interacted to produce today's affordability problem.

INCREASING CAMPUS COSTS

The aggregate costs of providing a quality higher education began to rise rapidly after 1980. New areas of study demanded new and expensive facilities. Students moved from lower-cost fields of study into higher-cost fields. Non-traditional students returned to college in greater numbers and brought with them a whole new set of needs, demands, and expenditures. The costs of providing benefits in a very labor-intensive industry shot upward. This drove total compensation costs up at colleges and universities even at times when the salaries of faculty and staffs were relatively stable.

Exacerbating these cost increases, was the decline in the number of 18–24-year-old Americans. This demographic change set off an expensive competition among colleges and universities for new students. In the 1980s both public and private colleges expanded their recruiting, retention, student services, and financial aid offices to keep enrollments up. This added new layers to college administrations. Accordingly, new buildings, new staff, and new expenses were necessary to maintain stable enrollments. As a consequence, the cost of providing any single student with a quality college education was higher in 1990 than it had been in twenty years and was continuing to rise.

As campus costs were going up rapidly, the non-tuition revenues available to colleges to pay those costs were increasing much more slowly. State governments, long the principle revenue source for public colleges, were in their own financial squeeze. Facing new responsibilities and pub-lic demands for tax relief, states began shifting dollars away from higher education into other areas of need. In order to fill the resulting revenue shortfall, colleges undertook new and aggressive fund-raising and devel-opment programs. They also expanded their government relations and lobbying efforts in the state capitals and in Washington to seek additional funds and to protect themselves from further budget cuts. These initia-tives required colleges to develop still larger administrative structures on campuses. Such expenditures may eventually produce substantial new revenues. In the short term, however, the costs of these additional pro-grams must be absorbed into the operating budgets of the college.

Caught between rising costs and stable revenues, colleges had to either reduce programs, increase productivity, or raise tuitions. Perhaps because many were concerned with losing their ability to attract new stu-dents, few chose to reduce programs. Many colleges did, however, attempt to improve productivity. These efforts have met with some success.[5] But expanding class sizes, hiring more part-time faculty, and increasing the teaching loads of faculty are also dangerous in times of increased competi-tion for new students. If these moves reduce, or are perceived to reduce, the quality of academic programs, any savings can be eaten up by enroll-ment declines. Indeed, the resulting damage to a college's reputation could be much more costly than an increase in tuitions.

For many campus leaders, the only viable option to fill the revenue shortfall appeared to be to raise tuitions. Every college, public or private, did this. Many have done it every year since 1980. Many also increased required fees and began charging for services which had previously been free. Implicitly, government was shifting the responsibility for paying for higher education to the colleges and, in turn, to the students and their families.

SCARCE GOVERNMENT RESOURCES

Rising educational costs account for only a part of the decline in college affordability since 1980. The scarcity of government resources also played an important role. The success of the federal student-aid programs in the 1970s was made possible because the federal government was willing and able to provide the vast resources necessary to give grants to needy stu-dents and to provide loans to almost all students. In many states, the success of the low-tuition policies was possible because state policy-makers were able to provide public colleges with the large subsidies necessary to keep tuitions low.[6]

But with increased demands on government budgets and public pressure to hold the line of tax increases, federal and state policy-makers were no longer willing to provide the substantial appropriations which are now necessary to cover the rising costs of providing a higher education. There are not enough government dollars to continue to fully fund a system of low tuitions, large federal grants, and widely available student loans. This, in turn, has had important political consequences. As David Longanecker describes it:

> Everyone's fighting over fewer and fewer dollars. In any environment where there is simply not enough to go around, people don't want to work together to ration resources, they want to work separately to create advantaged positions. It's not pretty.[7]

The 1980s and 1990s certainly brought fiscal pressures to the federal and state government. Yet it is important not to exaggerate the extent to which those pressures translated into real reductions in the levels of government support for higher education. Aggregate public spending on higher education, even when measured in constant dollars, was substantially higher in the early 1990s than it had been in 1970. Per-capita spending on higher education also increased during the two decades. Contrary to the cries so often heard on college campuses, the Reagan administration did not dramatically reduce federal spending on student aid. It simply slowed the rate of growth. Further, nearly every state increased their aggregate and per-capita appropriations for higher education since 1980. Given the political and budgetary pressures of the day, it is surprising the extent to which policy-makers were able to protect higher education from what otherwise might have been devastating funding reductions.

MISGUIDED RESPONSES TO SCARCE RESOURCES

Rising educational costs and the lack of sufficient government support for higher education are the most easily identifiable causes of the college-affordability problem. But they are not the only, perhaps not even the most important, factors in the rapid rise of college price barriers. In order to fully understand why these government efforts failed, it is necessary to look at how policy-makers at all levels responded to the pressures created by rising educational costs and declining government resources. When faced with such important decisions, policy-makers often made choices and followed strategies which served to exaggerate rather than reduce the impact of rising educational costs and limited government resources. It was these misguided political responses to fiscal stress, as much as the fiscal stress itself, which accounted for the growing gap between college prices and the resources available to families to meet those costs.

Misguided Responses in Washington

During the early 1970s, the federal government undertook a vast expansion of the college student-aid system. Congress supported that expansion with continually growing appropriations for both grants and loans. However, that growth in overall Pell grant spending did not produce larger grants for the most needy students. When measured in constant dollars, the maximum Pell grant was less in 1981 than it had been in 1974, the first year that the program was fully operational. Instead, Pell grant eligibility was expanded such that students from families with higher incomes could qualify for a federal grant.

The pattern of spreading out eligibility for federal student aid to an ever wider clientele rather than targeting that aid to the most needy can also be seen by the growth of the student loan programs. In 1970, there were more than $3.1 million dollars of guaranteed student loans awarded. By 1980, that amount had doubled. Thus, not only were a larger percent of total Pell grants going to middle-income students, but a larger percentage of the total student-aid budget was going to fund loans which were awarded, in large part, to middle- and upper-income students. As such, while there was more student aid each year, a smaller portion of that aid was finding its way to the most disadvantaged students.

In the early 1980s, the rapid growth of federal student-aid spending came to an abrupt end. Owing both to a deteriorating budget situation and a change in presidential administrations, the federal government was no longer willing to fund student aid at progressively higher levels. The student loan programs, in particular, were costing far more than had been anticipated and the Reagan administration placed a much lower priority on improving access to college. Thus, the president and his supporters began to focus their attention on ways to cut federal spending on student aid. Reagan sought to reduce student loan eligibility and target federal funds more effectively to the neediest students. He also wanted to freeze overall federal spending on student aid as part of a broader effort to reduce the overall scope of government and the size of the federal budget. But in spite of these efforts, the overall costs of the loan program continued to grow rapidly. The rapid tuition inflation of the 1980s notwithstanding, controlling government spending had become a greater priority than improving college affordability.

But fiscal scarcity alone cannot explain why federal policy-makers followed a strategy of taking money away from the foundation college-affordability program and diverting it to a loan program intended to ease the burden of up-front costs for middle- and upper-income students. The answer is found by looking at the different constituencies served by the two programs. The constituency that benefits most from the Pell grant program is politically weak. It is composed of the lowest-income college students and their families. They are poorly organized, have few resources to contribute to political activity, and most are poorly informed about such relatively invisible events in national politics as the reauthorization of the Higher Education Act. Moreover, the interest groups which represent these families were preoccupied in the 1980s fighting on other fronts. As the pressure accelerated to reduce spending on all social programs, saving the Pell grant was rarely their top priority.

The forces working to protect the Pell grant were further weakened because the cuts to the program occurred indirectly. The size of the grants was never reduced, instead they were just never increased, or expanded so slowly that their purchasing power was severely eroded. As such, there was never a focusing event which would serve to mobilize public support for the program.[8] In the end, the value of Pell grants to the most needy students was reduced significantly, but it had been done without the battle which might have followed a direct assault on the program.

Contrast this with the power and resources of those who benefit from the student loan programs. Banks and financial institutions have a substantial stake in the continuation and expansion of the program. Banks received billions of dollars each year in direct subsidies for participating in the program. The larger the program, the greater the subsidies they receive. Also benefitting from the loan programs were prestigious private colleges. With tuitions often in excess of $20,000 a year, few families would be able to cover four years of those prices from income and savings. Without a system to allow upper- and upper-middle-income students to borrow these large sums, many such colleges might face a difficult time attracting a sufficient enrollment to remain viable. Private colleges worried that reductions in the federal loan programs would make it less attractive for many students to attend private colleges and they would enroll instead at less expensive public colleges.

When budgetary pressures made it impossible to fully fund both the grant and loan programs, Congress responded by rewarding the advantaged interests at the expense of the disadvantaged. Cuts were made so that middle- and upper-income students would continue to have access to large loans, while the value of grants to needy students was allowed to erode. By taking this approach, the aggregate costs of student aid were contained, but at the expense of redistributing subsidies from the most needy to the less needy and, in turn, reducing the effectiveness of the programs.

It is not as if congressional supporters of the Pell grant program stood by passively as its value was eroded. Many, especially Sen. Claiborne Pell and Rep. William Ford, fought vigorously to protect the program. But recognizing this political mismatch, they developed a strategy of viewing the fate of the grant and loan programs as intertwined. Ford argued that targeting student aid money to needy students at the expense of restricting loans to middle- and upper-income students would destroy the political base of the Pell grant program. This would give it less support in the future and make it even more vulnerable in the annual appropriations process.

As such, many supporters of increased federal grants tacitly supported the growth in the loan programs even when it came at the expense of the Pell program. Given the way the forces were arrayed, and the limited dollars available for discretionary domestic programs, they felt as if they had little choice. As a result, by the mid-1980s, the federal dollars spent on student aid were awarded, in an ever larger percentage, as loans for middle- and upper-income students. At the same time, needy Pell grant recipients were left to pay higher tuitions with smaller grants.

By the mid-1990s, the debates in Washington over college affordability had become fully subsumed in the larger debate over how to best control federal spending. It is easy to see why. The federal budget deficit had increased to more than $300 billion in 1992. Social Security, Medicare, and interest payments were eating up an ever larger portion of the federal budget. Even President Clinton, who had made improving college affordability a priority of his new administration, could not marshall enough support to enact a comprehensive reform of the student loan program or to institute a full-scale version of his national service trust. Congress was not willing to spend the amounts necessary to improve college affordability in the existing policy framework. But neither were they willing to reform that framework to target resources more efficiently to the most needy students.

Misguided Responses in the States

As the 1970s began, most state governments were following a strategy of keeping tuitions within the easy reach of most families. To do this they provided public institutions with substantial appropriations. Increasing state funding produced stable tuitions for everyone and, when coupled with increasing federal student aid, the low-tuition funding model produced improved college affordability. While states were increasing their aggregate spending on higher education during the 1970s, relatively little was directed to need-based grant programs. Although there were significant federal incentives for states to expand their grant programs, more than half of the states provided less than $50/FTE in need-based grants in 1980.

Stable tuitions and expanding eligibility for state grants certainly benefitted the lowest-income students. But the improved affordability of the 1970s was produced at a very high price. Because a large portion of instructional subsidy dollars went to upper- and upper-middle-income students, large numbers of state dollars were necessary to achieve small reductions in the net price of higher education to lower-income students.

But the 1980s also brought fiscal scarcity to state governments. Federal cutbacks in public housing, social service, and public assistance programs forced states to take on expanded responsibilities.[9] Reductions in federal grants to state and local governments, plus the elimination of general revenue sharing, gave states fewer resources with which to provide those expanded responsibilities. Further, many of the conditions which were driving up federal expenditures, rising health care costs, increased need for prisons, and a deteriorating infrastructure, were increasing state expenditures as well. But since 1980 there have been countervailing public pressures for the states to limit tax increases. In this context, many states looked to limit the growth of their higher-education budgets. There was neither the money nor the political will to appropriate the sums necessary to keep tuitions low for all students and still meet the expanding responsibilities of state governments.

But the fiscal stress experienced by states since 1980 did not, by itself, create college price barriers. In aggregate, state governments spent substantially more on higher education in the 1990s than they had in the 1970s. However, when measured as a percent of total state expenditures, the portion directed to higher education has declined. As James Mingle describes it:

> The long-term trend is that higher education appropriations are becoming a smaller and smaller portion of state budgets. This fact was obscured in the 1980s by economic growth, but has been obvious with the recent recession.[10]

Given their difficult budget situations, and the increasing costs of providing a high-quality higher education, policy-makers in most states simply could not afford to dramatically increase their overall level of spending on higher education.

Like their federal counterparts, state policy-makers could have responded to these fiscal pressures by improving the efficiency of their college-finance systems. If they could find ways to provide a quality college education at a lower cost, they could have cushioned or even eliminated the need for price increases. Similarly, if states could have more efficiently targeted their subsidies to the students who needed the aid the most, they could have slowed the increases in net college prices facing their lower-income residents, which are, in turn, increasing the overall level of government spending on higher education. But like their federal counterparts, state policy-makers did not meet fiscal pressure with improved efficiency. Instead, they too made allocation decisions which served to exaggerate rather than minimize the impact of that fiscal stress on lower-income families.

To be sure, policy-makers in many states struggled to target their scarce resources more efficiency to lower-income students. These states began shifting the focus of their higher-education budgets away from instructional subsidies and toward need-based grants. Under other circumstances, this high-tuition/high-aid funding strategy might have produced an improvement in college affordability for disadvantaged students. But because public college tuition increased so rapidly after 1980, these increased grant-spending levels still resulted in reductions in the purchasing power of state grants. In most states, regardless of their funding strategy, the outcome was the frustrating combination of more state spending, higher public college tuitions, and the decreasing purchasing power of state grants.

In response to the rising prices facing all college students, many states began to turn their attention to programs to increase families' personal savings for college. By enacting these programs, policy makers were able to respond to public pressures to "do something" about the affordability problem without spending much money. But these savings plans have little impact on the most needy students. Moreover, if funding to improve college access is zero-sum, as it seemed to be in the 1980s and 1990s, any dollar in state aid which goes to upper-income students through a savings incentive is a dollar less that can go to grants for needy students.

THE FAILURE TO TARGET

When educational costs were stable and there were sufficient governmental resources, the college-affordability programs were able to achieve the desired outcome, despite their inefficiencies. But as costs rose and resources tightened, the effectiveness of these programs has declined correspondingly. If federal and state policy-makers were going to make these programs work in this new fiscal environment, they needed to either find new resources or make more efficient use of the existing resources. In most cases they did neither.

Sound economics suggests that the most efficient way to improve college affordability is to redistribute subsidies away from middle- and upper-income families to the more needy. In Washington, this would mean awarding larger grants and fewer loans and loan guarantees. In the states, it would mean shifting funds from instructional subsidies to need-based grants. Such changes would produce the greatest reductions in the net price of higher education for lower-income students at the lowest price.

Political concerns, however, demand that higher-education funding be distributed to the widest possible range of claimants. By expanded loan eligibility and increasing instructional subsidies, awards could be made to the advantaged as well as the disadvantaged. This allowed policy-makers to maximize the political gain from their higher-education appropriations rather than maximizing the value of those appropriations for needy students.

The distortion resulting from this spread-rather-than-target allocation strategy, was most evident in the way policy makers responded to the fiscal stress since 1980. Instead of redirecting the substantial subsidies they were providing to middle- and upper-income students to the most needy students, policy makers often responded by reducing the benefits they were providing to everyone in an across-the-board manner. The federal government did not reduce Pell grant eligibility for the newly eligible higher-income applicants, it slashed the size of grants to everyone. Many states continued to increase their appropriations to higher education, but most did not shift the emphasis of that funding to need-based grants.

This failure of policy-makers to target their scarce resources to the most disadvantaged students has diluted the effectiveness of the college-affordability programs. Year after year, federal and state policy-makers made appropriations and authorization decisions which favored upper- and middle-income families at the expense of the disadvantaged. By the mid-1990s, these decisions had undermined the original objective of bringing college within the financial reach of all Americans. Still worse, by raising price barriers for lower-income students, governments risked lowering college participation and suffering the negative economic and social consequences which will follow.

A FINAL FACTOR: MISGUIDED TIME HORIZONS

At its heart, any government effort to increase college affordability, and hence improve college participation, must be evaluated on a long time horizon. Public money spent today to remove college price barriers cannot be expected to produce an immediate payoff. Policy-makers, and the public more broadly, must recognize that such spending will bring benefits in future decades and to future generations. In this way, state efforts to keep tuitions low and provide need-based grants, as well as the federal grant and student loan programs, are really public investments by the citizens of the states and the nation.

With future labor markets demanding more skilled workers, and the growing gap between the wages of the college-educated and non-college-educated, the economic benefits of removing college price barriers are greater in the 1990s than they had been at any time in recent history. The private and the public value of that investment is increasing. But in the 1990s, many policy-makers are no longer willing to invest in improved college access. Moreover, public demands for lower taxes coupled with an unwillingness to support reductions in government services, have further encouraged policy-makers to search for budget cuts even when the cost will be paid in lost future benefits.

To be sure, it is easier for policy-makers to invest in higher education when the relative costs of providing that education were lower as they were in the 1970s. It is also easier for policy-makers to spend money on higher education when they have more discretionary funds to distribute. However, it is even more important to make that investment in the 1990s when incomes are stable, savings rates are lower, and the future promises a vastly more competitive labor market. Yet, as the value of public and private investment in higher education is rising, the willingness of policy-makers and the public to make that investment seems to be diminishing.

It is politically expedient for federal policy-makers to use the inefficient and costly loan programs as the principle mechanism to allocate expanded funding for student aid and to allow the maximum Pell grant to decline. Similarly, it is politically expedient for state policy-makers to attempt to maintain low-tuition policies even as cost increases and budget pressures made it impossible for them to keep those tuitions within the financial reach of lower-income students. However, these politically expedient funding strategies are shortsighted and counterproductive. When government's have fewer and fewer resources to devote to removing college price barriers, as they do in the 1990s, policy-makers must think in the long term and find ways to target those funds to the most needy and not to the most powerful. Not doing so risks accelerating the current spiral of higher college prices, lower college-participation rates, slowing economic growth, and the resulting reductions in government revenues which, in turn, bring further pressures to reduce government spending.

10

OPTIONS TO IMPROVE
COLLEGE AFFORDABILITY

The fact that previous government efforts to remove college price barriers have fallen short of their goal, does not mean that such efforts must inevitably fail. Today, many federal and state policy-makers, college administrators, and students and their families continue to believe that removing college price barriers is a goal that can, and should, be achieved. Toward that end, there are dozens of college-finance reform proposals circulating in Washington, in the statehouses, and among policy professionals ranging from technical adjustments in existing programs, to grand schemes to recast the entire college finance system. While each plan promises to achieve the objectives stated in Title IV of the Higher Education Act of 1965, none has been able to secure the political and public support necessary to win approval.

In this chapter I look at several of the leading reform proposals to reverse the decline in college affordability. These include proposals for student loan reform, loan repayment reform, a shift to the high-tuition/high-aid funding model, and allowing students to pay for college through national and community service. After reviewing these plans, I consider why, even as college affordability is continuing to decline, plans which promise to reverse that trend cannot be enacted.

REFORMING THE STUDENT LOAN SYSTEM

Perhaps the most straightforward approach to improving college affordability is to reform the student loans programs. Loan reform offers the potential to solve some of the most disturbing aspects of the affordability problem. Various reform plans promise to allow students to more easily borrow the funds needed to pay their rising tuitions, to streamline and ease the repayment burdens facing students, and lower the program's costs to the federal government by reducing or eliminating the subsidies now paid to lenders.[1] In other words, advocates of student-loan reform claim that it will make more money available to more students with less paperwork and at a lower total cost.

The direct lending plan which is being phased in during the mid-1990s will go a long way toward relieving some of the problems resulting from the loan guarantee programs. It will reduce the costs of student loans to the federal government, it should reduce the default rates for student loans, and it should simplify the administration of the program for colleges. In spite of these advantages, however, many reformers feel as though the direct lending program did not do enough to reduce program costs and simplify the process of lending to students. In this view, a better way to make and service student loans would be for the federal government to by-pass campuses and make loans directly to students. This would be done through the creation of a federal student loan bank.

The Student Loan Bank

Economists and social reformers as diverse as Milton Friedman,[2] Robert Reischauer,[3] John Silber,[4] and Barry Bluestone[5] have all proposed replacing the current system of campus-based direct lending and public guarantees with a federal student loan bank. The loan bank would be created with the federal government capitalizing a quasi-governmental trust. Students would then borrow from the trust and repay the loans at a level that allows a reasonable rate of return. The repayments are then added to the trust and lent out again. Thus, once it was established, the bank would be self-sustaining and the profits which lenders now make on the student loans would be used to increase the volume of funds available to lend. Such an institutional arrangement is alleged by its supporters to provide better service to students, reduce default rates, and lower the long-term costs of student loans to the taxpayer.

Like direct lending, a student loan bank holds the promise of reducing the volume of defaulted loans. Defaults occur primarily because borrowers are unable, or unwilling, to make their repayments. A loan bank would improve collections on both counts. For those borrowers who are unable to repay because of low income or financial emergencies, the present system throws them into default after only a few missed payments. However, an income-contingent repayment system, as included in most loan bank plans, would raise and lower monthly payments to correspond with the borrower's income. If they lose their job, their loan does not go into default. As soon as they begin working again, their payment continues to be deducted as a portion of their income.

Those students who are unwilling to repay their loans would be handled even more effectively by a loan bank. Collection of loans would be centralized, possibly under the Internal Revenue Service. Repayments would be made through withholding procedures, or through FICA payroll deductions. The correct payment would be withheld from the borrower's earnings automatically. Under such a system, the problem of the geographic mobility of borrowers would be of no concern.

Just as important as cost savings, creation of a student loan bank would allow the government to target federal subsidies more carefully to the most needy students.[6] As the federal loan guarantee programs expanded after 1978, that growth was often funded at the expense of the other federal aid programs. But if a loan bank could effectively reduce the dollars necessary to insure that all students have access to adequate capital, the additional funds could be channeled into the grant programs which provide the greatest assistance to low-income students.

A Loan Bank or Direct Lending?

Originating student loans from a federal loan bank, rather than from individual campuses (as is the case with direct lending), could produce the advantages of direct lending without exacerbating the current college-price spiral. Its supporters argue that colleges don't have experience in making and servicing loans. Direct lending requires campuses to assume this banking function that many schools are either unwilling, or unable, to perform effectively.

Under direct lending, even those campuses which can handle the responsibilities of lending will experience increased costs as they implement the program. It is unrealistic to expect campus financial-aid offices to take on these additional responsibilities without expanded staff and training. These may translate into higher administrative costs on campus and exacerbate the current price spiral. Larger campuses may be able to absorb the additional responsibilities resulting from direct lending, but smaller colleges, technical schools, and vocational institutes will find this a burdensome, and costly, addition.[7]

How It Might Work: HELP

In a variant of the student loan bank, Robert Reischauer, director of the Congressional Budget Office, has proposed a "social insurance approach" to student loans.[8] He calls his plan the "Higher Education Loan Program" (HELP). Under HELP, any student enrolled more than half-time at an institution of higher education would be able to borrow from the loan bank. The loan would be made to the student without regard to family circumstance. Students would repay their loans through the existing FICA payroll tax system. Each borrower's payroll tax rate would be increased by an amount that would vary according to the size of their loan.[9] The uniform loan repayment rate would be set so that each cohort of borrowers would repay the bank for the full costs of its loans. Reischauer estimates that the rate of about 0.24 percent per $1,000 borrowed (in 1989 dollars) would be sufficient. In other words, a one-percent payroll tax would be sufficient to repay a $4,000 loan and a three-percent tax would suffice for a loan of $12,000.[10]

The amount that could be borrowed per percentage point of payroll tax would be indexed to inflation to keep pace with the rising costs of education without threatening the integrity of the bank. This is possible because the average earnings of each new cohort will be higher than those of the previous cohort. Thus a constant tax rate would generate a higher stream of repayments. The low tax rates are possible because the burden of repaying student loans would be spread out over the borrower's full working life. Repayments would start immediately because the new payroll tax would be applied to wages that borrowers earned while they are in school and payments would continue to be deducted whenever and wherever the borrower worked.

Disadvantages of a Loan Bank

The most obvious shortcoming of any student loan bank proposal is that it would require a substantial injection of initial capital in order to build a self-sustaining fund. Reischauer estimates that if the total amount lent in the first year was $10 billion and the average volume of new loans grew at the same rate as average wages, the negative balance would be more that $300 billion in fifteen years. This balance would stabilize after forty years at about $280 billion.[11]

Barry Bluestone recently proposed the Social Security Trust as a potential source of capitalization for a student loan bank. These surpluses are being generated by the payroll tax increases of 1983 and are expected to generate annual surpluses of more than $100 billion by the mid-1990s.[12] He argues that such an approach "provides for a level of intergenerational equity not available through any other devise and furnishes the Social Security Trust with an investment opportunity second to none."[13]

Regardless of the source of the new funds, however, any loan bank would require substantial federal appropriations during the program's first few decades. Current federal budgetary constraints make the discovery of such a sum highly unlikely. Private capital markets are a possible source of capital, especially since the creation of the loan bank would mean that private capital markets would not be lending the billions of dollars that students borrow though the current student-loan programs. Still, the capital needs of such a program would be greater than the existing programs because the repayment period is so much longer. In addition, it is reasonable to expect that borrowing would increase under the new program. This would drive up the costs of the program and require additional federal appropriations. As such, long-term savings in operating costs might be offset by the short-term costs of capitalization.[14]

REFORMING THE LOAN REPAYMENT SYSTEM

Other reformers[15] argue that it may not be necessary to make major changes in the student loan programs in order to produce a better student lending.[16] This is because many of the problems that students, colleges, and the federal government now encounter are really problems with the repayment structure. If changes were made in the way student loans are repaid, even if no other changes were made in the loans, significant strides could be made to make them more accessible to disadvantaged students.

Currently, student-borrowers participating in the federal programs must repay their loans over a ten-year period beginning sixty days after the time they leave school or have finished their deferment. This can lead to prohibitively large post-collegiate payments for many borrowers even at relatively low interest rates. These payments put many students in a severe financial bind. They borrowed the money expecting that college would increase there lifetime earnings. But often the financial rewards of college do not appear for several years after graduation. This puts student-borrowers in the difficult position of paying large monthly payments out of small post-collegiate incomes. By the time they begin to see their incomes rise, their student loans may already be in default.

The second problem of the repayment system is that it discourages students from low-income backgrounds, and those seeking to enter low-paying professions, from participating in the programs. The fear of large post-graduation payments, coupled with uncertainty over their future income, may drive such potential students away from the program and thus out of college.

Lengthened Repayment Periods

The most simple way to solve these problems is to lengthen the period of repayment from ten to twenty years or longer. Much like the development of the thirty-year home mortgage allowed many families to afford to buy a home who otherwise could not, lengthening the repayment period for student loans would lower monthly payments and make them more attractive and financially viable to lower-income students.

In addition, by spreading the repayment over an entire working life-time, instead of ten years, the loan bank would make it possible for students to borrow much larger sums than are currently allowed. This would allow students to borrow a sufficient amount to attend any college to which they were admitted. From the perspective of the low-income student-borrower, such a reform makes it possible for them to enjoy the same benefits now available to students from middle- and upper-income families. These families, who often finance their child's education through a home equity loan, are able to spread the payments over many years. Moreover, the interest paid on such loans is tax deductible. For those students without access to such tax-advantaged home equity loans, lengthened repayment periods would add substantial flexibility to their post-collegiate repayment schedules.

Income-Contingent Repayment

Beginning in 1993, many student loans allow borrowers to select a repayment plan which adjusts their repayment amounts to match their post-collegiate earnings. Called "income-contingent repayment," this reform allows borrowers to repay their loan as a percentage of income spread over their working lifetime. After completing their education, students repay their loans over a greatly extended period through a system of payroll deductions which take income and the amount borrowed into account. As such, income-contingent repayment provides students with both repayment flexibility and with a form of low-income insurance.

This approach offers significant advantages over the fixed-repayment approach currently used by lenders under the loan guarantee programs. First, no borrower would have to worry about a large debt that he or she could not repay. Those students who entered low-income occupations would have their monthly obligation proportionally decreased. This might make students from lower-income families more willing to borrow. As long as they were willing to make payments over many years, they would be almost as free as students from wealthy families to choose from among the entire range of colleges they are academically qualified to attend. As a consequence, the proportion of low-income students attending college might increase.

Disadvantages of Flexible Repayment Plans

Not everyone believes that such flexible repayment plans are a good idea. Lengthening repayment periods would increase the real cost of many student loans. Longer-term loans might mean smaller monthly payments, but they also mean increased interest charges. By increasing the aggregate debt burden, such payment plans may allow some students to take on a debt that would dramatically skew their post-collegiate opportunities and choices. Additionally, such plans can create enormous administrative complexity.[17] Income information would need to be collected annually from every borrower in order to calculate the next year's repayment schedule. Divorce, remarriage, and bankruptcy all present difficult challenges to efforts to calculate acceptable repayment schedules.

But even if these administrative problems can be overcome, flexible repayment plans make it easier for the government to shift the burden of paying for college on to the student.[18] Since such plans reduce the possibility that a student will be crushed under the burden of high loan payments, policy-makers may feel that lower-income students can now afford to pay a larger share of the costs of college. State legislatures may feel less obligated to provide institutional subsidies. Congress may see less need to maintain or expand the Pell grant program or other non-loan financial aid programs. Even families may feel less obligated to save for their children's education.

In the end, easing repayment burdens is counterproductive if it accelerates the shifting of a larger portion of the responsibility of paying for college from the government to lower-income students. This is especially true if the reform substitutes the short-term hardship of a high monthly payment with the long-term hardship of an unmanageable debt burden.

HIGH-TUITION/HIGH-AID PRICING

High-tuition/high-aid is a comprehensive reform of college funding in which governments reduce their subsidies to public colleges and allow then to raise tuitions to close to the real cost of providing an education. Governments then channel the increased revenues into expanded need-based aid programs. Upper- and upper-middle-income students, who can afford to pay more for higher education, will be expected to pay a greater share of their real educational costs. But lower- and lower-middle-income students will have the higher tuitions offset by increased grants based on their financial need.

While the concept of high-tuition/high-aid funding has been around for more than three decades, it only emerged as a leading reform option in the early 1990s.[19] This rise to prominence was driven largely by the fiscal pressures facing state governments. As states searched for ways to reduce spending without producing negative social consequences, high-tuition/high-aid made sense. By expecting upper-income students to pay more, states could reduce their spending on higher education without necessarily reducing college access for lower-income students.

Supporters of high-tuition/high-aid argue that low-tuition policies are both inefficient and ineffective ways to fund higher education.[20] State instructional subsidies allow public colleges to charge students the same low tuitions regardless of their need. Students who can afford to pay the full cost of their education pay the same price as those who cannot. Further, low-tuition policies insulate public higher education from the discipline of the marketplace. Many students, especially low-income students, have little choice but to attend a nearby public college. Thus, public colleges do not face the competitive pressures which serve to increase performance and improve quality. They have a captive audience of lower-income students who, even with federal financial aid, cannot afford to attend a private college or even another state institution.

Advocates of the high-tuition/high-aid funding model see it as a way to simultaneously reduce government spending and increase educational quality. By reducing instructional subsidies state governments save money. By increasing student aid, lower-income students experience no declines, or perhaps even increases, in college access. And public colleges are forced to raise standards to compete with private colleges based on quality of education and not price.

How it Might Work: Federalizing College Finance

In *Keeping College Affordable* Michael McPherson and Morton Schapiro suggest that public-college tuitions should be encouraged to rise to more closely reflect the actual price of providing that education.[21] Then, the government should use the resulting revenues to fund a grant program for those students who cannot meet these higher prices. But recognizing the difficulties state governments would have in instituting an equitable high-tuition/high-aid reform, they suggest instead a comprehensive reform of college finance which federalizes the funding of higher education for low-income students.

To do this, they propose shifting the responsibility for paying for the higher education of lower-income students from the states to the federal government. The key is a plan to recast federal student aid so that all higher education subsidies are combined into a single grant program. The federal government would provide these grants to all students who need subsidies. They estimate that the maximum grant could be increased from its current $2,300 level to about $8,000. The total cost of their expanded grant program to the federal government would be between $10 billion and $15 billion.[22] Part of these costs would be offset by the elimination of nearly all of the other federal need-based student-aid programs including College Work-Study, SEOG, SSIG, and Perkins loans as well as the elimination of interest subsidies to banks in the loan guarantee programs. The rest would be borne by upper- and middle-income students in the form of higher tuitions at public colleges.

Such a dramatic change in funding responsibilities would give public colleges a powerful incentive to raise their tuitions to cover a larger portion of their costs. Public colleges could raise tuition without fearing that lower-income students would be able to afford the higher prices. Those colleges which raised tuition enough to capture the increased federal spending fully, would see their revenues increase because higher tuitions would be paid by all students not receiving federal aid.[23]

In addition to more efficient use of resources, McPherson and Schapiro argue that their plan would expand the choices available to low-income students. Since most private colleges currently charge more than the maximum proposed grant, they would have no incentive to raise prices. Low-income students would thus have less financial incentive to select public over private higher education.

Disadvantages of Federalization

It is easy to see why McPherson and Schapiro's plan has found little support in the higher-education community. While they seem to recognize the enormous political obstacles their plan would face, they suggest no strategy to overcome them. This is especially important since the model offers something to offend nearly every higher-education interest. Public colleges oppose efforts to reduce their government subsidies. Private colleges worry that the maximum federal grant will be too small to allow students to afford them. Banks oppose efforts to remove subsidies for student loans. And most families will be angered by higher posted college prices even if the amount they later actually must pay remains unchanged.[24]

Additionally, the swap holds little appeal to the political interests of either federal or state policy-makers. In Washington, the obvious concern is over how to pay for the costs of the program at a time when there are substantial pressures to reduce spending in all program areas. States, on the other hand, are concerned that federal support will lag behind the growth in the real costs of college just as the Pell grant spending did after 1980. States also object to the implicit shifting of enrollments and dollars from public to private colleges. This substantially reduces the opportunity for state officials to shape decisions governing higher education and produces a dramatic shift of state resources from public to private hands.

In the end, the appeal of any high-tuition/high-aid funding model, including this one, is not that it provides an ideal solution to the college-affordability problem. Rather it draws its support from those who recognize that government funding for higher education is limited. High-tuition/high-aid pricing is simply a more efficient way to allocate those limited funds. Such a strategy insures that more public funds are targeted to the most needy students. The danger is that such targeting undermines the support necessary to maintain a high-quality educational system. This could, over time, erode the public higher education system which has been so important in expanding college access to lower-income and disadvantaged students.

THE NATIONAL COMMISSION COMPROMISE

The National Commission on Responsibilities for Financing Postsecondary Education was created to study problems in the college finance system. In 1993 the commission issued a report recommending a comprehensive reform plan which suggests changes at all levels of the college finance system. But it would also maintain the basic structures and responsibilities of the present student-aid programs.[25]

The central feature of the commission's recommendations is the creation of the Student's Total Education Package (STEP) to be available to all Americans. Under the STEP plan, all full-time students, regardless of income level, would be eligible for about $14,000 of financial aid each year. But while the amount of aid would be the same for all students, the type of aid any student would receive would vary widely based on their family income. Students from the lowest-income families would receive a mixture of grants, work-study, and subsidized loans. For middle-income students the aid package would be composed of a combination of subsidized and unsubsidized loans. Upper-income students would only be eligible for unsubsidized loans. The sliding scale of government support is presented in table 10.1.

Table 10.1

"The Student's Total Education Package, as Proposed by the National
Commission on Responsibilities for Financing Postsecondary Education

		Federal Dollars		
Family Income	Pell Grant	College Work-Study	Subsidized Loan	Family Contribution[1]
$ 0	$4,000	$4,000	$ 6,000	–
20,000	3,500	3,500	7,000	–
40,000	500	3,000	9,000	500
60,000	–	2,000	6,000	6,000
80,000	–	–	2,000	12,000
100,000	–	–	–	14,000

Source: *Making College Affordable Again: Final Report* (Washington D.C.: National
Commission on Responsibilities for Financing Higher Education, 1993).

In order to make the STEP concept work, the commission recommends important changes to both the student-loan and the Pell grant programs. The entire system of federally guaranteed student loans would be replaced by a system of campus-based lending, much like direct lending. All of the federal loan programs would be streamlined into a single program in which colleges would originate loans. Those loans would then be serviced and collected in a central location. Students would have the option of repaying the loan through a conventional or an income-contingent payment schedule with up to twenty-five years to repay.

While the commission plan incorporates several of the best features emerging from the debate over student-loan reform, its recommendations go well beyond the mechanics of lending. The commission also recommends strengthening the Pell grant program by consolidating it with the SEOG program and raising the maximum annual grant from $2,300 to $3,700 a year. The commission recommends that, eventually, the size of the maximum Pell grant be fixed at an amount equal to 75 percent of the median cost of attending a public four-year college.[26]

In order to reduce the need for lower-income students to borrow for college, the commission argues that this level of Pell grant funding should be viewed by the federal government as an "unbreakable promise that promotes greater opportunities for postsecondary education."[27] Making the Pell grant such an unbreakable promise would be a substantial step towards improving college access for lower-income students.[28] In the current fiscal environment, if a proposal to increase the Pell grant does not also increase congressional appropriations, it will not have any impact on affordability.

Disadvantages of STEP

By combining the reformulated direct-loan program with the strengthened Pell grant program, the commission envisioned an entirely new student-aid system. But the report creates some new problems even as it is solving some old ones. Under the STEP plan, everyone would be eligible for federal aid, albeit unsubsidized aid for the more affluent students. Indeed, everyone would be entitled to a substantial amount of federal aid. This creates an incentive, or at least opportunity, for less expensive colleges to raise tuitions to capture more of the federal aid dollars. Similarly, cash-strapped states may see this as an opportunity to reduce their state student-aid programs or cut other subsidies to higher education. If this happens, the result might be an increased federalization of college finance similar to that suggested by McPherson and Schapiro.

While their plan may encourage higher tuitions, the commission explicitly rejects the high-tuition/high-aid approach. Instead they warn that a headlong rush into such a funding strategy would be a mistake. Without the political support to maintain the high levels of student aid necessary to make the model work, students could find tuitions rising without the corresponding increases in student aid to offset those increases. They note that between 1991 and 1993, ten states raised tuitions *and* cut student aid.[29] If this pattern was to become widespread the high-tuition/high-aid strategy could easily be transformed into a high tuition/low-aid strategy with disastrous consequences for college access.

The STEP plan thus promises to be much more expensive, as well as more effective, than the present system. The savings from the shift to direct lending might be substantial, but it will certainly not be enough to cover the increased cost of expanding the grant and work-study programs. The commission also endorsed the creation of a system which would allow students to repay their loans through two years of national service. As will be discussed next, the national service plan will greatly increase the costs of the commission's recommendations while doing little to improve college affordability.

NATIONAL SERVICE AND COLLEGE FINANCE

Recently, the most widely discussed of the reforms to improve college price barriers is the linking of national service to college grants or loan forgiveness.[30] But the push for programs to encourage national and community service is much broader than concerns over rising college prices. Community service is seen as a way to integrate the values of service and citizenship into the fabric of American life, as a mechanism to develop the infrastructure necessary for citizens to change their communities, and as providing the human capital to rebuild deteriorating structures in urban and rural areas.[31]

The term national service is now used to describe a wide variety of activities. To George Bush it was largely voluntary service by individuals, or a series of small locally run programs. His vision of national service involved facilitating the emergence of "a thousand points of light." But Bill Clinton brought to the presidency a much larger vision of the government's role in encouraging service. He favored using government action to greatly expand the number of opportunities available for citizens to provide service and to increase the rewards paid to those who serve.

In 1993, at the urging of President Clinton, Congress enacted a national service program that will, by 1998, place 100,000 Americans in community service jobs.[32] These will range from teachers, to health service workers, to construction workers and safety officers. The plan attracts participants by offering a threefold compensation package. Participants get the psychic benefits of contribution to the regeneration of their communities. They receive a small stipend, health benefits, and child-care benefits while they are engaged in their service projects. Finally, those who have not been to college receive educational grant to help pay them cover their future college costs and those who have already graduated will receive loan forgiveness to reduce their college debt.[33]

For those who participate, the program improves college affordability in several ways. By providing grants to pre-collegiate participants, the program gives them new resources from which to pay their college bills. By providing loan forgiveness to post-collegiate participants, it reduces their student-loan debt burden. But the program also allows participants to defer repayment of their loans, giving them the opportunity to work at lower-paying service jobs and not have the loans go into default or have interest accumulating during their service period.

Solving a Different Problem

Because the program has not yet been fully implemented, it is difficult to fairly evaluate the impact of the National and Community Service Trust Act of 1993. It is clear, however, that even a fully functioning national service program would only be available to, and appropriate for, a small percentage of the more than 4 million students now receiving federal student aid and the more than 10 million students now enrolled in some form of higher education. Moreover, the amount a participant could earn under the program is less than $10,000 for two years of service. This amount is less than the cost of two years at a public university and less than one year at a private college. Thus, even those who are able to participate in the program may face significant college price barriers after they have completed the program.

Ultimately, the rationale for a national service program has little to do with college finance. Such plans are designed to build better citizens, rebuild deteriorating communities, and/or regenerate the moral purpose of the nation. These are noble objectives for national policy. But if the goal of the college finance system is to provide access to college for the broadest number of students, national service plans are far less cost-effective that grants or even guaranteed loans. As such, while the debate over national service may be an important one, it is only coincidentally related to the problem of college affordability. It is also likely to be only a small part of any effort to remove cost barriers to college.

Moreover, the cost of using national service as a mechanism for college finance is vastly higher than it would be for the Title IV student-aid programs. Each student who participates in the program receives a payment (around minimum wage) for their services during the period in which they are performing their service obligations. They also receive health and child-care benefits during their service period. Many will also receive some training to prepare then to perform their service more effectively. Then, after their service has been completed, they receive $4,750 to pay for college. As such, the government must pay as much as $20,000 per year for each student who participates in the national service program.[34]

In this light, national service is an even more inefficient way to improve college affordability than the highly inefficient student-aid system now in place. Even when fully operational, less than 2 percent of all college students could participate in the program in any particular year. Many nontraditional students would find it impossible to participate in the program without disrupting their lives. At the same time, the cost of each service worker would be the same as the cost of providing the maximum Pell grant to five disadvantaged students. In a time when the purchasing power of the Pell grant is eroding rapidly, and the federal government is unable to fully fund these grants, it may not make sense to spend such large sums to provide an education to such a small number of students.

Ultimately, because national service plans are not college-affordability programs at all, they must be judged by different standards. Like the G.I. bill, they use college grants as a benefit to entice people to participate in providing an important public service. Accordingly, the debate over the value of such programs should revolve around the value of the service provided and not the impact it has on college access. For even the largest national service program would be too small and too costly to have any meaningful positive impact on the growing college affordability program.

WHY LARGE-SCALE REFORM HAS FAILED

While none of these reforms have been fully adopted, neither have they been rejected out of hand. In fact, several features of these reforms have already been incorporated into the student aid system. The new direct-lending program has an income-contingent repayment plan for up to 30 percent of all borrowers. The high-tuition/high-aid model has been adopted in a few states and is under consideration in several others. A national service plan has been put into place and will enroll up to 100,000 students by 1998. Still, aside from the enactment of the direct-lending program in 1993, every effort to reform the system has rejected major new initiatives in favor of tinkering with existing programs. In spite of their many flaws and widespread dissatisfaction with their operation, the basic structure of the major federal student-aid programs look very much the same today as they did in 1972. What, then, explains this seeming contradiction between the simultaneous demand for, and the failure of, student-aid reform?

Class Politics Again

The principle reason for the failure of any comprehensive student-aid reform is the same combination of political and economic forces which has driven the shift in program dollars from lower- to middle- and upper-income students since 1980. Inasmuch as each of these reforms seek to create a more efficient student-aid system, they redistribute benefits from financial intermediaries and less-needy students to more-needy students. They thus seek to redistribute resources from the more politically powerful to the less politically powerful. Such a combination does not bode well for the enactment of any comprehensive reform effort.

The current scarcity of government resources exacerbate the always difficult task of targeting funds to the disadvantaged. During times when funds are relatively plentiful, it is possible to assemble the coalition necessary to extend benefits to the disadvantaged. A reform plan can distribute more aid to the disadvantaged without reducing benefits to middle- and upper-income families. This was the case in the 1960s and 1970s. But as government's resources became scarce, as they have since 1980, politics become zero-sum.[35] In these more difficult circumstances, reformers have been unable to build the support necessary to take benefits away from those at the top and redirect them to those on the bottom.

Blame, Mistrust, and Stalemate

But there is more involved here than just class politics. The failures of recent reform efforts point out a fundamental dilemma facing any new college-finance plan. If a reform is to be effective, it must substantially increase the resources now available to disadvantaged students to pay for college. But at the same time those reforms which require substantial new resources, whether they are to be generated through new taxes or by shifting funds away from existing programs, seem unable to attract the political support necessary to be enacted. The result is that any plan which is limited enough to be passed, is unlikely to be effective. Any plan which is large enough to be effective, cannot be passed.

This dilemma is rooted in the very different ways that campus leaders and public policy-makers perceive the college-affordability problem. To campus leaders, the value of higher education is self-evident, and rapidly rising tuitions are seen as an obvious consequence of a lack of government support for higher education. Many blame this inadequate support on a lack of understanding by political leaders of the critical role colleges play in the development of the economy, the culture, and society. Rising college prices simply underscore the need for governments to increase their appropriations to higher education.

In Washington and in the statehouses, however, the college-affordability problem looks very different. Here, colleges themselves are seen as sharing the blame for rising prices. Federal and state policy-makers, faced with stable revenues, mounting social problems, escalating health-care costs, and accelerating demands for public services, must struggle to limit all types of discretionary spending. They argue that colleges have not been singled out for special cutbacks. Higher education in general, and student aid in particular, have experienced smaller reductions than other areas of discretionary spending. As such, many public officials see themselves as already providing colleges with all the support that their tight budgets will allow. In return, they expect colleges, like other state agencies, to tighten their belts, streamline their operations, and improve their productivity.

In this context, policy-makers are often frustrated by the magnitude of the gap between changes in government appropriations for higher education and changes in the tuitions charged at colleges and universities. In the last half of the 1980s, in particular, federal spending on student aid increased by 30 percent and state appropriations for higher education increased by 20 percent. Yet public college tuitions still increased by 50 percent. This gap caused many policy-makers to wonder whether colleges were making genuine efforts to control prices and, in some cases, to even question the commitment of higher-education leaders to the cause of college affordability.

This frustration is clearly seen in some recent statements by state officials. In 1990, Maryland Governor William Donald Schafer warned public college leaders in his state not to raise tuitions to make up for cuts in the states higher education budget.[36] In Virginia, Governor Douglas Wilder demanded that the state's public colleges "get their fiscal house in order" before they raise tuitions. Wilder went on to suggest that college presidents would be wise to "streamline programs, cut unnecessary expenses and—in appropriate cases—to curtail programs or services in order to meet the states budget constraints."[37] New York Governor Mario Cuomo was even more blunt when he said that public colleges in his state "can't manage their own affairs" during difficult fiscal times.[38]

This lack of trust between those responsible for providing higher education and those who supply the endeavor with its principle financial support, creates the dilemma which makes redistributive reform so difficult. Policy-makers are hesitant to allocate additional revenues to higher education because they are not convinced that those appropriations are being spent wisely. Colleges respond by claiming that their rising costs demand additional appropriations and that stable government funding has left them with no choice but to increase tuitions.

These recriminations and mistrust have produced a stalemate. Until federal and state policy-makers are confident that additional resources allocated to higher education will be spent wisely, they will not be willing to fund new or expanded college-affordability programs. But until governments are willing to make that commitment of new resources, there is little that colleges can do to improve affordability without reducing quality or restricting enrollments.

THE NEXT STEP

The failure of college finance reform is not the product of a lack of good ideas. There are plenty of reasonable and well-developed reform plans now circulating. Instead, advocates of improved college affordability have been unable to rebuild the public and political support necessary to enact a reform. This requires breaking the deadlock which now blocks comprehensive reform. That cannot happen until colleges are able to persuade government that they will make prudent use of any new public resources they receive. Similarly, governments must persuade the public that there are compelling reasons to use public funds to target aid to the most disadvantaged and not simply distribute subsidies to powerful interests and wealthy constituents.

11

A Plan to Remove
College Price Barriers

An effective program to achieve universal college affordability must do at least two things. First, it must insure that all potential students have access to the capital necessary to cover the full price of any college they have the ability and desire to attend. This requires, at the very least, the development of a broadly available student loan which will allow potential students to borrow without requiring collateral or co-signers. The development of the federally guaranteed student-loan programs, and now the direct-lending program, has achieved this first objective to a remarkable degree. But it has done so at a very high price to students, colleges, and taxpayers.

Second, an effective affordability program must fairly apportion the costs of college among the various parties who benefit from higher education. Since students receive a large return from an investment in a college education, they should be expected to pay a commensurate portion of the cost. But the state and the nation also benefit when more of its citizens go to college. The public, acting through the government, thus has a substantial interest in increasing college participation by subsidizing its costs. In doing so, they must insure that potential students from disadvantaged families do not face pre-enrollment "sticker shock" or post-collegiate debt burdens. Finally, needy students must know that these grants will be available to them many years before they can enter college. Only then will such students be certain that college will be within their financial reach and be encouraged aspire to college and to select the courses which will best prepare them for college.

249

It is here in achieving this second objective, that the current programs and policies break down. Today, the grants provided by the federal government are far too small to allow lower-income students to cover the costs of attending even a modestly priced college without taking out a loan. As a consequence, even the most disadvantaged students must borrow large sums. But the prospect of large debts discourage many such students from entering college and place heavy burdens on those who do.[1] As it stands today, government is asking students and their families to pay a larger and larger portion of their education. The result is a national underinvestment in higher education in which all parties are hurt.

In this regard, there are a number of plans which would be an improvement over the current badly flawed system. If properly implemented and funded, several of the reforms discussed in the previous chapter, and many others, offer the possibility of significantly reducing college price barriers. But, despite their substantial merits, none of these reforms has been able to secure the public and political support necessary to replace the current system.

In this closing chapter I outline a politically and fiscally feasible alternative which can achieve the two important goals of universal college affordability. This plan mixes the most attractive features of several prominent reform plans with the basic structures of the current college-finance system. The result is clearly not the best of all possible programs. The current fiscal and political constraints make that an unrealistic goal. It is, instead, a compromise which recognizes that, in the years ahead, the costs of providing a quality higher education are likely grow faster than either the incomes of disadvantaged families or the revenues available to governments. This accelerating fiscal squeeze, coupled with the recent declines in the confidence of policy-makers in higher education, will make it difficult for colleges to secure the new revenues necessary to hold down college prices and for governments to increase the availability of student aid.

REFOCUSING ON AFFORDABILITY:
ACCESS BEFORE CHOICE

The central objective of Title IV of the Higher Education Act of 1965 was to insure broad access to college for potential students from families at all income levels. Insuring that students from more financially well-off families would have a choice of schools, or that everyone would have access to even the highest priced colleges, were clearly secondary. But over the past three decades, these goals have been reversed. Today, insuring that middle- and upper-income students have a choice of colleges, through the availability of federal student loans, has replaced providing lower-income students access through grants as the fundamental value advanced by the student aid programs.

During the 1960s, when government resources were relatively plentiful, it was possible, perhaps even desirable, for policy-makers to advance the causes of access and choice simultaneously. But such an approach is simply too expensive to follow when public resources are scarce. By attempting to serve these two goals, and also to control aggregate government spending on higher education, federal and state policy-makers have managed to create a system in which many low-income students do not have the money to attend even a moderately priced college without incurring substantial debt. At the same time, middle-income students still find the price of private colleges to be beyond their reach. As such, the current system produces the undesirable combination of insufficient access *and* constrained choice for all but the most wealthy students.

Solving the college-affordability problem must begin with the return to one simple rule: providing lower-income students access to a four-year college is a more important value than providing all students with a choice among different types of colleges. During times when there are too few resources to provide all potential students with both access and choice, limited funds should first be used to insure all qualified lower-income students with access to the resources necessary to attend a moderately priced four-year college. Only after universal access has been achieved, is it appropriate for policy-makers to shift their focus to advancing the cause of college choice. In short, government must refocus the college-affordability programs on achieving their original goal and reverse the transformation which has occurred since 1980.

The assertion that access is a more fundamental policy goal than choice is, ultimately, a statement of personal values. But it has its roots in empirical economic reality. All else being equal, the difference in post-collegiate earnings between those who have earned a bachelor's degree and those who have not is substantial. Similarly, the difference between the earnings of those who have a bachelor's degree and those who only have an associate's degree is also large.[2] Yet, the earnings differential between those who attended lower-priced colleges and those who attended higher-priced colleges is quite small. Indeed, many studies find no earnings differential at all.[3] Public dollars spent to increase college access produce increases in the earnings of the student and in revenue for the government. But dollars spent to send a student to a higher-priced college rather than a lower-priced college produce little or no measurable economic return. As a consequence, utilitarian as well as egalitarian principles suggest that access be the principle goal of the college finance system.

Certainly, the decision to refocus the government effort on universal affordability at the expense of universal choice carries a substantial price. Some deserving students will find elite colleges beyond their financial reach. More students will be forced to attend state colleges. But these costs must be balanced against the benefits which flow from the elimination of price barriers to modestly priced colleges.

A FEASIBLE REFORM PROPOSAL

Given the combination of scarce public resources, the rising cost of providing a quality higher education, the declining pool of college-age students, and the growing mistrust between colleges and policy-makers, achieving universal college affordability will be a difficult matter. But it is not impossible. By taking four simple steps, policy-makers can redirect the college-affordability programs and finally begin to realize the grand vision of the Higher Education Act of 1965.

STEP #1: REVITALIZING THE PELL GRANT

To make the most of these limited resources, the federal government needs to more efficiently target their funds to the most needy students. Ironically, the program which does this best is also among the oldest: the Pell grant. Indeed Pell grants may be the single most effective program ever devised to keep college affordable to lower-income students. It targets money efficiently to the most needy students, it produces no debt to discourage potential students or burden graduates, and it provides a solid foundation upon which a program of equal college opportunity can be built.

The problem with the Pell grant program today is not its design, but the inadequate funding it has received from Congress since 1980. This underfunding has happened in two ways. First, even as government spending on student aid has increased over the past two decades, the size of the maximum Pell grant has lagged badly behind college prices. As a consequence, the grants available to the most needy students today purchase far less higher education than they did in 1975. Second, in recent years Congress has failed to appropriate enough money to fully fund even these diminished grants. Many needy students thus now receive grants which are far smaller than their documented need. These constraints have turned the Pell grant into a shadow of the program it was designed to be.

Fully revitalizing the Pell grant will require three simple modifications. First, to insure that the grants are sufficiently large to assure lower-income students access to a reasonably priced college, and to insure that the real purchasing power of the grants do not again lag behind increases in college costs, federal policy-makers should tie the size of the maximum Pell grant to the actual price of attending college.

One proposal to do this was suggested by the National Commission on Responsibilities for Financing Postsecondary Education.[4] They recommended that the maximum Pell grant be fixed at 75 percent of the national median price of attendance at a public four-year college. In 1993, the median price of about $6,000 would produce a maximum Pell grant of $4,500. This strikes me as a reasonable amount from both the government's and the student's perspective. It provides those students who do not want to borrow with sufficient resources to attend a lower-priced college. Those students who are willing to take on additional debt could borrow the sums necessary to attend more expensive schools. The 75 percent level is also high enough to allow families with modest savings, and students willing to work part-time, to complete college with very little debt. But this level is also low enough to provide an incentive for individual colleges to moderate their tuition increases.

The second change which is necessary in the operation of the Pell grant program is the elimination of the half-cost provision (raised to 60 percent in 1993). This provision limits the size of the maximum Pell grant to 60 percent of the total cost of attending college. Originally, the half-cost provision was the result of a compromise in the creation of the BEOG in 1972 over how best to allocate the federal government's limited grant funds. It stipulates that the most needy students can receive either the maximum grant or half of the total annual cost of the college they are attending. The logic was that all students should be expected to pay for at least half the cost of their education either by working while they were in school or through loans which they would repay after graduation. No one would be provided a college education totally at government expense.

The half-cost provision may have made sense in 1972 when the constant-dollar price of both public and private colleges was less than 60 percent of their 1992 level. At that point, the half-cost provision required even the neediest student to contribute (through savings, work, or borrowing) less than $1,000 a year to the cost of a private college and less than $500 to the price of a public college.

But in 1994, the price of the average private college was $20,000 a year. The maximum Pell grant was $2,300. This forces even the neediest student to pay more than $17,000 a year either now or later. The same is true at public colleges. The average total annual cost of four-year public college or university is now more than $6,000. Even with the maximum Pell grant, a needy student would be forced to pay $3,700 a year to attend college full-time. Thus, in the vast majority of cases, the rising price of college has made the half-cost provision irrelevant.

The place where the provision does have an impact is on the low-income student attending a low-price two-year college. The total annual average price of a two-year college in 1994 was about $3,700. A student attending such a college would not be eligible for the full Pell grant of $2,300 because it would cover more than 60 percent of the total cost of attendance. Such students would have their grant reduced to $2,200, forcing them to pay the $1,500 difference. Students attending colleges which cost only $3,000 a year would have their grant reduced to $1,800.

It is reasonable that all students be expected to pay for a portion of their educational costs. But in a time of high tuitions and high tuition inflation, the half-cost provision requires the most needy students to pay too much. A much more reasonable method would be to expect all students to pay a fixed amount, perhaps $500, toward the annual cost of their education (or through private or institutional financial aid). Under such a system needy students would receive the maximum grant, or $500 less than the full cost of attendance, whichever was less. Such a change would affect only those low-income students attending low-cost colleges, but these are often the students in the greatest need of federal help. More important, it sends the clear message that the federal government is committed to the goal of insuring that all lower-income students have access to at least a lower-priced four-year public college.

The third and final change necessary to revitalize the Pell grant is to begin funding the program as an entitlement. This proposal, which was widely discussed in the Reauthorization of the Higher Education Act in 1992, would force the Congress to fully fund grants to all students who meet eligibility requirements. The fact that the guaranteed student loan programs (and now the direct loan program) are funded as entitlements, but the Pell grant is not, is one of the factors responsible for the shift in federal funding from grants to loans after 1980. Until the Pell grant is put on an equal footing with the loan programs, it will never be a reliable college-affordability program.

By providing the dual guarantee of full funding of the Pell grant and the promise that there will be no decline in the purchasing power of the grant over time, Congress can finally send the clear message that anyone who has the skills and the qualifications to be admitted to college will be able to afford to go. There is simply nothing else which policy-makers at any level could do which would produce such a significant improvement in college affordability for lower-income students.

The certainty of opportunity that would result from a guaranteed Pell grant would have both a short- and a long-term impact on college-participation rates. As soon as it is enacted, many lower-income students who are now forced out of school because they cannot afford the high price of tuition, or are frightened away by the prospect of large post-collegiate debts, would see those price barriers substantially removed. Secondarily, many students in middle school and high school will see that college is not beyond their financial reach and begin raising their aspirations and changing their course-taking behavior.

The development of a guaranteed Pell grant would also go a long way toward solving several of the other problems now plaguing the federal student-aid system. Lower-income students would need to borrow less to enroll in college and would thus face lower post-collegiate debts. As grants replaced loans as the principle mechanism of student aid, federal subsidy dollars would be more effectively targeted to the most needy students. Because disadvantaged students are most likely to default on their loans, asking them to borrow less would almost certainly lower the student-loan default rate and reduce the costs of the loan program. And even if college prices continued to accelerate, lower-income students would know that the purchasing power of the Pell grant would hold steady.

The benefits of fulfilling the original promise of the Pell grant are easy to see. But because of the cost, and the configuration of political forces, these benefits will be very difficult to achieve. The CBO estimates that increasing the size of the maximum Pell grant from the present

$2,300 to $3,700 would be about $6.5 billion in 1993.[5] If the grant were to be increased to the $4,500 level, that price-tag could be closer to $12 billion.

At the same time, these changes in the Pell grant should also produce some important savings. Such an expansion in the Pell grant program would allow many states to reduce or restructure their grant programs. If the Pell grant is covering 75 percent of college prices for the most needy students, states would find filling in the remainder of the funding package to be a much less burdensome task.

These savings notwithstanding, the cost of the revitalized Pell grant will be high and there are few dollars available to fund such a large new initiative, even if it is simply to reestablish the original purpose of the program. Some funds could be found by merging the SEOG with the Pell grant. But that generates less than $1 billion. The best place to look for the new Pell funds, however, is in the place where those funds have been shifting in the 1980s and 1990s: the student loan programs. Indeed, shifting money out of the loan programs and back to the grant programs, presents the best hope of securing the funds to rebuild the Pell grant to achieve its original promise.

STEP #2: REPAIRING STUDENT LOANS

Revitalizing the Pell grant is an important first step to removing college price barriers, but it is only a first step. As discussed in chapter 10, there are large and important inefficiencies inherent in the federal guaranteed student-loan programs. They award too many dollars to support students who do not need government support and too few dollars are left to go to those families that need them.[6] Indeed, just as the Pell grant program is a well-designed program which has been tragically underfunded, the FFEL are poorly designed programs which have been wastefully overfunded. Many of the dollars which went to pay the costs of loan guarantees to the children of wealthy students could, and indeed should, have been used to fully fund the Pell grant program.

There are a number of alternatives to the current student-loan mess. But direct lending offers the greatest promise of generating the kind of support necessary to replace the costly and cumbersome guaranteed student-loan programs. In fact, since many schools are now in the process of shifting to direct lending it is an ideal time to extend the scope of the program to cover all, or nearly all, colleges. Direct lending will produce two important savings. By eliminating the role of private lenders, guarantee agencies, and secondary markets in all new loans, direct lending will greatly reduce the costs of interest subsidies and special allowance payments. By allowing more borrowers the option of income-contingent repayment, direct lending will keep many students out of default and thus lower default costs to the federal treasury.

Direct-lending supporters suggest that these changes will reduce the price of student loans by as much as $1 billion a year. While the immediate savings will be significant, such estimates are probably overstated. This is because of the high costs of starting up the new structures on campus, and because the savings from lower default rates will not be evident for many years. Still, even if the initial savings are small, reducing the number of players in the lending process will simplify the loan process and flexible repayments will reduce the post-graduation debt burden of borrowers.

If loan reform stops with the shift to direct lending, however, it will not improve the problem of declining college affordability. Direct lending will mean some savings for the federal government, and some simplification for students. But it will leave many of the most critical problems of the loan program unresolved. Students will still be borrowing the same amount of money, albeit from a different source. As college prices rise, those who are hesitant to borrow will still be discouraged from entering college and those who borrow will still face substantial post-collegiate debts. In both situations, the negative impact falls squarely on the backs of the most needy students.

An effective loan reform must go on to redirect those savings to the place it will have the most impact. That place is the guaranteed Pell grant. As the savings from loan reform begin to appear, there will be tremendous pressure to use those funds to expand the National Service Trust or other policy initiatives which benefit primarily middle- and upper-income families. The substantial benefits of national service notwithstanding, this would be a serious mistake. In an environment of scarce public funds, it is unreasonable to expect government to direct large new sums to improve college affordability. But it is not unreasonable to expect that the current level of federal spending be allocated in the way which will have the greatest impact.

Solving the Proprietary School Problem

A final component of an effective student-loan reform is that it must resolve the problems now presented by proprietary and for-profit schools. Clearly, many students at such schools have a substantial need for government help. But including them in the federal student-loan programs has produced a tremendous strain on the lending system. The student-loan default rate at proprietary schools is more than 40 percent. And while proprietary schools account for only about 20 percent of all FFEL borrowers, they constitute more than 40 percent of all defaults and more than 35 percent of the total cost of defaults.

Part of the reason that the federal government has had such a difficult time addressing the problem of proprietary schools is that they serve a fundamentally different purpose, and clientele, than do more traditional academic institutions. Currently, much of the government's effort to address the proprietary school problem has focused on making schools with high default rates ineligible for the student loan programs. This has had some success at reducing default rates, but it may well do so at the cost of closing down some good schools or shutting some worthy students out of school.[7]

A more reasonable approach to the problem is to take proprietary schools out of the student-loan programs entirely and create a separate vocational loan program to lend money to anyone enrolled in vocational education. This new program would then be administered by the Department of Labor, rather than the Department of Education, and could become a part of an expanded national job training initiative in which the determinations of loan eligibility would be coupled with pre-enrollment career counseling and post-enrollment placement assistance.[8]

Ideally, the creation of this new program would serve as a catalyst for a comprehensive reorganization of the federal programs to assist non-college-bound students. Economist Lester Thurow observes that:

> The United States is unique among industrial countries in that it does not have an organized postsecondary education system for the non–college bound. Relative to their respective sizes, for every dollar in taxpayer's money invested in the education of the non-college bound, fifty-five dollars is spent subsidizing those going to college—, a ratio that in neither fair or efficient. Other nations' governments invest heavily in the postsecond-

ary skills of the non–college bound. Britain, France, and Spain spend more than twice as much as the United States; Germany, more than three times as much, and Sweden, almost six times as much.[9]

It is this absence of an educational system for the non-college-bound or a widely available job training program, which is fueling the growth of proprietary education. Today, many high school graduates who would like to enter the work-force see little choice but to go to college (even if they have little interest in academic study), or to enroll in a proprietary school. In Thurow's view the result is "that there are too many people in college and not enough qualified workers."[10]

Removing proprietary schools from eligibility for the present college loan programs would save as much as 25 percent of their current costs. But saving money should not be used as an excuse for reducing the vocational opportunities available to disadvantaged students. Proprietary schools are an essential component of the nation's job training network. Many of the students who benefit from these programs have very few other options and, upon completing their program, find a productive place in the work-force.

But there is also enormous fraud, confusion, and wasted resources in the way the federal government helps students to attend proprietary schools.[11] By making these schools a valued part of the government's effort to train and retrain the labor force, rather than a mismatched partner in the college-loan program, students seeking vocational education would benefit and the college-loan programs could be refocused to better serve most conventional two- and four-year colleges.

Reversing the Transformation

Revitalizing the Pell grant and repairing the loan program would reverse the transformation in federal student aid which has occurred since 1980 and reestablish the proper balance between grant aid and student loans. Moreover, much of the additional cost of expanding the Pell grant program could be funded with the savings produced by reforms of the loan program.

Still, building the coalition necessary to pass this combination of federal program changes will be difficult. It will require policy-makers to shift subsidies away from advantaged groups and toward disadvantaged groups. This will be made more difficult because even accounting for the savings produced by loan reform, the guaranteed Pell grant will still require new federal spending. As a consequence, funding universal college affordability for students from disadvantaged groups will mean that students from advantaged groups will be forced to pay more and get less. Banks and financial intermediaries will complain that direct lending cuts into their profits. Expensive private colleges will complain that even the expanded Pell grant is too small to allow lower-income students to attend their schools without incurring large debts. Proprietary schools will complain that some needy students will be hurt in the shifting of loan program. And those who seek to reduce the size of the federal government will complain that the expanded and guaranteed Pell grant program is too costly.

In spite of the powerful forces lined up against it, enacting such a mildly redistributive reform is not unprecedented. Indeed, this is not a revolutionary plan which will cost hundreds of billions of dollars. Instead, it is a refocusing of the existing aid programs which leaves the basic structures largely intact. It does not carry the high capitalization costs of the loan bank. It does not require the complex and disruptive intergovernmental transfers necessary to federalize the college finance system. It does not include a costly national service component. In fact, it proposes no new federal program (apart from the division of the loan program) and its price-tag is modest compared to many other reform plans. Put simply, this plan asks nothing more than to return to the original spirit of the Higher Education Act of 1965.

STEP #3: ENCOURAGING STATE EXPERIMENTATION

By guaranteeing disadvantaged students a Pell grant which would cover 75 percent of the cost of the median-priced four-year college, the federal government will solve much of the affordability problem facing lower-income students. But the states also have a role. By adjusting the level of subsidy they provide to public colleges, or the grants they provide to students, they can raise or lower the net price of higher education for their residents.

If a state is willing to hold their public college tuitions down to 75 percent of the national median price of attending a four-year college, the maximum federal grant would cover the entire price their lower-income residents would pay to attend college. This low-tuition/low-aid strategy, while relatively costly to a state, would virtually eliminate price barriers for low-income students without any state grants at all. It would also provide low public college tuitions for all state residents.

Those states which favored the high-tuition/high-aid strategy would also benefit. The federal grant would not purchase as much higher education in these states as it would in the low-tuition states. But the additional revenue generated by those higher tuitions would be more than enough to fund a generous grant program to supplement the federal program. The high-tuition/high-aid strategy would continue to be the most efficient way for a state to improve college affordability. But the changes in the federal programs would further reduce the cost of such an approach.

There is great diversity in the systems of higher education from state to state. Any effort to federalize funding for the college-affordability programs would risk reducing that diversity. But under a revitalized Pell grant and a reformed federal loan program, states would be encouraged to tailor their affordability program to their individual needs and resources. Those states with a vital private sector might choose to provide large grants which could be used at any in-state school. Those states seeking to encourage students of all ages to attend college, and willing to devote more resources to that end, could focus most of their efforts on keeping tuitions low. States seeking to achieve broad college affordability at the lowest price could still let tuitions rise and focus their funds on a grant program to compensate for the fraction of college price not covered by the expended Pell grant.

No two states have the same needs or the same resources. By deciding how much they are willing to spend to make higher education affordable to its residents, and how those funds will be allocated, states could tailor their funding mechanisms to their unique needs. The federal government cannot and should not be expected to pay the whole cost of educating lower-income students. But by providing a reasonable framework, it can insure that every state which is willing to make a moderate effort will be able to provide affordable higher education to their lower-income residents.

STEP #4: REBUILDING CONSENSUS

In the short run, a revitalized Pell grant and repaired loan program will substantially reduce the net college prices facing most disadvantaged students. But over the longer term, the success of any effort to remove college price barriers must rest on the willingness of the nation's taxpayers to pay the high cost of universal college affordability. The responsibility for building this long-term public support rests, in large measure, on the shoulders of college presidents and other higher-education leaders. They must aggressively and relentlessly make the case that, just as a college education has become a requirement for an individuals financial success, a highly educated work-force has become a requirement for a sound and healthy national economy.

Advocates of universal college affordability must also make the more difficult, but no less compelling case, that increased access to higher education brings important non-economic benefits to communities, states, and the nation. Going to college enhances an individual's life in fundamental ways. It also enhances the lives of that person's family, neighbors, and co-workers. Middle- and upper-income families are already convinced that it is important to send their children to college. They must now be convinced that it is equally important to insure that the children of their disadvantaged neighbors are also able to go to college. It is no longer enough to provide a high-quality higher education at a reasonable price. Colleges must spread the word of their wide-ranging benefits to potential students and to the public.

If the goal of college affordability is ever to be fully achieved and maintained, a national consensus over the value of higher education must be reestablished. This will only happen if college leaders are able to persuade federal and state policy-makers, and the public, of the economic and non-economic value of an educated nation. Until the nation recognizes the importance of sending every talented children to college, just as they now embrace the value of sending all children to elementary and secondary schools, the problem of college affordability will persist. In the end, rebuilding the national consensus on the value of removing college price barriers, will be much more important than the provisions of any government program or the details of any reform package.

COLLEGE AFFORDABILITY AND EQUAL OPPORTUNITY: THE MISSING PIECE OF THE PUZZLE

Providing all Americans with an equal educational opportunity must be the final goal of any college-affordability program. Removing college price barriers is a prerequisite to insuring that all American's have an equal opportunity to attend college. Equal educational opportunity is, in turn, a prerequisite to making full use of each individual's ability and of the nation's human capital. As long as these price barriers remain, equal opportunity will never be achieved.

But improving college affordability is not the same thing as providing an equal opportunity to attend college. Price barriers are by no means the only obstacles which deny the children of disadvantaged families the higher education they need. Declining incomes, lack of employment opportunities, race and gender discrimination, the breakdown of the family, and the deterioration of the public schools in many communities all stand between disadvantaged students and the promise of college. Providing an equal opportunity for college, will require efforts to effectively address these very difficult social problems. The current college-affordability system can never bring about equal opportunity. Neither can the proposal I have outlined here.

Ultimately, much of what must be done to insure an equal opportunity to go to college has little directly to do with college prices. Programs which increase family income or decrease unemployment may, over several years, add as much to the resources available to disadvantaged families as would a revitalized Pell grant. Carefully developed incentives to encourage savings could increase the resources available to middle-income families and thus lessen their need to participate in the federal student-aid programs. Similarly, improvements in elementary and secondary education would help to insure that students will be prepared for college. Creation of a national apprenticeship program, to provide students who don't want to go to college with a viable employment option, would reduce the demand for vocational education which has fueled the growth of the proprietary sector. Such steps should all be part of a comprehensive effort to achieve equal educational opportunity.

Still, the long journey to equal opportunity must begin with the first step of removing college price barriers for disadvantaged students. Today, these barriers are large and growing. The widening gap between the price of college and the resources available to lower-income families to meet those prices has placed college beyond the financial reach of too many potential students. Many other potential students are discouraged by those high prices and abandon college ambitions when they are very young. Others are scared away by the potential of large debts. The chilling impact of declining college affordability on the college-going behavior of disadvantaged students, in turn, hurts everyone. Individuals are denied the opportunity to develop their abilities and expand their earnings potential. Communities and states are denied the benefits of a fully educated and fully productive citizenry and, increasingly, the failure to develop its critical human capital will place the nation at a disadvantage in the international economy. An effective effort to make college affordable will be an important step toward achieving the substantial benefits which flow from increased participation in higher education.

Notes

INTRODUCTION

1. President's Commission on Higher Education, *Higher Education in American Democracy*, vol. 2 (Washington, D.C.: GPO, 1947), p. 3.
2. Ibid.
3. "Democratic Party Platform: 1964," in *National Party Platforms, Vol. II, 1960–1976*, compiled by Donald Bruce Johnson (Urbana, IL: University of Illinois Press, 1978), p. 644.
4. "Republican Party Platform: 1968," in ibid., p. 752.
5. The College Board, *Trends in Student Aid: 1983–1993* (Washington, D.C.: The College Entrance Examination Board, September 1993), table 3, p. 6.
6. National Center for Education Statistics, U.S. Department of Education, *Digest of Education Statistics* (Washington, D.C.: GPO, 1993), table 37, p. 40.
7. The College Board, *Trends in Student Aid: 1983–1993* (Washington, D.C.: The College Entrance Examination Board, September 1993), table 1, p. 4.
8. The National Center for Education Statistics, U.S. Department of Education, *Digest of Education Statistics* (Washington, D.C.: GPO, 1993), table 306, pp. 308–9.

CHAPTER 1. WHY COLLEGE MATTERS

1. Quoted in L. Leslie and P. Brinkman, *The Economic Value of Higher Education* (New York: Macmillan, 1988), p. 77.

2. Quoted in "New Secretary Sees Many 'Ripped Off' in Higher Education," *New York Times,* 12 February 1985, p. A1.

3. All dollar figures in this chapter have been converted to constant 1994 dollars using CPI-U.

4. Among the most widely cited of these earnings differential studies are: J. Mincer, *Schooling, Experience, and Earnings* (New York: Columbia University Press, 1974); R. Freeman, "Overinvestment in College Training," *The Journal of Human Resources* 10 (1975): 287–311; and R. Rumberger, "The Changing Economic Benefits of College Graduates," *Economics of Education Review* 3 (1984): 3–11.

5. For a detailed discussion of this "screening hypothesis," see M. Blaugh, "Where Are We Now in the Economics of Education?," *Economics of Education Review* 4 (1985): 17–28.

6. Earnings data in this chapter are from, U.S. Census Department, *Current Population Reports P-60-184* (Washington, D.C.: GPO, 1992).

7. It is interesting to note that female workers did not experience the same decline in college wage premiums during the decade. In 1970, female college graduates earned 82 percent more than female high school graduates. By 1980, that gap had widened to 86 percent.

8. C. Bird, *The Case against College* (New York: McKay, 1975). Bird's figures are expressed in 1972 dollars.

9. R. Freeman *The Overeducated American* (Orlando, FL: Academic Press, 1976).

10. The W.T. Grant Foundation, *The Forgotten Half* (Washington, D.C.: The Grant Commission on Work, Family, and Citizenship, 1988).

11. M. Blackburn, D. Bloom, and R. Freeman, "The Declining Economic Position of Less Skilled American Men," in G. Burtless (ed.), *A Future of Lousy Jobs? The Changing Structure of U.S. Wages* (Washington, D.C.: Brookings Institution, 1990).

12. F. Levy and R. Michel, *The Economic Future of American Families* (Washington, D.C.: Urban Institute Press, 1991), p. 65.

13. Ibid.

14. Ibid.

15. Ibid, p. 115.

16. J. Bishop and S. Carter "The Worsening Shortage of College Graduate Workers" *Educational Evaluation and Policy Analysis* 13 (1991): 237.

17. The evidence presented in this section is drawn largely from the encyclopedic efforts of Leslie and Brinkman, *The Economic Value of Higher Education* and Ernest Parcarella and Patrick Terenzini, *How College Affects Students* (San Francisco: Jossey Bass, 1991).

18. G. Duncan, "Earnings Function and Nonpecuniary Benefits," *Journal of Human Resources* 11 (1976): 462–83.

19. R. Lucas, "Hedonic Wage Equations and Psychic Wages in the Returns to Schooling," *American Economic Review* 67 (1983): 549–58.

20. L. Lee, "Health and Wage: A Simultaneous Equation Model with Multiple Discrete Indicators," *International Economic Review* 23 (1982): 199–222.

21. I. Erlich "On the Relation between Education and Crime," in F. Juster (ed.) *Education, Income, and Human Behavior* (New York: McGraw-Hill, 1975).

22. M. Lando, "The Interaction between Health and Education," *Social Security Bulletin* 38 (1975): 16–22.

23. L. Solmon, "The Relation between Schooling and Savings Behavior," in F. Juster (ed.) *Education, Income, and Human Behavior.*

24. For a summary of the numerous studies on this subject see Pascarella and Terenzini, *How College Affects Students,* pp. 62–114.

25. C. Pace, *Measuring Outcomes of College: Fifty Years of Findings and Recommendations for the Future* (San Francisco: Jossey Bass, 1979).

26. Pascarella and Terenzini (*How College Affects Students,* pp. 162–214) provide an excellent overview of the studies examining the impact of college on identity, self-esteem, and self-concept.

27. L. Wolfle and D. Robertshaw, "Effects of College Attendance on Locus of Control," *Journal of Personality and Social Psychology* 43 (1982): 802–10.

28. K. Feldman and T. Newcomb, *The Impact of College on Students* (San Francisco: Jossey Bass, 1969).

29. R. Thomas and A. Chickering, "Education and Identity Revisited," *Journal of College Student Personnel* 25 (1984): 392–99.

30. P. Heist and G. Yonge *Omnibus Personality Inventory Manual* (New York: Psychological Corporation, 1968).

31. M. Grossman, *Determinants of Children's Health* (Washington, D.C.: National Center for Health Services, 1982).

32. G. Psacharopoulos, "Returns to Education: A Further International Update and Implications," *Journal of Human Resources* 20 (1985): 583–604.

33. R. Hill and F. Stafford, "Family Background and Lifetime Earnings," in F. Juster (ed.) *The Distribution of Economic Well-Being* (Cambridge, MA: Ballinger, 1977).

34. Pascarella and Terenzini, *How College Affects Students,* p. 415.

35. D. Schuman, *Policy Analysis, Education, and Everyday Life* (Lexington, MA: D.C. Heath, 1982).

36. Ibid., p. 77.

37. Ibid.

38. E. Denison, *Trends in American Economic Growth: 1929–1982* (Washington, D.C.: The Brookings Institution, 1985).

39. Ibid., p. 15.

40. Ibid., p. 81.

41. Leslie and Brinkman, *The Economic Value of Higher Education,* p. 82.

42. G. Psacharopoulos, "The Contribution of Education to Economic Growth: International Comparisons," in J. Kenkirk (ed.) *International Comparisons of Productivity and Causes of the Slowdown* (Cambridge, MA: Ballinger, 1984).

43. For a complete account of this argument, see R. Reich, *The Work of Nations* (New York: Knopf, 1991) and L. Thurow, *Head-to-Head* (New York: Morrow, 1992).

44. About 2,000 of these institutions are four-year colleges and universities and the remaining 1,500 are two-year colleges.

45. The data used in this section are based on the estimates made by Leslie and Brinkman in *The Economic Value of Higher Education*.

46. B. Bluestone, "UMass/Boston: An Economic Impact Analysis," unpublished manuscript, January 1993.

47. Ibid, pp. 3–4.

48. This issue is discussed in detail by Leslie and Brinkman, *The Economic Value of Higher Education*, especially pp. 69–105.

49. Erlich, "On the Relation between Education and Crime.

50. I. Garfinkel and R. Haveman, *Earnings Capacity, Poverty, and Inequality* (New York: Academic Press, 1977).

51. H. Haygne, "Volunteers in the U.S.: Who Donates Their Time?" *Monthly Labor Review* 114 (February 1991): 17–23.

52. R. Wolfinger and S. Rosenstone, *Who Votes?* (New Haven: Yale University Press, 1980).

53. M.M. Conway, *Political Participation in America* (Washington, D.C.: Congressional Quarterly Press, 1991.

54. The Carnegie Commission on Higher Education, *Higher Education: Who Pays? Who Benefits? Who Should Pay?* (New York: McGraw-Hill, 1973), p. 80.

55. D. Hecker, "Reconciling Conflicting Data on Jobs for College Graduates," *Monthly Labor Review* 115 (1992): 2–12.

56. T. Amirault, "Labor Market Trends for New College Graduates," *Occupational Outlook Quarterly* 34 (Fall 1990): 10–22.

57. K. Murphy and F. Welch, "Wage Premiums for College Graduates: Recent Growth and Possible Explanations," *Educational Researcher* 18 (May 1989): 17–25.

58. Bishop and Carter, "The Worsening Shortage of College Graduates," p. 273.

59. Hecker, "Reconciling Conflicting Data on Jobs for College Graduates."

60. Ibid., p. 10.

61. W. Johnson, *Work Force 2000* (Indianapolis: Hudson Institute, 1987).

62. Ibid., p. 96.

63. R. Kutchner, "Outlook 2000," *Occupational Outlook Quarterly* 34 (Spring 1990): 2–8.

64. Bishop and Carter, "The Worsening Shortage of College Graduates," p. 232.

65. Ibid., p. 237.

66. Thurow, *Head-to-Head*, p. 160.

67. For a discussion of the link between family background variables and college participation see "Factors Associated with College Attendance of High School Seniors," *Economic of Education Review* 3 (1984): 169–76; and S. Christensen, J. Melder, and B. Weisbrod, "Factors Affecting College Attendance," *Journal of Human Resources* 10 (1975): 174–88.

68. For a more detailed discussion of why private credit-markets are unwilling to provide sufficient capital for student loans, see M. McPherson, "Appearance and Reality in the Guaranteed Student Loan Program," in Lawrence Gladieux (ed.) *Radical Reform or Incremental Change? Student Loan Policy Alternatives for the Federal Government* (Washington, D.C.: The College Board, 1989), pp. 11–24.

69. M. McPherson and M. Schapiro, *Keeping College Affordable* (Washington, D.C.: Brookings Institution), p. 157.

70. It is important to note that such government actions need not involve the provision of public subsidies. All the government must do is to insure that these loans, which are privately and publicly beneficial, are made. Individual initiative and private credit-markets can be left to take care of the rest.

71. For a discussion of the difficulties of balancing private and social benefits in college pricing, see the Carnegie Commission on Higher Education, *Higher Education: Who Pays? Who Benefits? Who Should Pay?*, especially pp. 79–88.

72. A. Ostar, "State Tuition Policies and Higher Education," in Leonard Goodall (ed.) *When Colleges Lobby States* (Washington, D.C.: American Association of State Colleges and Universities), 133–49.

CHAPTER 2. UNDERSTANDING COLLEGE PRICES

1. All dollars figures in this chapter have been converted to constant 1994 dollars using the CPI-U.

2. T. Hartle, "Are College Costs a Problem?," *Public Opinion* 10 (1987): 48–50.

3. Gallup poll data from the Gallup Organization *Attitudes about American Colleges 1991* (Washington, D.C.: Council for Advancement and Support of Higher Education, 1991), p. 8.

4. J.B. Quinn, "The Middle Class Melt," *Newsweek* 17 (1990): 49.

5. Cited in S. Tift, "Sticker Shock at the Ivory Tower," *Time* 25 (1989): 72.

6. A. Trachtenberg, "Achieving High Marks Can Be Costly," *Northwest*, October 1991, pp. 20–21.

7. The data on college prices are from the National Center for Education Statistics, *Digest of Education Statistics*, section on "College Charges."

8. D. Martin, "Understanding the Costs of College," *Phi Delta Kappen* 69 (May 1988): 675.

9. Data on college expenditures are from the *Digest of Education Statistics* section on "College Expenditures.".

10. These concerns have led to an on-going national debate over appropriate faculty workloads. Obviously, one way for a college to compensate for increasing faculty salaries is to demand increased productivity in return. Often this has translated into administrative demands for faculty to teach more courses, or expand the size of their courses. Such workload adjustments may thus risk lowering the quality of instruction.

The many issues of faculty workload and instructional quality are clearly related to the problem of rising college prices. But to address them would take require more space and attention than is appropriate for my more limited purposes here. For an overview of the issues involved in adjusting faculty workloads, see J. Waggaman, *Strategies and Consequences: Managing Costs in Higher Education* (Washington, D.C.: ERIC Clearinghouse on Higher Education, 1991).

11. Waggaman, *Consequences and Strategies*, p. 42.

12. A. Hauptman, *The College Tuition Spiral* (Washington, D.C.: The College Board and the American Council on Education, 1990), p. 12.

13. C. Francis, *What Factors Affect College Tuition?* (Washington, D.C.: American Association of State Colleges and Universities, 1990), p. 13.

14. Ibid.

15. It is interesting to note that much of the shifting from low- to high-cost majors occurred between 1970 and 1985. But the increases in tuition did not begin until 1980 and have continued even as student interests seems to be shifting back to such lower-cost fields as education, letters, and the social sciences. Indeed, between 1986 and 1991, degrees awarded in these lower-cost areas grew more rapidly than did business and engineering degrees.

The reasons for this lag between the shifts in student demands and colleges costs are not clear. Certainly a part of the difference can be explained by the slow rate at which college curriculum and faculty change over time. As demand for business and computer programs expanded in the 1970s, many colleges, unable to hire large numbers of new faculty quickly, may have shifted existing resources away from other areas to fill those courses in the short term. While faculty are not always substitutable across disciplines, some math faculty can be shifted to computer science and some economics faculty can shift to business. Then, over the next several years, these colleges began to incrementally expanded their departments and facilities in these growing programs to meet student demand. As such, it may not have been until the 1980s that the largest part of the expensive additions in faculty and equipment were finally made.

16. Waggaman, *Strategies and Consequences*, pp. 33–34.

17. Ibid., p. 51.

18. B. Bergmann, "Bloated Administration, Blighted Campuses," *Academe* 77 (November/December 1991): 12.

19. The broad problem of unfunded government mandates is clearly explained in M. Derthick, "Federal Government Mandates: Why the States Are Complaining," *Brookings Review* 10 (Fall 1992): 50–53. The more narrow issue of how mandates are affecting colleges is discussed in Waggaman, *Strategies and Consequences: Managing Costs in Higher Education* (Washington, D.C.: ERIC Clearinghouse on Higher Education, 1991), pp. 35–60.

20. Francis, *What Factors Affect College Tuition?*, p. 13.

21. K. Halstead, *Higher Education Tuition* (Washington, D.C.: Research Associates, 1989), p. 68.

22. The data on institutionally funded student aid used in this section are from the College Board, *Trends in Student Aid: 1983–1993* (Washington, D.C.: The College Board, 1993).

23. Francis, *What Factors Affect College Tuition?*, p. 32.

24. J. Zuckerman, "Dollars and Degrees: U.S. Higher Education," *National Journal* 23 (7 September 1990): 1685.

25. T. Sowell, "The Scandal of College Tuition," *Commentary* 95 (August 1992): 24.

26. Ibid.

27. Waggaman, *Strategies and Consequences*, pp. 28–31.

28. Halstead discusses changes in tuition setting policies at private colleges in *Higher Education Tuition*, pp. 50–57.

29. M. O'Keefe, "Where Does the Money Really Go? Case Studies of Six Institutions," *Change* 19 (November/December 1987): 11–34.

30. Halstead, *Higher Education Tuition*, p. 55.

31. Halstead discusses this shift in the responsibilities for paying for college in *Higher Education Tuition*, pp. 74–76.

32. The data on voluntary support of higher education used in this section are from Council for Aid to Education *Voluntary Support of Higher Education, 1992* (New York: Council for Aid to Education, 1992).

33. Hauptman, *College Tuition Spiral*, p. 93.

34. Waggaman, *Strategies and Consequences*, p. 15.

35. Ibid., p. 94.

36. Francis, *What Factors Affect College Tuition?*, p. 15.

37. This is not a new argument. It goes back at least to W.L. Hansen and B. Weisbrod, "A New Approach to Higher Education Finance," in M. Orwig (ed.), *Financing Alternatives for Higher Education* (Iowa City: American College Testing Service, 1971), pp. 117–43.

38. H. Bowen, *Financing Higher Education* (Washington, D.C.: Association of American Colleges, 1974), p. 14.

39. The President's Commission on Higher Education, *Higher Education in American Democracy* (Washington, D.C.: GPO, 1947).

40. Carnegie Commission on Higher Education, *Higher Education: Who Pays? Who Benefits? Who Should Pay?* (San Francisco: McGraw Hill, 1973).

41. The most persuasive of these criticisms is made by M. McPherson and M. Schapiro, *Keeping College Affordable* (Washington, D.C.: Brookings Institution, 1991).

42. F. Fisher, "State Financing of Higher Education: A New Look at an Old Problem," *Change* 24 (January 1990): 49.

43. Thomas Mortenson, "Low Tuition Has Become an Enemy of Opportunity," in *Post-secondary Education Opportunity*, March 1993, p. 10.

44. Fisher, "State Financing of Higher Education: A New Look at an Old Problem."

45. McPherson and Schapiro, *Keeping College Affordable*, pp. 133–52.

46. M. Lopez, "High Tuition, High Aid Won't Work," *Chronicle of Higher Education*, 7 April 1993, p. B-1.

47. Ibid.

48. National Commission on Responsibilities for Financing Higher Education, *Making College Affordable Again: Final Report* (Washington, D.C.: National Commission on Responsibilities for Financing Higher Education, 1993).

49. Francis, *What Factors Affect College Tuition?*, p. 49.

50. Waggaman, *Strategies and Consequences*, pp. 62–63.

51. Ibid., p. 65.

CHAPTER 3. THE CHANGING COURSE OF COLLEGE AFFORDABILITY

1. All dollar figures in this chapter have been converted to constant 1994 dollars using the CPI-U.

2. T. Hartle, "Beneath the Surface: College Is Not As Costly As It Seems," *Educational Record* 67 (Spring-Summer 1986): 16–19.

3. J. Wittstruck and S. Bragg, *Focus on Price Trends in Higher Education: Tuition and State Support* (Denver: State Higher Education Executive Officers, July 1988), p. 37.

4. Ibid., p. 10.

5. A. Astin, K. Green, and W. Korn, *The American Freshman: Twenty Year Trends 1966–1985* (Los Angeles: Higher Education Research Institute, University of California, Los Angeles, 1987); A. Astin, K. Green, W. Korn, M. Schalit, and E. Berz, *The American Freshman: National Norms for Fall 1988* (Los Angeles: Higher Education Research Institute, University of California, Los Angeles, 1988).

6. G. Burtless, "Introduction and Summary," in G. Burtless (ed.), *A Future of Lousy Jobs?* (Washington, D.C.: Brookings Institution, 1990), pp. 1–30.

7. F. Levy, *Dollars and Dreams* (New York: Russell Sage Foundation, 1987), pp. 13–22.

8. F. Levy and R. Michel, *The Economic Future of American Families* (Washington, D.C.: Urban Institute, 1991), p. 11.

9. D. Gillespie and N. Carlson, *Trends in Student Aid: 1963–1983* (Washington, D.C.: The College Board, 1983), p. 18.

10. All family income data in this section are from U.S. Bureau of the Census, *Current Population Reports*, series P-60 (Washington, D.C.: GPO, 1992).

11. Data on family savings rates are from Council of Economic Advisors, *Economic Indicators*, A Report to the Congressional Joint Economic Committee, published monthly.

12. All data in this section are from College Board, *Trends in Student Aid: 1983–1993* (Washington, D.C.: The College Board, 1993); and Gillespie and Carlson, *Trends in Student Aid: 1963–1980*.

13. T. Mortenson, *The Impact of Increased Loan Utilization Among Low Family Income Students* (Iowa City: ACT Student Financial Aid Research Report Series, February 1990).

14. T. Mortenson, *Pell Grant Program Changes and Their Effects on Applicant Eligibility, 1973–74 to 1988–89* (Iowa City: ACT Student Financial Aid Research Report Series, May 1988), p. i.

15. L. Gladieux, "Introduction," in L. Gladieux (ed.), *Radical Change or Incremental Reform: Student Loan Policy Alternatives for the Federal Government* (New York: College Board, 1989), p. 1–7.

16. Mortenson *The Impact of Increased Student Loan Utilization Among Low Family Income Students* (Iowa City: ACT Student Financial Aid Research Series, 1990), pp. 8–9.

17. Gladieux, "Introduction."

18. M. Mumper, "The Transformation of Federal Aid to College Students: Dynamics of Growth and Retrenchment," in *Journal of Education Finance* 16 (Winter 1991): 332–47.

19. Mortenson, *The Impact of Increased Loan Utilization*, p. i.

20. T. Mortenson and Z. Wu, *High School Graduation and College Participation of Young Adults by Family Income Background 1970–1989* (Iowa City: ACT Student Financial Aid Research Reports, September 1990).

21. This is the figure for the maximum Stafford loan. There are other loans now available which would allow a student to borrow even more money. The differences among those loan programs will be discussed in Chapter 6.

22. Mortenson *The Impact of Loan Utilization*, p. ii.

23. C. Francis, "Student Aid: Is It Working Like It Is Supposed To?," *Change* 22 (July/August 1990): 35–43.

24. Ibid.

25. Data in this section are from R. Fensky and J. Boyd, *State Need-Based College Scholarship and Grant Programs: A Study of their Development, 1969–1980* (New York: College Board, 1981); and the National Association of State Scholarship and Grant Programs, *Annual Survey Report* (Harrisburg: Pennsylvania Higher Education Assistance Agency, published annually 1980–1993).

26. Fensky and Boyd, *State Need-Based College Scholarship and Grant Programs*.

27. In can be argued that because loans do not need to be repaid for several years, a borrowed dollar should be discounted as against a dollar which must be paid now. But loan dollars must be repaid with interest, even if that interest is below market rates as it is with the Stafford loan. In this analysis, borrowed dollars and current dollars are considered to have an equal value. Additionally, the responsibility for repaying loans often falls to the student, while current dollars are often paid by the family. The analysis here makes no distinction between the resources of the student and the resources of the family.

CHAPTER 4. CREATION OF FEDERAL STUDENT AID PROGRAMS

1. The programs discussed in this chapter changed names several times over the years. To avoid conflict, I use the name currently used for the program. As such, the BEOG is called the Pell grant, the NDSL is called the Perkins Loan, and the guaranteed student loan programs, PLUS, and SLS programs are referred to here under the umbrella title of the Federal Family Education Loan (FFEL) Program.

The dollar figures in this chapter, unlike those in previous chapters, are expressed in current-year dollars. This is done to maintain the proper historical context which shaped the debate over the student aid programs.

2. For a discussion of the changing relationship between colleges and the federal government, see L. King, *The Washington Lobbyists for Higher Education* (Lexington, MA: Lexington Books, 1985).

3. R. Lykes, *Higher Education and the United States Office of Education* (Washington, D.C.: GPO, 1975).

4. King, *The Washington Lobbyist for Higher Education*, pp. 65–70.

5. This relationship is discussed in L. Goodall, *When Colleges Lobby States*, (Washington, D.C.: American Association of State Colleges and Universities, 1987).

6. It is no coincidence that these programs are reviewed by the Veteran's Affairs committees in Congress and administered through the Department of

Veteran's Affairs. This is discussed in N. Thomas, *Education and National Politics* (New York: McKay, 1975).

7. Quoted in J. Hansen, "The Politics of Federal Scholarships: A Case Study of the Development of General Grant Assistance for Undergraduates," Ph.D. dissertation, Princeton University, 1977, p. 89.

8. The enactment of the NDEA is discussed more fully in J. Sundquist, *Politics and Policy: The Eisenhower, Kennedy, and Johnson Years* (Washington, D.C.: Brookings Institution, 1968).

9. P.L. 85–864, p. 1.

10. Thomas, *Education and National Politics*, pp. 24–25.

11. Ibid.

12. These developments are chronicled by Sunquist, *Politics and Policy: The Eisenhower, Kennedy, and Johnson Years*.

13. The equal opportunity rationale is clearly developed by Hansen, "The Politics of Federal Scholarships," pp. 145–48.

14. U.S. Congress Higher Education Act of 1965, S. Report no. 673, 89th Congress, 1965.

15. F. Hechinger, "Challenge to Colleges," *New York Times*, 9 December 1965, p. 29.

16. S. Davenport, "Smuggling in Reform: Equal Opportunity and the Higher Education Act 1965–1980," Ph.D. dissertation, Johns Hopkins University, 1983.

17. Hansen, "The Politics of College Scholarships," pp. 166–70.

18. The fascinating story of how LBJ worked his way through college is recounted in R. Dallek, *Lone Star Rising: Lyndon Johnson and His Life and Times* (New York: Oxford University Press, 1991), pp. 62–90.

19. The Johnson administration's original proposal in 1965 would have replaced the Perkins loan program with a broader student loan operated by private lenders. The president had hoped that such a plan would increase the amount of credit available to college students without corresponding increases in the costs borne by the federal treasury. Congress, however, rejected Johnson's plan in favor of both keeping the Perkins loan and creating a new one.

20. F. Keppel, "The Higher Education Acts Contrasted, 1965–1986: Has Federal Policy Come of Age?," *Harvard Educational Review* 57 (February 1987): 49–67.

21. Hansen, "The Politics of College Scholarships," especially pp. 170–93.

22. U.S. Department of Health, Education and Welfare, Assistant Secretary for Planning and Evaluation, *Towards a Long-Range Plan for Federal Financial Support for Higher Education: A Report to the President*, January 1969.

23. Hansen, "The Politics of College Scholarships," pp. 166–70.

24. Ibid., p. 168.

25. Thomas discusses these limits in *Education and National Politics*.

26. For the most complete discussion of the enactment of the Higher Education Amendments in 1972, see L. Gladieux and T. Wolanin, *Congress and the Colleges* (Lexington MA: Lexington Books, 1978).

27. The chief rival to Pell's reform plan was developed by Edith Green, chair of the House Education Subcommittee. Her plan was constructed around increasing federal support of higher education by giving more aid directly to colleges. It provided very little in the way of aid to increased student aid beyond continuing those programs which had been initiated in 1965. Federal assistance was to flow from Washington to the colleges themselves, which, in turn, would spend the funds as they saw fit. By rejecting the institutional-aid approach, Congress took a bold step toward providing college access to all Americans through federally funded financial aid.

28. Chester Finn notes that the half-cost provision served several purposes. First, it insured that no student would get a "free ride" through school. Even for the most needy students, loans and work-study funds were to be added to the grant. But it also was a subtle way of providing increased federal aid to high-priced private colleges. This is because the disallowing of full coverage for costs at a low-cost institution reduced the financial disincentive to attend high-price schools. If an absolute dollar limitation had been adopted, low-income students would have been able to use their grants to cover their full cost at a low-price institution. It was reasoned that the financial penalty for choosing a high-cost institution would not be so great since any choice would still require extra financial effort. Finally, the half-cost limitation allowed policy-makers to spread a limited number of dollars among more students than could be covered if individual grants were larger.

29. Gladieux and Wolanin, *Congress and the Colleges*, p. 304.

30. Davenport, "Smuggling in Reform: The Higher Education Act, 1965–1980."

31. A. Astin, K. Green, and W. Korn, *The American Freshman: Twenty Year Trends 1966-1985* (Los Angeles: Higher Education Research Institute, University of California, Los Angeles, 1987).

32. R. Fensky and J. Boyd, *State Need-Based College Scholarship and Grant Programs: A Study of Their Development, 1969–1980* (New York: The College Board, 1981).

33. The College Board, *Trends in Student Aid: 1983–1993* (Washington, D.C.: The College Board, 1993), table A, p. 12.

34. D. Gillespie and N. Carlson, *Trends in Student Aid: 1963–1983* (Washington, D.C.: The College Board, 1983), table 7, p. 16.

35. Nixon's attention, and inattention, to education is discussed in C. Finn, *Education and the Presidency* (Lexington, MA: D.C. Heath, 1977).

36. L. Gladieux and T. Wolanin, "Federal Politics," in D. Brenneman and C. Finn (eds.), *Public Policy and Private Higher Education* (Washington, D.C.: Brookings Institution, 1978), pp. 199–230.

37. The debate over how to expand the student aid programs brought to the surface a long-standing, but often submerged, conflict between private and public colleges. Both sectors of higher education supported expanding eligibility for, and spending on, student aid. But they had very different ideas on how that expansion should take place. Private colleges favored increasing the size of the maximum Pell grant. They argued that, as the gap between tuitions at public and private colleges increased during the early 1970s, private colleges were in danger of losing their capacity to attract a diverse student body. Increasing the maximum Pell grant would enable many lower-income students to afford higher-priced private colleges.

Public colleges, on the other hand, favored lowering the floor of federal assistance by removing the half-cost provision in the Pell grant. Such a change would allow the student to receive the full amount of the grant for which he or she was eligible. Such a revision would benefit almost all public colleges, but it would especially help those with very low tuitions.

38. Gillespie and Carlson, *Trends in Student Aid: 1963–1980.*

39. There were several reasons for the growing public demand for increased college aid to middle-income students which emerged in the late 1970s. The objective of the Title IV programs had been specifically to improve access to higher education for low-income students. The Pell grant and most other federal student aid was simply not available to most middle-income families. Members of Congress thus found themselves caught between the promise of universal college affordability and the reality that many middle-income families were still unable to afford to send their children to the college of their choice. Moreover, the demographics of college attendance were changing. Members of the baby-boom generation, who had been told that education was the road to economic success, were attending college in record numbers. Simultaneously, the college participation rates of women were increasing rapidly. The parents of this growing student population were demanding that government now provide them with some of the tuition relief now exclusively reserved for those with lower incomes.

40. R. Packwood, "Should Tax Credits for Tuition Payments to Colleges and Nonpublic Schools Be Enacted?," *Congressional Digest* 58 (January 1979): p. 10.

41. Ibid., p. 20.

42. Ibid.

43. H. Donnelly, "Carter Asks More Aid For College Students," *Congressional Quarterly Weekly Report* 36 (11 February 1978): 2205–7.

44. Ibid.

45. Califano, *Governing America*, p. 303.

46. One change was made in the president's bill in the Senate. The family income limit was removed entirely from the GSLP. The logic was that since the president's plan only excluded about 6 percent of all students, eliminating the income cap would significantly reduce paperwork without adding much to the

costs of the program. This change would make guaranteed and subsidized loans available to *all* students regardless of family income.

47. D. Gillespie and N. Carlson, *Trends in Student Aid: 1963–1983* (Washington, D.C.: The College Board, 1983).

48. L. Gladieux, "What Has Congress Wrought?," *Change* 12 (October 1980): 26–27.

49. Cited in Gladieux, "What Has Congress Wrought?," p. 27.

50. Editorial, *New York Times*, 19 March 1980, p. A19.

51. The archaic methods used in the implementation of the student aid programs had been a concern even during the years of program expansion. But now that the costs of the program were growing so quickly, and the need to cut government spending was becoming more acute, the management of the programs became the subject of extended attention from both the White House and the Congress. After careful study, Secretary of HEW Joseph Califano termed the administration of the student loan program a "monumental mess." He charged that virtually no student had ever been sent a bill for repayment when a loan went into default. Fewer than one in eight schools were independently audited each year. Moreover, he admitted that HEW regularly certified schools as eligible to participate in the programs without imposing any fiscal or administrative standards on them.

52. J. Califano, *Governing America* (New York: Simon and Schuster, 1981), p. 310.

53. Ibid., pp. 310–11.

54. The problems resulting from MISAA's creation of universally available subsidized student loans were a central part of the problem. This was made obvious in a description of the loan program on CBS television news in 1980 by business columnist Jane Bryant Quinn. She pointed out that under the guaranteed student loan program, families could borrow up to $5,000 a year at low interest rates, and put off repayment until graduation. She touted this action as a wise financial move for families at all income levels. This report, widely cited in congressional debate, revealed the degree to which the major student loan program had become a costly subsidy awarded to students who had little need for government help.

55. Quoted by C. Saunders in "Sorry, This Commitment May be Canceled—Higher Education and Ronald Reagan," *Change* 14 (January 1982): 8.

56. Gladieux, "What Has Congress Wrought?," p. 26.

57. The first evidence of this drift occurred that same year when a supplemental appropriation bill was passed for $650 million to cover unanticipated expenses for the GSLP. At the same time, $140 million in cutbacks were made to the Pell grant program achieved by cutting every award by $50. The result was a redistribution of federal subsides away from the lowest-income families toward middle- and upper-income families. Wealthy borrowers got their full loans, but needy grant recipients had their awards reduced.

58. D. Stockmam, *The Triumph of Politics* (New York: Harper & Row, 1986), p. 112.

59. "College Student Aid," *Congressional Quarterly Almanac 1981* (Washington, D.C.: Congressional Quarterly, 1981), p. 493.

60. Ibid., p. 494.

61. Ibid.

62. E. Fenske, "Education Secretary Plans Cutback in Student Aid," *New York Times*, 29 January 1981, pp. A1, A20.

63. The provisions of the 1981 budget reconciliation bill which applied to higher education are discussed in "College Student Aid," *Congressional Quarterly Weekly Report*, pp. 493–94.

64. Specifically, they voted to continue to pay the in-school interest subsidy, and they rejected the needs-test for families earning below the $30,000 limit.

65. J. Wilson, *Academic Science, Higher Education, and the Federal Government, 1950–1983* (Chicago: University of Chicago Press, 1983), pp. 82–83.

66. These cuts, included making graduate and professional students ineligible for GSLs, doubling the 5 percent origination fee charged by banks when a loan is taken out, applying the needs test to all students borrowing under the GSLP, and raising the amount families were expected to provide for their child's educational expenses. The 1982 proposal would also have eliminated the Supplemental Educational Opportunity Grant (SEOG) and slashed Pell grant spending from $2.2 billion in 1982 to $1.4 billion in 1983 and to $1 billion in 1984 and 1985. The administration estimated that such a cut would reduce Pell grant eligibility by 700,000.

67. "Congress Rejects Proposed Student Aid Cuts" *Congressional Quarterly Almanac 1982* (Washington D.C.: Congressional Quarterly, 1982) p. 485.

68. Ibid.

69. The story of how the higher-education associations mobilized to fight the proposed cuts in 1983 is told in R. Pear, "Colleges as Lobbyists: Fast Learners," *New York Times* 5 May 1983.

70. This process is discussed in more detail in "The Transformation of Federal Aid to College Students: Dynamics of Growth and Retrenchment," *Journal of Education Finance* 16 (Winter 1991): 315–31.

71. J. Hook, "Congress Faces Hard Choices over Aid to College Students," *Congressional Quarterly Weekly Report* 43 (14 September 1985): 1821.

72. "Five Year Higher Education Bill Cleared," *Congressional Quarterly Almanac 1986* (Washington, D.C.: Congressional Quarterly, 1986), pp. 236–39.

73. Ibid., p. 236.

74. The final provisions of the 1986 act are discussed in "Five Year Higher Education Bill Cleared," *Congressional Quarterly Almanac 1986*, pp. 231–38.

75. Freshman and sophomores were now allowed to borrow $2,650 a year (up from $2,500) and upperclassmen were allowed to borrow $4,000 (up from

$2,500). The aggregate maximum for undergraduates was also raised to $25,00 (from $17,500)

76. This effort was outlined in a speech given by William Bennett on college costs in November 1986. The text of that speech is reprinted in the *Chronicle of Higher Education*, 26 November 1986, p. A20.

77. E. Fiske, "New Secretary Sees Many 'Ripped Off' in Higher Education," *New York Times* 12 February 1985, pp. A1, B24.

78. Ibid., p. B24.

79. Ibid.

80. Quoted in E. Feske, "Bell Assails Reagan's Proposal to Cut Student Aid," *New York Times*, 14 April 1985, p. L31.

81. S. Palmer, "Bush Proposes 'College Savings' Plan, Indicates He Would Reverse Efforts to Slash Student Aid," *Chronicle of Higher Education*, August 5, 1987 p. A18.

82. In 1991, for example, Bush proposed reducing by the number of Pell grant recipients by 400,000. In exchange, he proposed boosting the size of the maximum grant from $2,400 to $3,700.

83. Ibid., p. 919.

84. Quoted in J. Zuckman, "Cherished Student Loan Program Plagued by a Tattered Image," *Congressional Quarterly Weekly Report* 49 (16 March 1991): 674.

85. J. Zuckman, "Nunn Blasts Loan System in Long Awaited Critique," *Congressional Quarterly Weekly Report* 49 (18 May 1991): 1288.

86. C. Saunders, "The Broadest Changes in 25 years Could Be Part of Education Amendments of 1992," *Chronicle of Higher Education* 3 April 1991, pp. B1–B2.

87. J. Zuckman, "Democrats Push to Give Loans to Middle Income Students," *Congressional Quarterly Weekly Report* 49 (8 June 1991): 1506.

88. Specifically, the plan sought to alter eligibility criteria in such a way as to allow students from the average four-person family earning up to $50,000 a year to receive a Pell grant and exclude the value of a family's home from the calculation of eligibility for those grants. The size of the maximum grant would also be increased over several years to $4,500 from the existing $2,400.

89. Rep. William Ford's tactics are discussed in J. Zuckman, "Courting the Middle Class: Congress and Student Aid" *Congressional Quarterly Weekly Report* 50 (4 January 1992): 20–24.

90. J. Zuckman, "Fight Looms over Priorities for College Loans, Grants," *Congressional Quarterly Weekly Report* 49 (5 October 1991): 2871–72.

91. A similar funding shortfall had forced Congress to reduce the size by the maximum Pell grant for $2,400 to $2,300 the previous year.

92. Ibid.

93. Ibid.

94. J. Zuckman, "Trying to Make Dollars and Sense Out of the Student Loan Program," *Congressional Quarterly Weekly Report* 49 (1 June 1991): 1446–49.

95. The argument is favor of direct loans is most clearly stated in "AASCU Offers Analysis of Direct Lending Issue," *Special Report* (Washington, D.C.: American Association of State Colleges and Universities, 26 March 1993).

96. The advantages of direct lending are discussed more fully in chapter 6 and in P. Simon, "Direct Loans to Students: A Bold Innovative Program," *Chronicle of Higher Education*, 12 May 1993, pp. B1–B2.

97. L. Hough, "Direct Loans to Students: An Unproven Experiment," *Chronicle of Higher Education* 12 May 1993, pp. B1–B2.

98. T. DeLoughry, "Final Draft of Higher Education Bill Draws Veto Threat over Student Loans," *Chronicle of Higher Education*, 24 June 1992, p. A21.

99. It broadened eligibility by eliminating consideration of home or farm equity in the calculation of a student's need. It also extended grants to students who attend college less than half-time and provided for the costs of child care be included in the calculation of aid eligibility.

100. The final provisions of the act are explained in "The Higher Education Amendments of 1992," *Chronicle of Higher Education*, 5 August 1992, pp. A20–A23.

101. The new "Unsubsidized Stafford Loan for Middle Income Borrowers" was guaranteed, but the government would not pay the interest on the loan while the borrower was in school. It also increased the amount an undergraduate student could borrow in any single year to $5,000 and the $23,000 total.

102. Indeed, in 1993–94, the first year the more generous limits were in place, Congress continued to fund the maximum award at the $2,400 which prevailed before the act was passed.

103. J. Zuckman, "President's Call to Service is Clear but Undefined," *Congressional Quarterly Weekly Report* 51 (30 January 1993): 218.

104. W. Clinton, *Putting People First* (New York: Times Books, 1992).

105. Clinton's position in favor of using community service to change the public ethos is described in T. Kolderie, R. Lerman, and C. Moskos, "Educating America: A New Compact for Opportunity and Citizenship," in W. Marshall and M. Schram (eds.), *Mandate for Change* (New York: Berkeley Books, 1993), pp. 129–52.

106. Ironically, while pressures to control the growing federal budget deficit were largely responsible for the twelve-year legislative deadlock over student aid, the same budget pressures played a major role in breaking the deadlock in 1993. In order to meet their deficit reduction targets, the House Education and Labor Committee needed to find almost $6 billion in spending cuts. They naturally wanted to find a way to absorb those spending reductions without reducing ben-

efits or eliminating programs. In this light, the full-scale shift to direct lending seemed a simple way to painlessly meet that deficit reduction target. The idea also had a renewed appeal since the threat of a presidential veto had been removed and a recent study by the General Accounting Office had praised direct lending and estimated that its implementation might save as much as $4.3 billion over the next five years.

107. J. Katz, "Republican Restraint Wins Out: Senate Committee Opts for Slower Approach to Direct Lending," *Congressional Quarterly Weekly Report* 51 (12 June 1993): 1481.

108. Ibid.

109. J. Zuckman, "Both Sides Hope to Be No. 1 in Dual Loan System Test," *Congressional Quarterly Weekly Report* 51 (14 August 1993): 2230–31.

110. Dean was quoted in J. Zuckman, "Both Sides Hope to Be No. 1 in Dual Loan System Test," *Congressional Quarterly Weekly Report* 51 (14 August 1993): 2230–31.

111. Longanecker was quoted in ibid.

112. McCurdy is quoted in J. Zuckman "President's Call to Service is Clear But Undefined," *Congressional Quarterly Weekly Report* 51 (30 January 1993): 218.

113. G. Seib and C. Trost, "Clinton Is Fervent about Tying College Loans to National Service, but Cold Realities Set In," *The Wall Street Journal*, 30 November 1992, p. A14.

114. The text of Clinton's speech at Rutgers University in New Brunswick, N.J. is reprinted in "Clinton Urges Participation in National Service," *Congressional Quarterly Weekly Report* 51 (6 March 1993): 544–46.

115. Initially, Clinton wanted to provide education awards of $6,500 a year for two years to each national service participant. But even before this plan was submitted to Congress, it was judged to be too generous and reconsidered. Veterans groups objected that $13,000 total would be almost as large as the $13,200 that military people can receive under the G.I. bill and Republicans objected to the high aggregate cost of the plan. In response, Clinton reduced the size of the awards in this initial project to $5,000 a year.

116. J. Zuckman, "Paring Funding Speeds Passage of National Service," *Congressional Quarterly Weekly Report* 51 (7 August 1993): 2160.

117. Molinari is quoted in "Will National Service Funding Cut Into Student Aid?," *Congressional Quarterly Weekly Report* 51 (24 July 1993): 1959.

118. Goodling is quoted in "Will National Service Funding Cut Into Student Aid?," *Congressional Quarterly Weekly Report* 51 (24 July 1993): 1959.

119. Kolderie, Lerman, and Moskos, "Educating America: A New Compact for Opportunity and Citizenship," pp. 143–51.

CHAPTER 5. COSTS OF FEDERAL
STUDENT AID PROGRAMS

1. M. Morehouse, "Student Loan Defaults: A $1.6 Billion Drain," *Congressional Quarterly Weekly Report* 46 (21 May 1988): 1369.

2. B. Bosworth, A. Carron, and E. Rhyne, *The Economics of the Federal Credit Programs* (Washington, D.C.: Brookings Institution, 1987), p. 131.

3. For a description of the utility of such a market-based approach to student lending, see J. Cronin, "Improving the Guaranteed Student Loan Program," in L. Gladieux (ed.), *Radical Reform or Incremental Change? Student Loan Policy Alternatives For the Federal Government* (New York: The College Board, 1989), pp. 57–74.

4. D. Gillespie and N. Carlson, *Trends in Student Aid: 1963-1983* (Washington, D.C.: College Board, 1983).

5. *FY 1991 Guaranteed Student Loan Programs Data Book* (Washington, D.C.: U.S. Department of Education, 1993).

6. College Board, *Trends in Student Aid: 1983–1993.*

7. This description of the student loan process is drawn largely from *The Student Guide to Financial Aid from the U.S. Department of Education: 1993–94* (Washington, D.C.: U.S. Department of Education, 1993); and *Timely Information for Parents and Students* (Washington, D.C.: National Association of Student Financial Aid Administrators, 1993).

8. The Stafford loan program provides both a grace period and a set of deferments for specific activities. PLUS and SLS loans provide no grace period and allow no deferments.

9. *FY 1991 Guaranteed Student Loan Program Databook*, p. 42.

10. Ibid., p. 37.

11. The financial data in this section are drawn from the *FY 1991 Guaranteed Student Loan Program Databook.*

12. While there are five different programs, they are all referred to here by their umbrella title, the Federal Family Education Loan (FFEL) program.

13. Because consolidated loans are not really new loans, but rather a restructuring of previously guaranteed loans, they are not considered to be new loans in the data presented here. However, these loans were initially included as Stafford, PLUS, or SLS loans in the fiscal year they were originated.

14. *FY 1991 Guaranteed Student Loan Program Databook*, pp. 25–26.

15. This point was made by L. Gladieux, J. Hansen, and M. Wolfe, in *Issues and Options in the Guaranteed Student Loan Program* (Washington, D.C.: The College Board, 1985), p. 2.

16. This figure is adapted from the National Commission on Responsibilities for Financing Postsecondary Education, *Making College Affordable Again: A Final Report,* February 1993, p. 45.

17. For a discussion of the risks inherent in the shift to direct lending, see Lawrence Hough "Direct Loans to Students: An Unproven Experiment," *The Chronicle of Higher Education* 12 May 1993, p. B-1.

18. General Accounting Office, *Direct Loans Could Save Billions in First 5 Years with Proper Implementation* (Washington, D.C.: GPO, November 1992).

19. B. Miles and D. Zimmerman, *Federal Family Education Loans: Reduced Costs, Direct Lending, and National Income* (Washington, D.C.: Congressional Research Service, Library of Congress, February 1993).

20. Hough, "Direct Loans to Students: An Unproven Experiment."

21. F. Keppel, "The Higher Education Acts Contrasted, 1965–1986: Has Federal Policy Come of Age?," *Harvard Educational Review* 57: 49–67.

22. It is noteworthy that while both the number of loans and the dollar volume of loans were growing rapidly, the real dollar size of the average loan was actually smaller in 1990 than it had been at any time since 1970. As such, in spite of the rising net college costs, students were not taking out larger loans. The increases in federal spending on the FFEL went to fund loans to more students, not to make larger loans to those students.

23. Indeed, up until the mid-1970s, the major problem of the FFEL was getting banks to make loans to low-income students. It is easy to see why lenders were so hesitant to participate. In 1968, for example, the prime rate on commercial loans was 8.5 percent. But student loans paid only 7 percent. Even with a federal guarantee, many banks were unwilling to accept this lower return in order to participate in the FFEL.

24. *FY 1991 Guaranteed Student Loan Program Databook* p. 4.

25. J. Hook, "Congress Faces Hard Choices over Aid to College Students," *Congressional Quarterly Weekly Report* 43 (14 September 1985): 1819–22.

26. *FY 1991 Guaranteed Student Loan Programs Databook*, p. 60.

27. Ibid., p. 53.

28. A. Astin, *The Black Undergraduate: Current Status and Trends in the Characteristics of Freshmen* (Los Angeles: Institute for Research in Higher Education, University of California, Los Angeles, July 1990).

29. Ibid., p. 11.

30. T. Mortenson, *The Impact of Increased Loan Utilization among Low Family Income Students* (Iowa City: ACT Student Financial Aid Research Report Series, February 1990), p. 8.

31. Ibid.

32. Quoted in J. Kosterlitz, "Losers by Default," *National Journal* 47 (15 April 1989): 924–25.

33. Ibid., p. 925.

34. The most comprehensive study of proprietary schools is R. Apling, "Proprietary Schools and Their Students," *Journal of Higher Education* 64 (July/August 1993): 379–415. Apling includes a discussion of the implications of the growth of proprietary education for federal student-aid policy.

35. *FY 1991 Guaranteed Student Loan Program Databook*, pp. 53–59.

36. Ibid., p. 4.

37. L. Gladieux describes the entire creation and development of federal student aid this way when he writes that the system "was not devised, it happened." L. Gladieux, "Introduction," in L. Gladieux (ed.), *Radical Reform or Incremental Change? Student Loan Alternatives for the Federal Government*, p. 1.

38. F. Keppel, "The Higher Education Acts Contrasted, 1965–1986: Has Higher Education Come of Age?," p. 57.

39. L. Gladieux discusses this potential problem in "The Future of Student Aid," *College Board Review* 126: 12–22.

40. These repayment figures are from *The Student Guide to Financial Aid from the U.S. Department of Education, 1993–94*, p. 35.

41. T. Mortenson *The Impact of Increased Loan Utilization*, p. i.

42. Astin, *The Black Undergraduate*.

43. Kosterlitz, "Losers By Default," p. 921.

44. A. Oster, "State Tuition Policies and Public Higher Education," in *When Colleges Lobby States* (Washington, D.C.: American Association of State Colleges and Universities, 1987), p. 138.

45. John Heileman, "Debt 101," *The Washington Monthly* 25 (March 1993): 42.

46. R. Reischauer, "HELP: A Student Loan Program for the Twenty-First Century," in L. Gladieux (ed.), *Radical Reform or Incremental Change? Student Loan Policy Alternatives for the Federal Government*, p. 40.

47. J. Hansen makes this point in *Student Loans: Are They Overburdening a Generation?* (Washington, D.C.: The College Board, 1987) and it remains true today.

48. These estimates were made by R. Reischauer in 1988 ("HELP: A Student Loan Program for the Twenty-First Century," p. 35). But changes made by Congress during the 1992 reauthorization of the Higher Education Act, especially those changes which allow the exclusion of the value of a home or farm from the determination of student need, may allow students from families with even greater net worth to receive federal student aid.

49. Ibid.

50. M. Mumper, "The Transformation of Federal Aid to College Students: Dynamics of Growth and Retrenchment," *Journal of Education Finance* 16: 315–31.

CHAPTER 6. THE STATES AND COLLEGE AFFORDABILITY

1. The data in this chapter are drawn largely from three sources. The data on college tuition are from *Tuition and Fee Rates: A National Comparison* (Higher Education Coordinating Board, State of Washington, Annual Editions, 1980–81 to 1990–91). This source has calculated average tuition and fee rates in a consistent way each year since 1970. These data represent the average undergraduate

charges at 213 state colleges and universities. For most states, the data are based on tuitions at comprehensive four-year colleges. For Alaska, Delaware, Hawaii, and Wyoming, the data represent tuitions at research universities.

The data on state need based grants are from the *Annual Survey Report* (National Association of State Scholarship and Grant Programs, Annual Editions, 1980–81 to 1990–91).

The data on state appropriations for higher education and FTE enrollments in the states are from Kent Halstead, *State Profiles: Financing Public Higher Education 1978 to 1992* (Washington, D.C.: Research Associates, 1992).

All dollar figures in this chapter have been converted to constant 1992 dollars using the CPI-U.

2. D. Henry, *Challenges Past, Challenges Present* (San Francisco: Jossey Bass, 1975), p. 98.

3. National Center for Education Statistics, *Digest of Education Statistics* (Washington, D.C.: GPO, 1993).

4 M. O'Keefe "What Ever Happened to the Crash of '80, '81, '83, '84, '85?," *Change* 17 (1985): 37–38.

5. Carnegie Commission on Higher Education, *The Capitol and the Campus* (New York: McGraw-Hill, 1971), p. 75.

6. The benefits of a low-tuition policy are forcefully stated by J. O'Hara, "It's Time to Blow the Whistle," in K. Young (ed.), *Exploring the Case for Low Tuition in Public Higher Education* (Washington, D.C.: American Association of Community and Junior Colleges, 1974), pp. 141–152.

7. E.T. Jones, "Public Universities and the New State Politics," in L. Goodall (ed.), *When Colleges Lobby States* (Washington, D.C.: American Association of State Colleges and Universities, 1987), pp. 110–22.

8. S. Gove, "Governors and Higher Education" pp. 41–53.

9. For an examination of the impact of prison construction on state higher education budgets, see K. Lively, "Competition from Prisons," in *The Chronicle of Higher Education*, 29 June 1994, p. A22.

10. The focus of this analysis, as well as the rest of this chapter, is limited to the period after 1981 for two reasons. First, as shown in chapter 2, college affordability did not begin to decrease until 1980. As such, it was not until after 1980 that most states and colleges felt forced to address the problem of college price barriers. Second, prior to 1980, maintaining and ensuring access to higher education was viewed as a federal responsibility. Indeed, as discussed in chapter 4, it was the federal government which developed and expanded the various student aid programs during the 1960s and 1970s. But in the early 1980s, with the transformation of the federal student aid programs coupled with the rising costs of providing higher education and the decline in the number of traditional college-age students, the states were first forced to address the problems of college affordability.

11. A. Hauptman, *The College Tuition Spiral* (Washington, D.C.: The College Board and the American Council on Education, 1990), pp. 59–67.

12. For a discussion of these different viewpoints, see "Legislators and Academicians," in L. Goodall (ed.) *When Colleges Lobby States*, pp. 88–99.

13. Rather than judging what is affordable, we evaluate whether college has become more or less affordable to state residents when both tuition levels and state grant appropriations are considered. A careful examination of these figures should reveal which of the many roads proved to be the most effective at keeping public colleges affordable.

14. R. Fenske and J. Boyd, *State Need-Based College Scholarship and Grant Programs: A Study of Their Development, 1969–1980* (New York: The College Entrance Examination Board, 1981).

15. National Association of State Scholarship and Grant Programs *Annual Survey Report*.

16. Grant per FTE must be viewed with some caution. It does not show the size of the actual grants given in each state. Indeed, the size of the actual grants given may vary widely between two states where the grant per FTE is the same. This occurs because states employ different eligibility requirements when allocating their grants. Some states provide large grants to a small number of the most needy students, while others give smaller grants to a larger number of students.

In addition, some grant dollars are provided to students who attend private and out-of-states schools. As such, grant per FTE inflates somewhat the amount each state spends to provide need-based grants to its public college students. Nonetheless, grant per FTE provides the best way to compare grant spending among the states and across time.

17. Since both tuitions and grant spending are nominal and not ordinal measures, all fifty states could be arrayed along the two dimensions to produce a more complete visual picture. But since only the states in the extreme corners of the grid are relevant to this discussion of strategy, the majority of states that fall in the middle of the grid are left out of table 6.5. It is important to note, however, that these four strategies are by no means the only ones which can be used to improve college affordability. Rather they represent the four archetypal strategies.

18. S. Hoenack, "Pricing and Efficiency in Higher Education," *Journal of Higher Education* 34 (1982): 403–18.

19. Since grant dollars per FTE inflate the amount of grant aid available to students at public colleges (some of the aid goes to students at private and out-of-state schools), this measure of net price may appear slightly lower than the actual price of a year of college. And since the states use many different eligibility requirements, this measure can not show the exact net price of higher education to lower-income students. But inasmuch as state grants are used to offset the price of college, discounting tuition by state grants is a rough approximation of how

much public colleges and universities in a state charge for a year of undergraduate instruction.

20. Because grants are not given in equal amounts to all students, need-based aid can be targeted more effectively than tuition subsidies to improve college affordability for needy students. A state which provides large grants to its lowest-income students, while increasing tuitions for everyone else, may increase the number of students who have the resources to attend college, even as net price of college in that state is rising.

21. In addition, our model considers not only state appropriations for higher education operating expenses, but also state spending on need-based grants. By using the ratio of total appropriations and need-based grants to per capita tax capacity, we develop a measure which estimates each state's effort to reduce the net price of college, relative to its tax wealth.

22. The growth of merit aid and its implications are discussed in A. Hauptman, *The Tuition Dilemma* (Washington, D.C.: Brookings Institution, 1990), pp. 62–65.

23. National Association of State Scholarship and Grant Programs, *Annual Survey Report*, 1992, p. 1.

24. Ibid.

25. Lange's experiment is discussed in R. Koff "Philanthropy, the Public Schools, and the University: The 'Albany Dreamers' Program as a Model for At-Risk Youth," in A. Hauptman and R. Koff (eds.), *New Ways of Paying for College* (Washington, D.C.: American Council on Education, 1991), pp. 110–21.

26. The Liberty Scholarship program is discussed in P. Keitel, "New York's Liberty Scholarship's Program" in Hauptman and Koff, *New Ways of Paying for College*, pp. 122–28. As of 1994, the Liberty scholarship had yet to be funded by the state legislature.

27. Hauptman, *The Tuition Dilemma*, p. 58.

CHAPTER 7. HELPING FAMILIES TO SAVE FOR COLLEGE

1. All data in this chapter are in constant 1994 dollars.

2. D. Bradford "What is National Savings? Alternative Measures in Historical and International Context" Walker, Bloomfield, and Thorning *The U.S. Savings Challenge* pp. 31-75.

3. For a detailed discussion of the theoretical and policy issues involved in the decline in U.S. savings rates see C. Walker, M. Bloomfield, and M. Thorning *The U.S. Savings Challenge: Policy Options for Productivity and Growth* (Boulder CO: Westview Press, 1990).

4. C.F. Bergsten "Domestic and International Consequences of Low U.S. Savings Rates" in Walker, Bloomfield, and Thorning *The U.S. Savings Challenge* pp. 89-113.

5. Ibid.

6. Ibid.

7. J. Immerwahr *Saving: Good or Bad? A Pilot Study of Public Attitudes Toward Saving, Investment, and Competitiveness* (New York: Public Agenda Foundation, 1989).

8. Bergsten "Domestic and International Consequences of Low U.S. Saving", p. 89.

9. These practices are discussed by M. Boskin "Policy Prescriptions for Raising U.S. Savings" In Walker, Bloomfield, and Thorning *The U.S. Savings Challenge* pp. 8-16.

10. Summers "Stimulating U.S. Personal Savings" p. 167.

11. The complex relationship between rates of return and U.S. savings rates is examined in D. Bernheim *The Vanishing Nest Egg: Reflections on Savings in America* (New York: The Twentieth Century Fund, 1991) pp. 43-48.

12. Ibid., p. 121.

13. Summers, "Stimulating U.S. Savings Rates," p. 167.

14. A. Hauptman notes, "Ironically, the PASS program was phased out in 1987 just as enthusiasm for college savings plans was growing." *The Tuition Dilemma* (Washington, D.C.: Brookings Institution, 1990), p. 28.

15. Ibid.

16. For a discussion of economic of the Duquesne plan, see J. Finnerty, "Commentary on Investment Issues," in *Invitational Conference on College Prepayment and Savings Plans: Proceedings* (New York: The College Board, 1988), pp. 25–31.

17. J. Merisotis, "An Inventory of Innovative Financing Plans to Help Pay for Higher Education," in Hauptman and Koff *New Ways of Paying for College* (New York: Macmillan, 1991), p. 57.

18. Aims McGuinness Jr., "The State's Role in Financing Higher Education: A Perspective," in Hauptman and Robert *New Ways of Paying for College*, pp. 184–97.

19. The many problems of the MET, both theoretical and practical, are reviewed in "Social Irresponsibility, Actuarial Soundness, and Wealth Redistribution: Lessons about Public Policy From a Prepaid Tuition Program," *Michigan Law Review* 88 (1990).

20. For a discussion of the many tax issues involved in tuition prepayment plans, see D. Williams II, "Taxation of Tuition Prepayment Plans and Other Forms of College Expense Assistance," in M. Olivas (ed.), *Prepaid College Tuition Plans: Promise and Problems* (Washington, D.C.: College Board, 1993), pp. 55–77.

21. Education Commission of the States, *1990 Survey of College Savings and Guaranteed Tuition Plans* (Denver: Education Commission of the States, 1990), p. 3.

22. The courts decision is reviewed and evaluated by Williams II in "Taxation of Tuition Prepayment Plans and Other Forms of College Expense Assistance," pp. 68–69.

23. Eureka Project, *Paying for College: Student Loans and Alternative Financing Mechanisms* (Sacramento: The Eureka Project, 1988), p. 21.

24. Finnerty, "Commentary on Investment Issues."

25. Education Commission of the States, *1990 Survey*.

26. These concerns are reviewed in G. Blumenstyk, "Florida's Prepaid Tuition Program Stirs Skepticism amid Success," *Chronicle of Higher Education*, 1 July 1992, p. A24.

27. J. Evangelauf, "Duquesne U. Suspends Pioneering Prepaid Tuition Plan: Nationwide the Concept Meets Growing Resistance," *Chronicle of Higher Education*, 16 March 1988, p. A35.

28. Lehman, "Social Responsibility, Actuarial Soundness, and Wealth Redistribution," p. 1113.

29. Hauptman, *The Tuition Dilemma*, pp. 28–29.

30. Education Commission of the States, *1990 Survey*.

31. Hauptman, *The Tuition Dilemma*, p. 29.

32. M. Olivas, "Introduction: Financing Higher Education," in Olivas (ed.) *Prepaid College Tuition Plans*, pp. 1–15.

33. Williams II, "Taxation of Tuition Prepayment Plans," pp. 57–58.

34. Minnesota Higher Education Coordination Board, "Minnesota College Saings Bonds with Coordinating Board Recommendations," a report published by the Minnesota Higher Education Cordination Board, January 1989.

35. Olivas, "Introduction: Financing Higher Education," p. 9.

36. Ohio Tuition Trust Authority, *Saving for College . . . Today*.

37. S. Baum, "Issues of Equity in College Savings," in Hauptman and Koff (eds.) *New Ways of Paying for College*, pp. 93–100.

38. Eureka Project, "Paying for College: Student Loans and Alternative Financing Mechanisms," p. 18.

39. Ibid.

40. Baum, "Issues of Equity in College Savings," pp. 93–100.

41. T. Bracken, "Developing a National Savings Agenda," in Hauptman and Koff (eds.) *New Ways of Saving for College*, pp. 73–74.

42. In an attempt to reach more lower- and middle-income families, the MET developed a program to allow participants to purchase contracts on a monthly installment plan. This was intended to reduce the price of contracts and make them more accessible to a wider range of families. But even purchasers of these monthly payment contracts were still biased toward upper-income families. By analyzing the ZIP codes of participants in the Michigan program, Jeffrey Lehman estimated the income of families who purchased contracts using the monthly-payment option (MPO). Even in the more widely accessible MPO, Lehman estimated that more than 60 percent of the purchasers are from the top 40 percent of income distribution. But the fact that 22 percent of those purchasers came from families in the bottom 40 percent of the income distribution is evidence that the program was not limited to the wealthy.

CHAPTER 8. FROM PRICE TO PARTICIPATION

1. This process is discussed by P. McDonough in "Windows of Opportunity: Equality of School Choice," UCLA: unpublished manuscript.

2. Even decisions made at an early age can place an unsuspecting child on a road which leads away from college in a way that can preempt any subsequent decision. There is strong evidence that, if disadvantaged students, even at a very young age, feel that they will not have the financial resources to go to college, it is unlikely that they will ever go. As such, creating the impression among young people that when they are ready to go, college will be within their financial reach, may be just as important as changes in the net price that those students will eventually face.

3. The most comprehensive analysis of the link between price and participation was done by L. Leslie and P. Brinkman, *The Economic Value of Higher Education* (New York: Macmillan, 1988).

4. McPherson and Schapiro provide an excellent review of this literature in *Keeping College Affordable* (Washington, D.C.: Brookings Institution, 1991), pp. 44–56.

5. C. Manski and D. Wise, *College Choice in America* (Cambridge, MA: Harvard University Press, 1983).

6. Ibid., pp. 119–28.

7. Leslie and Brinkman, *The Economic Value of Higher Education*, p. 155.

8. E. Savoca, "Another Look at the Demand for Higher Education: Measuring the Price Sensitivity of the Decision to Apply to College," *Economics of Education Review* 9 (1990): 123–34.

9. Ibid., p. 123.

10. M. Tierney, "Student Matriculation Decisions and Financial Aid," *Journal of Higher Education* 3 (1980): 14–25.

11. M. McPherson and M. Schapiro, *Keeping College Affordable* (Washington, D.C.: Brookings Institution, 1991), pp. 44–56.

12. G. Orfield, "Money, Equity, and College Access," *Harvard Education Review* 62 (Fall 1992): 342.

13. G. Orfield et. al., *The Chicago Study of Access and Choice in Higher Education* (Chicago: University of Chicago Committee on Public Policy Studies, 1984).

14. These trends are discussed by Mortenson in *Postsecondary Education Opportunity* 11 (May 1993).

15. These data are the bases of many studies including S. Pelavin and M. Kane, *Changing the Odds: Factors Increasing Access to College* (New York: College Board, 1990).

16. Ibid., p. 33.

17. Pelavin and Kans, *Changing the Odds*, pp. 37–79.

18. The data used in this section are from *Appalachian Access and Success*

(Athens, OH: Institute for Local Government and Rural Economic Development, October 1992).

19. Ibid., p. 150.

20. Ibid., p. 1.

21. Ibid., p. 150.

22. Because low-income students are more likely to drop out of college, this measure may actually overestimate the number of low-family-income students enrolled in college at any point in time.

23. In Orfield, "Money, Equity, and College Access," p. 340.

24. Ibid.

25. These reports are published several times a year in the Mortenson's *Postsecondary Education Opportunity* newsletter.

26. While the quartiles have always been defined in the same way, they *do not* represent constant-dollar income intervals. Because of the redistribution of family income over the past two decades, the incomes of the bottom quartile have dropped while those in the top quartile hav grown. For example, in constant dollars, the bottom income quartile in 1970 would end at $25,112. The highest income quartile would begin at $56,909.

CHAPTER 9. WHAT WENT WRONG AND WHY

1. All dollar figures in this chapter have been converted to constant 1994 dollars.

2. National Center for Education Statistics, *Digest of Education Statistics*, "International Comparisons: Higher Education Degrees Conferred," table 344, p. 418.

3. This point is clearly made with regard to state policies by F. Fisher, "State Financing of Higher Education: A New Look at an Old Problem," *Change* 24 (January 1990): 42–55. The same point in made about federal policy by T. Mortenson in *The Impact of Increased Loan Utilization among Low Family Income Students* (Iowa City: ACT Student Financial Aid Research Reports, 1990); and in *Pell Grant Program Changes and Their Effects on Applicant Eligibility, 1973–74 to 1988–89* (Iowa City: ACT Student Financial Aid Research Report Series, 1988).

4. This strategy is most vocally supported by Rep. William Ford, former chair of the House Education and Labor Committee. His views are described in J. Zuckman, "Courting the Middle Class: Congress and Student Aid," *Congressional Quarterly Weekly Report* 50 (4 January 1992): 20–23.

5. These state efforts are discussed in C. Eckl, "Joe College Pays the Tab," *State Legislatures* 19 (September 1993): 26–36.

6. Ibid.

7. Cited in Eckl, "Joe College Pays the Tab," p. 33.

8. J. Kingdon discusses the role of crises and focusing events in moving problems onto the government's agenda in *Agendas, Alternatives, and Public Policy* (Boston: Little Brown, 1984).

9. These intergovernmental changes since 1980 are discussed in R. Gage, "Key Issues in Intergovernmental Relations in the Post-Reagan Era: Implications for Change" *American Review of Public Administration* 20 (1990): 155–74.

10. In Eckl, "Joe College Pays the Tab," p. 33.

CHAPTER 10. OPTIONS TO IMPROVE COLLEGE AFFORDABILITY

1. For an excellent discussion of the principle issues and options in student loan reform, see L. Gladieux (ed.), *Radical Reform of Incremental Change? Student Loan Policy Alternatives and the Federal Government* (New York: The College Board, 1989).

2. M. Friedman, *Capitalism and Freedom* (Chicago: University of Chicago Press, 1963), chapter 6.

3. R. Reischauer, "HELP: A Student Loan Program for the Twenty-First Century," in Gladieux (ed.), *Radical Reform or Incremental Change?*, pp. 33–56.

4. J. Silber, "The Tuition Dilemma: A New Way to Pay the Bills," *Atlantic* 242 (July 1978); and "Tuition Made Easy," *New York Times* 4 February 1993, p. A15.

5. B. Bluestone, *Financing Opportunity for Post-secondary Education in the U.S.: The Equity Investment in America Program* (Washington, D.C.: The Economic Policy Institute, 1990).

6. The savings resulting from a loan bank are discussed in Reischauer, "HELP: A Student Loan Program for the Twenty-First Century."

7. J. Cronin, "Maintaining and Improving the GSL Program," in Gladieux (ed.), *Radical Change or Incremental Reform?*, p. 125.

8. Reischauer, "HELP: A Student Loan Program for the Twenty-First Century."

9. The increased tax rate would apply only to the employee, and not the employer portion of the payroll tax.

10. Ibid., p. 49.

11. Ibid., p. 46.

12. Bluestone, *Financing Opportunity for Post-secondary Education in the U.S.*, p. 12.

13. Ibid., p. 11.

14. Cronin, "Maintain and Improve the GSL," p. 125.

15. The major issues in repayment reform are laid out in W. Simpson,

"Income Contingent Student Loans: Context, Potential, and Limits," *Higher Education* 16 (1987): 699–721.

16. Ibid.

17. For a summary of the difficulties, see J. Merisotis, "Income Contingent Loans: A Hot 'New' Idea and Its Cold Realities," *Change* 19 (March/April 1987): 10–11.

18. This problem is examined by D. Long, "Income Contingent Loans: A Student Life Indenture Program," in L. Eiser (ed.), *A Call for Clarity: Income, Loans, Cost* (American Association of State Colleges and Universities, 1988), pp. 33–43.

19. W. Hansen and B. Weisbrod, "A New Approach to Funding Higher Education," in M. Orwig (ed.), *Financing Alternatives to Higher Education* (Iowa City: American College Testing Service, 1971), pp. 117–43.

20. S. Hoenack, "Pricing and Efficiency in Higher Education," *Journal of Higher Education* 34 (1982): 403–18.

21. This section is based on M. McPherson and M. Schapiro, *Keeping College Affordable* (Washington, D.C.: Brookings Institution, 1991).

22. Ibid., pp. 209–10.

23. Ibid.

24. M. Lopez, "High Tuition, High Aid Won't Work," *Chronicle of Higher Education*, 7 April 1993, p. B1.

25. National Commission on Responsibilities for Financing Higher Education, *Making College Affordable Again* (February, 1993).

26. Ibid., p. 40.

27. Ibid., p. xviii.

28. While the commission does explicitly recommend making Pell grants an entitlement, the spirit of the plan is clearly to insure future generations of students a reliable foundation of federal funding to pay for college.

29. Ibid., p. 57.

30. The most widely discussed of these reform plans is the Report of the Commission on National and Community Service, *What You Can Do for Your Country* (January 1993).

31. Ibid., p. ix.

32. The final version of the National and Community Service Trust Act of 1993 is described in detail in *Serve! America: The Newsletter of the Commission on National and Community Service* 2 (Fall 1993).

33. Ibid.

34. G. Seib and C. Trost, "Clinton Is Fervent about Tying College Loans to National Service, But Cold Realities Set In," *The Wall Street Journal*, 30 November 1992, p. A14.

35. M. Mumper, "The Transformation of Federal Aid to College Students: Dynamics of Growth and Retrenchment" *Journal of Education Finance* 16 (Winter 1991): 315–31.

36. "State Notes," *Chronicle of Higher Education*, 28 November 1990, p. A25.

37. "State Notes," *Chronicle of Higher Education*, 11 April 1990, p. A29.

38. Ibid.

CHAPTER 11. A PLAN TO REMOVE
COLLEGE PRICE BARRIERS

1. Moreover, Pell grant funds are not guaranteed from year to year and students do not know how large a grant they are eligible for until a few months before school starts. This uncertainty further diminishes the value of the federal grant.

2. T. Mortenson, "Economic Welfare and Educational Attainment," in *Postsecondary Education Opportunity*, January 1994, p. 13.

3. The findings of these studies are carefully summarized by E. Pascarella and P. Terenzini *How College Affects Students* (San Francisco: Jossey Bass, 1991), pp. 511–15.

4. National Commission on Responsibilities for Financing Higher Education, *Making College Affordable Again* (February 1993).

5. Ibid.

6. Manski and Wise *College Choice in America* (p. 23) note that a large portion of Pell grants went to students who would have attended college without the grant. While they explicitly draw no conclusions from this observations, they estimate that 59 percent of grants recipients would have gone to college had they not received the grant.

7. The dilemma of reducing defaults and insuring that disadvantaged students have access to vocational training programs is discussed by G. Orfield, "Money, Equity, and College Access," *Harvard Education Review* 62 (Fall 1992): 337–72.

8. The argument against such a split is made in S. Blair, "Congress Should Reject 'Separate but Equal' Aid Programs," *Chronicle of Higher Education*, 7 March 1990, p. A52.

9. L. Thurow, *Head-to-Head* (New York: William Morrow, 1992), p. 275.

10. Ibid.

11. While there are numerous government studies and reports documenting different types of abuses, two particularly interesting accounts are "Stafford Student Loans: Millions of Dollars Awarded to Ineligible Borrowers" (Washington, D.C.: General Accounting Office, December 1990) and "Guaranteed Student Loans: Analysis of Student Loan Default Rates at 7,800 Postsecondary Schools" (Washington, D.C.: General Accounting Office, July 1989).

Index